The "Hindered Hand"

Recent Titles in
Contributions in Afro-American and African Studies
Series Adviser: Hollis R. Lynch

Blacks in the West
W. Sherman Savage

Frederick Douglass on Women's Rights
Philip S. Foner, editor

Travail and Triumph: Black Life and Culture in the South Since the Civil War
Arnold H. Taylor

Red Over Black: Black Slavery Among the Cherokee Indians
R. Halliburton, Jr.

New Rulers in the Ghetto: The Community Development Corporation and
Urban Poverty
Harry Edward Berndt

Black-Ethos: Northern Urban Life and Thought, 1890–1930
David Gordon Nielson

The FLN in Algeria: Party Development in a Revolutionary Society
Henry F. Jackson

Africans and Seminoles: From Removal to Emancipation
Daniel F. Littlefield, Jr.

American Socialism and Black Americans: From the Age of Jackson to
World War II
Philip S. Foner

Black Academic Libraries and Research Collections: An Historical Survey
Jessie Carney Smith

Trabelin' On: The Slave Journey to an Afro-Baptist Faith
Mechal Sobel

Revisiting Blassingame's *The Slave Community:* The Scholars Respond
Al-Tony Gilmore, editor

Schooling for the New Slavery: Black Industrial Education, 1868–1915
Donald Spivey

THE "HINDERED HAND"Cultural Implications of Early African-American Fiction

ARLENE A. ELDER

Contributions in Afro-American and African Studies, Number 39

GREENWOOD PRESS
WESTPORT, CONNECTICUT • LONDON, ENGLAND

59889

Library of Congress Cataloging in Publication Data

Elder, Arlene A.
   The "hindered hand".

(Contributions in Afro-American and African
studies; no. 39 ISSN 0069-9624)
   Bibliography: p.
   Includes index.
   1. American fiction—Afro-American authors—
History and criticism. I. Title. II. Series.
PS374.N4E4 813′.009   77-95358
ISBN 0-313-20323-7

Library of Congress Catalog Card Number: 77-95358
ISBN: 0-313-20323-7
ISSN: 0069-9624

First published in 1978

Greenwood Press, Inc.
51 Riverside Avenue, Westport, Connecticut 06880

Printed in the United States of America

10 9 8 7 6 5 4 3 2 1

For Richard

Contents

Acknowledgments

This study began at the University of Chicago in 1970. Therefore, first thanks must be offered to Professors Hamlin Hill and Robert Streeter, without whose interest and encouragement neither my degree nor this book would have been completed. Here in Cincinnati, Connie Spurlock and Alvena Stanfield, who nursed the text through seemingly endless "visions and revisions," deserve special mention for all those hours of careful typing and their never failing good humor. The work would never have reached the typing stage, of course, without support from the University of Cincinnati Research Council and the Taft Fund, through whose generosity I was able to use the excellent resources of the Charles Waddell Chesnutt Collection in the library at Fisk University, Nashville, Tennessee, and to afford the final costs of manuscript preparation. I am also grateful to the helpful staff of the Schomburg Collection of the New York Public Library, the Public Library of Nashville and Davidson County, Tennessee, and the Tennessee State Library and Archives. Special thanks are due the anonymous outside reader, secured by Greenwood Press, whose incisive criticism helped me to make this a better work than it would have been otherwise. Finally, a blessing on my dear relatives and friends who, in the course of seven long years, must have become unspeakably weary of hearing me enthuse or despair about this project, but never let on.

Introduction: The Tensions and the Traditions

The controversies in Black literature remain the same. William Wells Brown, the earliest African-American novelist, would have agreed in principle with poet Don L. Lee, who, attempting to define a Black aesthetic, asserted in 1968 that "black poetry not only gives positive direction to the community, but shows people black beauty and black substance. . . . Black poetry will give the people a future; will show visions of tomorrow." [1] This educative, inspirational intent has never been far beneath the surface in Black writing. Sometimes, as in nineteenth-century Black fiction, it formed the core around which all other themes were molded.

Throughout the history of African-American literature, when the desires to educate and protest were superseded by the artistic need to express truthfully the complexities and ironies of being Black in America (as, for example, in Claude MacKay's *Home to Harlem* [1928] and Langston Hughes's Simple stories), this instructive urge for change provided an energy, an impetus for showing both the comedy and the tragedy of Black life. When, however, as in most of the earliest Black novels, didacticism and propaganda became ends in themselves, they drew Black artists away from their own tradition of oratory, narrative, and folklore and, ironically, aligned them with the artificialities of secondary white writing—specifically, the nineteenth-century sentimental novel.

In any consideration of the development of the American novel during the 1800s, the names of Cooper, Hawthorne, Melville, Twain, James, and Howells immediately come to mind. At first glance, the earliest Black novelists do not appear to fit into the same category as these writers, not only in extent of talent and accomplishment, but also in terms of intent. They seem to be exotic, out of the mainstream of major American fiction.

Unlike Cooper, they explored no new fictional territory; southern slave life and the northern caste system had been the subjects of scores of white abolitionist and plantation novels. Because of the artificialities of their major protagonists, they plumbed few psychological and philosophical depths in the manner of Hawthorne and Melville. Although many Black novelists were well acquainted with the mores of Twain's southern and frontier locales, these middle-class writers accepted too many of the values of white nineteenth-century America to produce satires. James's wry and subtle analyses of social intercourse were clearly unsuited to their propagandist intent. And, since they accepted to such a large degree the literary standards of their period, their energy was not directed, like Howells's, toward refining contemporary critical tastes. All of this is simply to say that the earliest Black writers were not the shapers of American fiction. It is clear, however, that they were asking many of the same questions as their better-known contemporaries about the recurring American theme of individual possibility and social responsibility.

Don L. Lee states further in his essay that besides moving "that white boy toward righteousness," Black poets must "show him what a human being *is*." [2] William Wells Brown and Lee would probably have disagreed vehemently about what, exactly, a Black human being is and, especially, about how one relates to the white power structure. Nevertheless, they would have agreed that one of the primary functions of their writing was to define the individual within the context of American society. In this aim, both nineteenth- and twentieth-century Black authors clearly follow the path carved by major American novelists.

These writers show a common interest in the position of the individual in society and the consequences of a culture's preachments in forming a self-image. Hester Prynne's growing acceptance of her ornately embroidered *A,* which she wore both defiantly and contritely as an appropriate symbol not only of her sin but also of her strength; Huck Finn's judgment that he was a social outcast and his intriguing, if deceptive, decision to go to hell rather than return Jim to a life of slavery; and Lambert Strether's rebirth in Europe, where he arrived as a self-confident "ambassador"—all are cogent examples of the American writer's concern with the effects of society's dictates on an individual's understanding of himself.[3] The development, acceptance, and consequences of identity are inescapable topics, needless to say, for a country emerging from the warring traditions of Puritan predestination and Enlightenment perfectionism. The subject of self-image is even more appropriate for Black artists because of the unique and frequently contradictory position of their people in the social structure of the United States. W. E. B. DuBois's quarrel with Booker T. Washington, after all, suggests conflicting views about the very nature of the Black, reflected in their differences about education, job opportunities, and voting rights.[4]

The long-standing problem of Black citizens to determine their worth and place in a society dominated and defined by whites could not possibly escape examination in their earliest literary efforts. Despite the weaknesses caused by their propagandist intent, the nineteenth-century Black novels are rich and interesting precisely because of this theme of social and psychological conflict. It is in terms of this motif, the problem of Black identity, then, that the earliest novels are most clearly in the mainstream of American fiction as well as most inextricably entwined with the needs of the Black community. As Richard Wright knew, the "Negro is," indeed, "America's metaphor."

The first novel written by an American Black, Brown's *Clotel*; or, *The President's Daughter,* was published in London in 1853. This earliest-known attempt at a fictional representation of American life from a Black viewpoint went through several versions and retitlings. Finally given recognition on American soil, it was issued in 1864 as part of Boston abolitionist James Redpath's Campfire Series, a collection of propaganda pieces and reprints of popular British novels intended for the Union troops. Between 1853 and 1910, no less than eighteen more novels written by Black American authors were published in this country.

As one would expect, they concern men and women trapped by either slavery or caste and were intended to serve as inspirational guides for Black readers and as primers in the Black experience for whites. The overriding concern of most of the novelists was to show the "true" nature of Blacks and to reveal the actual conditions of their lives. The writers wished to inspire pride and determination in African-Americans and to arouse understanding, sympathy, and a desire for political reform in their white audience.

These novels are historically valuable because they provide the earliest fictional portrait of Black people in America drawn by Blacks themselves. Yet, only occasionally do they succeed in presenting complex characters whose lives compel a recognition of social or psychological truth. Most of the characters are unbelievable and their stories melodramatic and predictable. Ironically, it is through the artistic decisions of the writers—choices in characterization, tone, and plotting, which, for the most part, falsify their novels—that the destructive complexity of the Black's position in American society is most clearly revealed. Their acceptance of the techniques of the sentimental novel, rather than the devices of Black oratory, narrative, and folklore, indicates both the weakness of their conception and the distance between these early writers and the masses of their people.

Ralph Ellison's formula for good fiction is fiction "made of that which is real, and reality is difficult to come by. So much of it depends upon the individual's willingness to discover his true self, upon his defining himself—for the time being at least—against his background." [5] This "true self" was precisely what the early African-American writers found almost impossible to define and reveal. The reasons for this failure can be traced to their need for professional acceptance in a white society on white terms. The consequences of being Black in a white society constitute the entire content of most of these books. Ironically, the Black novelists themselves, by their inability to transcend the limitations of white popular fiction and their failure to draw heavily from the Black literary tradition, are their own best proof of the seriousness of the problem. Therefore, even the artistic shortcomings of the books can be seen as eloquent testimony to the conditions that their authors wished to portray.

If, however, these early novels unconsciously testify to the insecurity of the race in the nineteenth century, they also contain occasional piercing insights into the realities of the Black experience. Their conflict between the need to portray experience accurately and the conscious or unconscious decision to reinforce or refute wildly the white traditions about the Black is what makes these novels fascinating evidence of the complexity of man's attempt at truth telling. It is this tension that marks the books as revealing records of a people's survival and provides both their literary and historical interest. The schizophrenic conflicts in these novels are a direct result of the clash between their authors' attempts to conform to the accepted social, literary, and economic standards of their day and their almost antithetical need to portray their own people with honesty and imagination.

The focus of this study, then, is twofold. It critically examines, in a systematic, comprehensive, and detailed way, the earliest African-American authors' exploration of the social and psychological clashes between individuals and their society—a typically American theme. Moreover, to illuminate this conflict and to reemphasize to present-day readers the seriousness of the struggle, it attempts to show that by the very artistic choices that these writers made, by the difficulty that they encountered in their efforts to be published, and by the brief, abortive nature of their professional careers, they were living, breathing exempla of the dangers about which they wrote.

In this context, the title of one of Sutton Griggs's novels, *The Hindered Hand,* seemed a particularly apt designation for a work demonstrating the chains binding the first makers of African-American fiction. Like their slave forebears, they were bound and limited by preconceptions denying their humanity and could find spiritual and artistic strength only through their occasional acceptance of the liberating, subversive weapon of African-American folklore.

The study is divided into two parts, the first setting the literary and cultural backgrounds out of which the fiction grew and against which it must be measured, the second focusing in a chronological way upon the development of the three major Black fiction writers of the period: Sutton Elbert Griggs, Paul Laurence Dunbar, and Charles Waddell Chesnutt. Hopefully, this division and the resultant shift in critical approach from a thematic to a generally chronological emphasis is more illuminating than confusing. I am humbled by the multitude of threads—artistic, psychological, economic, political, cultural, sociological—that are interwoven in the earliest African-American fiction. Such is the complex tapestry of all American art. I only hope that the images in the picture are sharp despite their multitude of colors and that the work succeeds, to a degree at least, in fulfilling the old slave's admonition to "hit a straight lick with a crooked stick."

Part 1
THE BACKGROUND

1
Popular Myths and the Audience

As she stood there, the full moon cast its bright rays over her person, giving her an angelic appearance and imparting to her flowing hair a still more golden hue. Suddenly another change came over her features, and her full red lips trembled as with suppressed emotion. The muscles around her faultless mouth became convulsed, she gasped for breath, and exclaiming, "Is it possible that man can be so false!" again fainted.

William Wells Brown, Clotelle

The literary models chosen by nineteenth-century African-American novelists were those of white sentimental and propaganda fiction and, to a lesser degree, Black anti-slavery oratory and autobiographical narrative. The sentimental novel, which had been popular in America since the publication of *The Power of Sympathy* in 1789, was embraced wholeheartedly, even though melodramatic techniques shrouded these books in a romantic haze and riddled them with unreal characters and incredible incidents. Black oratory and narrative, on the other hand, while reinforcing some of the damaging influences of the devices of popular fiction, offered as well a solid foundation for Black writers by providing them with stories of actual Blacks as studies for their fictional characterizations. The Black tradition of oral narrative and abolitionist protest, which had a definite, but less easily observable, effect on the earliest Black writers, was also a rich source of folklore and humor. Most of the incongruities of character and action within the first African-American novels can be directly traced to the conflict between these two traditions. Jarring elements force the tales in opposite directions, diminishing their artistry and effect, but, in a fascinating way, powerfully suggesting the destructive atmosphere under which the early Black artists strove for a concept of their people's identity.

It is not necessary to reiterate the fictional banalities that induced literary critic Fred Lewis Pattee, in the pre-women's liberation era of the 1940s, to dismiss the decade preceding the Civil War as the "Feminine Fifties." Nor is it necessary to provide a detailed defense for the momentary misogyny in Hawthorne's tirade of

1855 against that "d——d mob of scribbling women," whose domestic romances strode manfully to the head of the best-seller lists while his *Mosses from an Old Manse* limped feebly behind. Nevertheless, certain prominent themes and ·conventions found in popular novels of the 1800s must be reviewed in order to fill in the background against which the Black novels should be examined.

When the Black artists searched for a fictional form suited to their aims, they quickly saw the appropriateness of the propaganda novel employed by British authors such as Charles Dickens and Mrs. Gaskell. In the United States, this genre was being used by such writers as Timothy Shay Arthur in behalf of the temperance crusade and Harriet Beecher Stowe for the abolitionists. The form appeared relevant because of its revelation of social ills and, especially, its strong moral tone. In addition, propaganda novels seemed effective models because, along with their more purely romantic counterparts, they were reaching the widest segment of the American public.[1]

However, the weaknesses of popular nineteenth-century fiction are painfully clear. Whether in the form of domestic romances of the earlier part of the century, of "novels with a purpose" enlisted in the temperance, abolitionist, and pro-slavery crusades, or, later, of prolific dime novels and Horatio Alger stories, this writing was framed with an obvious and, most often, clumsily executed didactic intent. It was crowded with easily identifiable character types representative of Good and Evil; its melodramatic conflicts inevitably built toward a thrilling climax, after which poetic justice blessed the good and banished the bad.[2] Furthermore, the values extolled and shown as triumphant in these accounts were invariably those of white middle-class America: industry, ambition, thrift, patriotism, and religious devotion. In the Black novels, the sincere espousal of these same qualities now seems surprising.

Their use of popular forms does not necessarily mean that the Black novelists were ignorant of the more imaginative fiction being written by their contemporaries. Walter Stowers and William Anderson, the authors of *Appointed* (1894), were well acquainted with the work of Howells and James. Two young white girls, members of a book club, are portrayed in the novel as discussing the merits of different kinds of fiction:

> "Yes," added Marjorie, "books like *Ben Hur* that are based on historical events are certainly great helps in the study of history, for they invest dull facts with the pleasing dress of romance, and many become acquainted with them who would not otherwise pour over dusty details. But, by the way, what was the opinion of the club in regard to our American novelists, Howells and James. . . .?"
>
> "Well, it was rather unsatisfactory, although it was generally conceded that they were the greatest of our novelists. Some were of the opinion that James was too analytical, and others that Howells was too prosy; yet while most of them thought that their novels were models of realism, they did not think that their style would meet the acceptation of the masses. For in

action and love, their characters are tame, everyday sort of people, and but served as a glass in which one sees himself reflected. They said that people read novels because they desire something out of the ordinary life."[3]

Speaking for the nineteenth-century white reading public and, it appears, for Stowers and Anderson as well, the girls recognize, but reject, the "realism" and "analysis" found in Howells and James. They prefer romantic characters and thrilling incidents. Another revealing feature in their conversation is their acceptance of fiction, in this instance a historical novel, *Ben Hur,* as a proper instrument for instruction. "Although critics were generally silent upon matters of technique," Herbert Brown has noted, "they were fond of affirming that the primary function of the novelist was to teach. . . . The prefaces to many novels were filled with disarming declarations of a desire to inculcate morality by precept and example." [4]

The warnings in these books ranged from threats of death and dishonor to young women who allowed themselves to be seduced by handsome villains (and of a similar fate awaiting young men lured into barrooms by the equally misleading charms of alcohol) to predictions of the downfall of an entire nation that callously blinked at the enslavement of a large segment of its population. Whatever the message, the instructional intent of sentimental and propaganda novels was clear to reader and writer alike. It is no wonder, then, that the established traditions of such a literary form would appeal to the Black writers, who felt an even greater urgency than most of their white counterparts to proclaim their racial and social message.

Another aspect of the contemporary popular fiction that must be taken into account is its ambivalent portrayal of the few Black characters who did find their way into its pages. Blacks were seldom given center stage; and when they were, they were usually disguised so thoroughly that Black readers would have had a difficult time recognizing them as members of their own race.[5] Some early nineteenth-century novels, *The Valley of the Shenandoah* (1824) by George Tucker, for example, admitted that slavery was sometimes an unhappy situation for those involved. In other aspects, however, *The Valley of the Shenandoah* is representative of the manner in which Black characters were handled by subsequent southern authors. Tucker's slaves are sentimentalized and shown to be extremely loyal to their masters. Moreover, Blacks are present only as background figures and are given no significant narrative function.

Writers such as W. A. Carruthers and John Esten Cooke filled their books with mammies, butlers, and coachmen who, despite their various outlandish classical names, were essentially interchangeable. The hostler in Kennedy's *Swallow Barn* (1832) is noteworthy because individual Blacks were seldom singled out for attention. They generally provided local color and comic relief in a peaceful background against which dramas of chivalry and adventure were performed by the white aristocrats.

This vaguely sympathetic portrayal of docile, satisfied Black servants persisted until the slavery controversy in the middle of the century led novelists either to attack or to become apologists for the southern system. White as well as Black stereotypes developed. Discussing the repetition of characters in plantation writing, Sterling Brown has noted:

> The characters are as constant as the cotton bolls: the courtly planter, the one hundred percent southern belle, the duelling cavalier, the mammy or cook, "broadbosomed . . . with vari-colored turban, spotless apron, and beaming face," the plantation uncle, black counterpart "of the master so loyally served and imitated," and the banjo plunking minstrel of the quarters.[6]

The intent of the antebellum southern writers was to show the childlike joy of the slaves and their loyalty to Ol' Massa and Ol' Miss. Frequently, these novelists would even portray slaves testifying to the "joys of their blessed bondage." [7] Obviously many aspects of plantation life were avoided or easily glossed over. Such facts as the hardships of working in the cotton fields and rice paddies, the complexities of miscegenation, and the cruel separation of slave families on the auction block seldom appeared in their pages.

Of course, the abolitionist novel *Uncle Tom's Cabin* (1852), despite its melodramatic excesses, forced the reading public to face up to the consequences of slavery for both Blacks and whites. Few modern readers, however, even the most ardent admirers of the abolitionists, would judge Stowe's work to be much better than the usual sentimental and sensational conceptions of her day. Unfortunately, even Augustine St. Clair and George Harris, the most complex characters in the book, take second place in the reader's attention to Simon Legree's brutal flogging of saintly Uncle Tom or to Little Eva's tear-shrouded apotheosis as an angel. The exciting image of Eliza crossing the icy Ohio, her terrified child clutched to her bosom, the rabid slave trappers and their dogs at her heels, stuck in the minds not only of white readers and theatergoers but of subsequent Black novelists as well.

Despite their humanitarian concern, their general inability to portray the Black as much more than a symbol in a controversial economic and political struggle hampered many a well-intentioned northern writer. Taking their lead from Stowe, other abolitionist authors proved to be just as propagandist and sensational in their approach to the slave as were their counterparts on the other side of the question. Books such as *Slavery Unmasked* (1856) established the tradition of Black fugitives, insurrectionists, helpless victims, noble savages, perfect Christians, and "tragic octoroons."

The ill-starred, beautiful mulatto was particularly appealing to the public imagination in novels and stage plays both before and after the Civil War. With Dion Boucicault's immensely successful melodrama *The Octoroon* (1859), the type was firmly established in the public mind. Zoe, his unfortunate heroine, the "victim" of a racially mixed alliance, dispatches herself with poison when her love for the white hero, George, proves legally hopeless. Such was the popular fate of many a subsequent olive-skinned heroine.

The abolitionist feeling engendered by Stowe's book was countered to some degree by works like *Aunt Phillis's Cabin; or, Southern Life as It Is* (1852) and *Uncle Robin in His Cabin in Virginia and Tom Without One in Boston* (1853), which through the use of a contrast of conditions in the North with those in the South attempted to demonstrate the superiority of life for Blacks under slavery. In novels such as these, there is no suggestion of Blacks as individuals with problems basic to them as human beings, but not inextricably bound up in race or social and economic status. Nor are they ever pictured as having personalities at least as complex as their white counterparts.

Moreover, as the Civil War approached and tempers grew hotter, certain kinds of Blacks came under heavier and heavier fire. Although dramatists such as Boucicault and J. T. Trowbridge, in his *Neighbor Jackwood* (1857), presented idealized and sympathetic portraits of the mulatto, white southern novelists like Thomas Nelson Page and, later, Thomas Dixon, Jr., portrayed the man or woman of mixed blood as evil, embodying the worst qualities of both whites and Blacks. As Hugh Gloster observes: "To these propagandists the mulatto woman is the debaser of the white aristocrat, while the mulatto man is the besmircher of white virginity and the dangerous intruder in the political scene." [8] Even writers sympathetic to mulattoes usually felt pity for them because of their white ancestry, which, it was believed, raised them above other Blacks. The mulattoes' beauty, pride, defiance, ambition, and intelligence were all traced to their white forebears, and their lowly station was considered pitiable because they were part white.

Even the more realistic postwar fiction, that of the local-color movement, contained traditional elements of romance. The myth-making tendency of many local-color writers shrouded their portraits of different sections of the country in nostalgia and glossed over unpleasant realities. Postwar humor, which reached its vogue in the 1860s and 1870s, pierced through many of the country's pretensions, but was itself guilty of condescending and misleading portrayals of Blacks.

Most of the humorous portrayals of African-Americans strengthened the concept of their inferiority to whites. One of the most frequent subjects of amusement was the carefree, irresponsible, and improvident freedman who depended upon his "white folks" to get him out of trouble. In appearance, he often resembled a baboon and was generally shown making his lazy way through an unreflective life as best he could—usually by lying and stealing.

In his extensive study of southern humor after the Civil War, Wade Hall notes:

> The humorist depicted the Negro stealing not only watermelons, but chickens from the chicken house, hams from the smokehouse, roasting ears from the cornfield, and anything else that was not tied or nailed down. . . .
> The Negro who refused to go on playing the role of Uncle Tom was

usually pilloried. If he attempted to get an education, he was ridiculed as an upstart and an asserter of equality with the white man.[9]

Educated Blacks whose speech was depicted as loaded with malapropisms, generally suffered ridicule in these works not only from whites but also from the old-fashioned "uncles" and "aunties" of their race. The white humorists obviously felt more at ease with these compliant, conservative, and congenial servant types. Traditionally loyal Uncle Tom changed his martyr's rags in postwar humor for the patches of Uncle Remus, "whose dominant traits are pride in Miss Sally and her boy and contempt for poor white trash and freed niggers." [10]

The Blacks' emotional and anthropomorphic religion was a particular target of postwar satire. Sketches dealing with this subject concentrated on their fondness for carnivallike camp meetings and revivals, their love of ritual, their frequent emotional conversions and backslidings, the weaknesses of their ministers, and their childlike, literal interpretation of the Bible.

Claims of realism were served to a certain extent, however, in the local colorists' interest in an accurate reproduction of the different dialects of the southern regions. Nevertheless, although the regional vogue inspired a careful rendering of dialects and speech patterns of ethnic groups in every part of the country, the dialect of the Black was frequently employed almost solely for humorous purposes.

Despite the occasional attempts at a realistic portrayal of Blacks, then, as in the novels of Albion Tourgee, for example, for the most part they served nineteenth-century popular novelists as symbols for propaganda purposes or as stereotypes for low comedy. Some writers, however, saw in the newly liberated freedman the source of continued political, economic, and social discord and painted him in melodrama's darkest hues.

Unfavorable portraits concentrated on the newly freed slaves unable to cope with their privileges, lazy, and easily manipulated by every carpetbagger sent down from the North. The freedmen in the works of Thomas Nelson Page, for instance, "idly hovered about railway stations . . . ; they were discourteous to the white gentry . . . and they supported the most abhorrent Republican leaders." [11] As the political climate in the South became increasingly tense, the image worsened. Sterling Brown notes that "in Reconstruction, when threatened with such dire fate as Negroes' voting, going to school and working for themselves . . . Southern authors added the stereotype of the brute Negro." [12] It was not, however, until the apologias for the Ku Klux Klan by Thomas Dixon, Jr. after the turn of the century that the Black man was portrayed as a whiskey-crazed beast, eager to wreak his vengeance upon a defenseless South in an orgy of riot and rape. Dixon made no attempt to conceal his hope for a pure Aryan civilization in America and his virulent, anti-Black bias. An indication of the public interest in his views is the popularity of his three novels, *The Leopard's Spots* (1902), *The Clansman* (1905), and *The Traitor* (1907). The fact that *The*

Clansman served as the basis for D. W. Griffith's famous film *The Birth of a Nation* and sold forty thousand copies in ten days after its publication suggests immense public curiosity, if not actual acceptance.

In summary, the popular fiction of the nineteenth century, including that portraying Blacks, was artificial and didactic, but generally representative of the values and goals of the American reading public. Stereotypes of characters as different as southern Black slaves and northern white orphans developed in these novels and were used to argue for the middle-class virtues of industry, piety, and ambition, as well as serving more specific propagandist purposes in the temperance and abolition crusades. With the exception of the best of the historical romances and local-color attempts, regional settings were also idealized in popular novels. While humorists added a touch of realism to nineteenth-century fiction, their portrayal of African-Americans served to increase, rather than decrease, the artificiality of their literary image. Blacks were shown either as loyal old retainers or as ludicrous, lazy freedmen indulging their "natural" bent for deception. Blacks who attempted to improve their lot degenerated by the turn of the century from the absurd, half-educated deacons of southern humor to Thomas Dixon's subhumans, seeking to destroy the "superior" white culture. Since it is largely from these white literary roots that the earliest Black fiction grew, its melodramatic and didactic excesses, particularly its insistence upon unrealistic counterstereotypes, can be readily understood.

While it was, perhaps, natural that the first Black novelists would succumb to the appeal of imitating the popular forms of the day, they did so at the peril of their artistry. The very devices that abounded in the white popular tradition dissipated the force of the Black novelists' insights about their people. These writers produced works populated with aristocratic heroes and heroines in blackface, who expressed themselves in the genteel diction of conventional white characters. Moreover, the didacticism and propaganda pervading the abolitionist and temperance novels became the predominant tone of the Black novel as well. The Black novelists' desire to succeed with the general reading public unfortunately produced not only characters but also plots typical of those in popular fiction. Their books, like those of their white counterparts, are filled with incidents of madness, betrayal, and death; they abound with families separated and lovers reunited, all accomplished with a liberal sprinkling of dank deathbeds, gloomy cemeteries, silvery moonbeams, and raging storms. Early Black fiction differs from most of the white domestic romances in being slightly more exotic, having, as it does, runaway slaves and tragic octoroons as its principal characters. It is also much more satiric than this sentimental genre, although its satire is limited to brief thrusts at social evils and is not sustained as a predominant tone. The novels are distinguished from the general run of abolitionist stories by their occasional, brief glimpses of imaginatively conceived Black folk characters, who are, unfortunately, subordinated to minor roles. Major emphasis is placed on the sufferings and triumphs of one or two "superior" protagonists.

While the Black artists were probably aware of the more realistic, imaginative, and experimental fiction of their period, these works had much less impact on them. As Robert Bone has pointed out, the African-American writer

> was not influenced by the incipient social realism of Howells and Garland, or the regionalism of Harte, Twain, and Sarah Orne Jewett, certainly not by the stylistic subtlety and urbane cosmopolitanism of James. For all of these idioms his experience was too limited and his own cause too compelling.[13]

Intent on countering the degrading southern image of the African-American and drawn by the abolitionist's middle-class aims and hopes for racial progress, the nineteenth-century Black authors wavered between artificial white models of heroes and heroines and the more genuine pictures of their people found in the slave narratives. Ultimately, popular fiction influenced them to write melodramatic and sentimental stories of stereotypic villains and heroes caught in the oppressive master-slave relationship or in a similarly restrictive caste system. In the writings of the abolitionists, the novelists found character types, like the eloquent, noble slave, that were favorable to their cause and that they imitated. The works of the southern writers offered other stock characters, created to show the necessity and benignity of slavery, characters which Black writers generally rejected and against which they established counterstereotypes.

The influence of popular fiction is greatest in the Black novelists' portrayal of their major protagonists. Their main characters derive their meaning through their relationship to the problems of their race: if they are the victims of slavery or caste and dedicate themselves to the furtherance of their people, they are good; if they impede the race's progress as in the case of some of the minor characters, they are evil. Since their qualities are made crystal clear, in almost all instances at their first appearance in the story, and since they do not change except to become even more aware of their people's sufferings and to pledge themselves more firmly to the solution of their problems, these protagonists remain one-dimensional. They are seldom shown as responding to other than external stimuli and receive their most extensive characterization by descriptions of their physical appearance and their manner of speech. Most of them suffer from being too good, too intelligent, too handsome, and too successful, the same handicaps that make so many of the white protagonists of nineteenth-century popular fiction completely unbelievable.

Howard, Kennett Young's hero in *Selene* (1898), is a brilliant student, accomplished in a rather amazing range of learning. ''He recites not only history and the dry sciences verbatim,'' Young reports in his stilted style,

> but no mathematical problem ever confuses him and the classics into fluent English he turns. Howard was an orator who gathered laurels wherever he

spoke. . . . His rapid Spenserian penmanship pronounced him one of the most proficient clerks that ever engrossed bill for the Secretary of State.[14]

Furthermore, Howard employs "invincible logic and masterly philippics" and exhibits unusual "control of the vocal organs and the preternatural gift of a rich melodious voice." [15]

One of the most surprising aspects of these male protagonists is their appearance. The sentimental prerequisite of outstanding beauty in the heroines of nineteenth-century romances is matched in the Black novels by an unusual kind of comeliness in the heroes. Like almost all the rest, Howard has strikingly un-Negroid features. He

was a handsome young man, of medium height, compact, open, affectionate eyes; shapely moulded nose; firm mouth; lips carved with nicety of precision; square cut chin, showing firmness of character. Then, too, the Socratic forehead, the most prominent feature of his well-poised cranium, stood out in philosophic conspicuousness in contradistinction to members of his class (p. 35).

Young's mention of Howard's difference from others of his "class," rather than from members of his race, is revealing, for although the reader is made vaguely aware that the characters are Black, Howard's skin color is never mentioned. Although his heroine is dark, Young wishes his characters accepted simply as human beings, uncomplicated by racial designations. The story itself has nothing explicitly to do with racial matters and could as easily have been about whites.[16]

Frank Webb's tale *The Garies and Their Friends* (1857)—which is definitely involved with problems of the African-Americans, particularly free Blacks in the North before the Civil War—introduces the unique Mr. Walters, a Black millionaire. Walters, the most financially successful of the characters in these books, is a force for racial justice, moving sympathetic whites into action against oppressors like Lawyer Stevens. He rallies Blacks into a unit for self-defense against Stevens's rampaging mobs, provides funds and shelter to the victimized, and urges militance of a self-defensive sort. These actions correspond with those of the hero of any adventure story and, since superhuman powers are not attributed to Walters, are entirely believable.

The source of his fortune, however, seems less likely. Although wealthy Blacks did exist in this country in the nineteenth century, they essentially made their money by catering to the Black community. Madame C. J. Walker, whose skin whiteners and hair straighteners brought her fortune and fame, is an example. John Hope Franklin also records that "in 1898 there were two real estate agents in New York City worth more than $150,000 each, and one in Cleveland had property valued at $100,000." [17] Walters, however, is depicted as an extremely successful realtor with hundreds of homes in all sections of Philadelphia, renting and selling to both white and Black.

However, it is in the area of personal appearance, not occupation or monetary worth, that the greatest idealization of this character occurs:

> Mr. Walters was above six feet in height, and exceedingly well-proportioned; of jet-black complexion and smooth glossy skin. His head was covered with a quantity of woolly hair, which was combed back from a broad but not very high forehead. His eyes were small, black and piercing, and set deep in his head. His aquiline nose, thin lips, and broad chin, were the very reverse of African in their shape, and gave his face a very singular appearance. In repose, his countenance was severe in its expression; but when engaged in agreeable conversation, the thin sarcastic-looking lips would part, displaying a set of dazzlingly white teeth, and the small black eyes would sparkle with animation (pp. 121-22).

Because of the novelists' own indoctrination with popular white standards of beauty, in all of these books, "woolly hair" and dark skin are acceptable for the males, but thick lips and flat noses are not. Perhaps, Walters's appearance is an extremely subtle indication of white blood somewhere in his ancestry, but if so, Webb never makes this explicit. More likely, Webb wishes his protagonist to be a convincing hero of a romance, and to be accepted, he had to conform as nearly as possible to the conventional white physical type.

A character similarly described, who definitely is not of mixed blood, is Jerome, the protagonist in *Clotelle*. "This slave," William Wells Brown reports,

> was of pure African origin, was perfectly black, very fine-looking, tall, slim, and erect as anyone could possibly be. His features were not bad, lips thin, nose prominent, hands and feet small. His brilliant black eyes lighted up his whole countenance. His hair which was nearly straight, hung in curls upon his lofty brow. . . . He was brave and daring, strong in person; fiery in spirit, yet kind and true in his affections, earnest in his doctrines.[18]

Jerome is presented as a superb representation of the American slave class because he is "of pure African origin" and "perfectly black," yet to be an acceptable popular hero, he is endowed with thin lips, small hands and feet, and "nearly straight" hair that curls poetically across his brow. Nowhere in these early novels is the tension between the novelists' desire to portray representative Blacks and their need to conform to white literary and social standards clearer than in *Clotelle*.

Yet even Frederick Douglass, whose narrative of his own escape is one of the most eloquently and powerfully written, succumbs to contemporary literary requirements that protagonists be larger than life when he constructs his historical novella, *The Heroic Slave* (1853). Madison Washington's appearance, nevertheless, is more successful than Jerome's, because Douglass employs a mythic, rather than a popular, description:

In his movements he seemed to combine with the strength of the lion, a lion's elasticity. His torn sleeves disclosed arms like polished iron. His face was "black, but comely." His eyes, lit with emotion, kept guard under a brow as dark and as glossy as the raven's wing. His whole appearance betokened Herculean strength; yet there was nothing savage or forbidding in his aspect. . . . A giant's strength, but not a giant's heart was in him.[19]

Unlike Jerome, with his thin lips and prominent nose, Madison's "broad mouth and nose spoke only of good nature and kindness" (p. 40). He exhibits the suppleness of the lion, the beauty of the raven, and the strength of a Hercules. While such qualities represent racial idealization, Douglass's story is grounded in fact, the actual mutiny aboard the slave ship *Creole;* therefore it is appropriate to emphasize his hero's strength and "genius" (p. 64).

Moreover, Douglass skillfully illuminates Washington's psychological turmoil, which explains his willingness to risk an escape attempt and a mutiny once he is recaptured. His realization of the possible consequences—"if I am caught, I shall only be a slave. If I am shot, I shall only lose a life which is a burden and a curse"—and his resolution, "I shall be free" (pp. 39, 40), are spoken as convincingly as Douglass's anguished probing of his own situation in his *Narrative.*[20]

A much more alarming indication of the influence of white models upon the black novelists is the fact that more than half of the male protagonists in the books are mulattoes. Such characterization was traditional in abolitionist works. Light-skinned George Harris, for example, easily steals Stowe's novel from Black Uncle Tom. As Sterling Brown notes, "some antislavery authors seemed to believe that submissiveness was a mystical African quality and used mulattoes for their rebellious heroes, attributing militancy and intelligence to a white heritage."[21]

This feeling may have prompted the relationship in J. McHenry Jones's *Hearts of Gold* (1896) between Clement St. John and his dark-skinned friend, Lotus Stone. Jones's attitude toward St. John's odd pigmentation is ambiguous. St. John is not only light; he is an albino and has the questionable distinction of being the only ugly protagonist in these books. Despite his colorless skin, marked here and there by "an ugly freckle," his shock of "stiff and bristly" reddish-brown hair, his "sickly mustache of faded red," and his "scanty row of disarranged eyebrows," he clearly belongs in the ranks of the idealized fighters for his race.[22]

Jones's intent in making him so repulsive is never clear. Perhaps he is meant to be symbolic of the race as a whole, to demonstrate the presence of talents never allowed to develop because of America's obsession with appearance. It is he, not Lotus, who performs most of the effective, courageous, and racially uplifting action in the novel. Besides being the editor and publisher of a successful Black newspaper, he is called upon to rescue Lotus from the convict labor camp where the doctor has been imprisoned after being falsely accused and convicted of malpractice. Regina, Jones's heroine, discovers Lotus's whereabouts and urgently writes to St. John for help. St. John responds immediately and travels to the camp, where there has been an uprising among the prisoners. He finds Lotus close to death and nurses him back to health, meanwhile feverishly writing newspaper accounts of conditions in the prison and successfully petitioning the governor for the doctor's release. Lotus, throughout all of this activity and to a large degree throughout the entire book, is completely passive. His one act of bravery, a personal one not related to racial betterment, comes early in the novel, when he rescues Regina during an accident aboard an excursion boat.

John Saunders of *Appointed,* also a mulatto, is not the chosen one of the title; his white friend, Seth Stanley, fulfills that role. He serves, nevertheless, as an educative force in Stanley's life. At the beginning of the book, Stanley is completely ignorant of the injustice faced by Blacks. Through his travels with his white friend and eventual martyrdom in the South, Saunders serves to educate both the reader and the young white man about racial oppression in both parts of the country.

The primary role of another mulatto, Dr. Frank Latimer in Frances E. W. Harper's *Iola Leroy* (1892), seems limited to marrying the heroine in the end. Nevertheless, he merits some attention by his frequent confounding of prejudiced whites who, fooled by the fairness of his skin, are favorably impressed with him until they discover his race. His white grandmother, a wealthy aristocrat, offers to adopt him legally on the condition that he sever all his connections with Blacks. This he refuses to do and, instead, dedicates his life to practicing medicine among the poor.

Unlike the other protagonists of mixed blood, Clarence Garie, in *The Garies and Their Friends,* is a weakling, driven to nervous exhaustion by his unsuccessful attempt to pass for white. While unheroic, he does not actively stand in the way of his race's progress. His action in the book is confined to the personal, not the political, realm, and he is definitely a forerunner of the unfortunate mulattoes caught up in the insecurity and guilt of "passing" who became popular character types in the Black novels of the 1920s.

Besides physical appearance and role in the action of the story, another feature of characterization that links the Black novels to the popular fiction of their day is the use of elegant and elaborate diction. Since most of the high-toned speeches issue from the mouths of slaves or former slaves, the language is incongruous and increases the artificiality of the books.

After his proposal of marriage is accepted, Howard in *Selene*—admittedly, a college student, not a slave—exclaims, "Unexpected joy! Am I myself; or is this scene another flitting image of a blank ideal? Relieve my suspense! Satisfy my bewildered brain! When do we marry?" (p. 64). It is hard to believe that even a college student in the nineteenth century could direct such arch diction at his ladylove without choking on the tongue in his cheek. Howard, nevertheless, expects to be taken seriously by both Selene and the reader.

Lotus Stone and Clement St. John, in *Hearts of Gold,* indulge in long conversations about racial prejudice, couching their despair and outrage in the most subdued and genteel of terms. In one of their high-flown conversations, they compare their status to that of sand castles buffeted by "the white caps of real life" and destroyed by tides that they cannot stem. It is inconceivable that any genuine feeling about the injustice of racism could be expressed in these delicate phrases. Consequently, the speakers appear as detached dilettantes, attempting to outdo each other with metaphors.

Jerome in *Clotelle* is also incongruously eloquent, although not as artificial in his expression as Lotus and Clement. After being jailed for attempting to escape from his master, Mr. Wilson, he announces in ringing tones:

"My liberty is as of much consequence to me as Mr. Wilson's is to him. I am as sensitive to feeling as he. If I mistake not, the day will come when the negro will learn that he can get his freedom by fighting for it; and should that time arrive, the whites will be sorry that they have hated us so shamefully. I am free to say that could I live my life over again I would use all the energies which God has given me to get up an insurrection" (p. 65).

Jerome's future as a militant slave leader never materializes. His impassioned speech, then, is not prophetic. It does not foreshadow future action in the novel, but exists primarily to paint Jerome as brave, eloquent, and intelligent, required attributes for any nineteenth-century hero of popular romance.[23] Such a portrayal, because of the language used to bolster it, rings hollow. Jerome is a field hand who was taught to read and write by Clotelle; she, in turn, was instructed by her octoroon mother, who received her education at the knee of an old freedwoman. While some excuse might be found for the high-flown eloquence of Jones's Lotus and Clement or Young's Howard, young men trained, after all, in the North after the Civil War, pleas for freedom couched in elegant, genteel diction drop with a thud from the lips of the haphazardly educated slave, Jerome. Despite his overall artistic superiority to Brown, Frederick Douglass is not above permitting his apparently uneducated hero to lament that "these birds, perched on yon swinging boughs, in friendly conclave, sounding forth their merry notes in seeming worship of the rising sun, though liable to the sportsman's fowling-piece, are still my superiors" (p. 39).

Obviously, then, one of the most difficult aspects of characterization with which the early novelists grappled was the realistic rendering of Black speech. Discussing the problems of recapturing the language of the nineteenth-century southern Black, Mike Thelwell, in *William Styron's Nat Turner,* observes:

The only vestiges we can find of the real language of the slaves are in the few spirituals which have come to us, which give a clue to its true tenor . . . .
Lacking complicated syntactical structure and vast vocabulary, it de-

pends on what linguists call para-language; that is, gesture, physical expression, and modulation of cadences and intonation which serve to change meaning—in incredibly subtle ways—of the same collection of words. It is intensely poetic and expressive, since vivid simile, creative and effective juxtaposition of images, and metaphor must serve in the absence of a large vocabulary to cause the audience to see and feel. It is undoubtedly a language of action rather than a language of reflection, and thus more available to the dramatist than the novelist.[24]

Unable to employ most of the elements of "para-language," the early Black novelists, in general, turned away from the rhythms, aphorisms, and poetry of Black speech. While these realistic elements are present to a degree in the dialogue of their minor characters, the language of the major protagonists imitates the artificial diction of white heroes and heroines. If such arcane speech is unbelievable in the mouths of white characters in popular fiction, it is doubly destructive when assigned to Blacks. Instead of speaking aphoristically, expressing the folk wisdom of their people, they spontaneously compose couplets; rather than observing and analyzing their situation, they deliver orations. Clearly, the propaganda motive reinforced the literary influence on the Black novelists' understanding of the "proper" diction for their characters. Blacks were ridiculed in white plantation and Reconstruction humor for the rough rhythms, slurred words, malapropisms, and quaint images in their language. In order to escape this degrading image, the Black novelists sped to the other extreme of creating cultured mulattoes or delicately featured, dark-skinned, male protagonists who expressed themselves in the arch tones of "respectable" white heroes.

The women in these novels are drawn in essentially the same exaggerated way as their male counterparts. Traditional white concepts of beauty are even more influential in their portrayal, however, as only one of the Black heroines is dark-skinned; all the rest are mulattoes. Only Kennett Young, cautioning that "beauty cannot be restricted to any particular color" (p. 6), portrays a dark woman who is central to his story. Selene, like the other heroines, is not only beautiful, however: she is extraordinarily beautiful. She and the others are also extraordinarily intelligent, extraordinarily talented, and extraordinarily virtuous. This excess of virtues results, needless to say, in extraordinarily unreal characters.

Selene plays the piano and violin, sings enchantingly, glides like a dancer, and is given to impassioned, multilingual expressions of feeling:

As she was quitting the room, she said, in soliloquy, "Ye temple of Learning, within whose walls I've looked wistfully on the fountain of knowledge; ye ghostly spectres, that flit upon the walls of my room; thou songster, that cometh to cheer my drooping heart; and thou, blushing beauty of the night, that hast ever come to dispel gloom with thy radiant

rays of light and love, I say to thee, one and all, for the time and place, farewell!''

Turning for a last glance, she says, ''Thou ghost of Virgil, if such thou art, and in his language, 'vale! vale! untrique, vale!' '' (p. 29).

This melancholy, sensitive creature, prone to apostrophes to nature and to Virgil ''in his language,'' was intended not as a caricature, as the modern reader might take her, but as a representation of the potential for refinement in the Black woman. She is both the ultimate in sentimental, romantic heroines and a propaganda device intended to educate whites to Black possibilities and to inspire Blacks to self-development. Young's concept of self-development is, of course, a reflection of the absurdities of popular white characterization.

All the other heroines are fair-skinned and practically interchangeable. Clotelle will serve as representative of the lot. Like Selene, she is gorgeous: ''Her tall and well-developed figure; her long silky black hair, falling in curls down her swan-like neck; her bright, black eyes lighting up her olive-tinted face, and a set of teeth that a Tuscarora might envy, she was a picture of tropical ripened beauty'' (p. 8).

Also like Selene, she is given to poetic expression. As a matter of fact, when sufficiently aroused, Clotelle speaks in couplets! To her first husband, the Frenchman Antoine Devenant, who helps her to escape slavery and takes her to France, she whispers, ''Away, away, o'er land and sea / America is now no home for me'' (p. 82). This spontaneous ability does not fail her when, years later, after Devenant's death, she is found in France by Jerome. She boldly assures him, ''No power in death shall tear our names apart / As none in life could rend thee from my heart'' (p. 98).

Clotelle, of course, is completely virtuous. She is ''open, frank, free, and generous to a fault'' and ''always thought of others, never of her own welfare'' (p. 70). This generosity is demonstrated when she exchanges places with Jerome in his jail cell, allowing him to escape. Like the male protagonists, she is eloquent in defense of racial equality. To her white father, who rebukes her for marrying Jerome, she asserts: ''I married him . . . because I love him. Why should the white man be esteemed better than the black? I find no difference in men on account of their complexion. One of the cardinal principles of Christianity and freedom is the equality and brotherhood of man'' (p. 103).

Interestingly, several of the middle-class African-American writers themselves appear not entirely convinced that the popular concepts about Black people were completely false. They, too, sometimes accept common racial stereotypes. Although the banjo-picking, hand-clapping, happy darky of conventional plantation fiction appears in none of their books as a major figure, Kennett Young, for one, makes sure that his heroine demonstrates the race's traditional musical ability. Predictably, Selene's taste runs to classical music, which she performs on both the piano and the violin. Only her ability to play two instruments equally well, but not her natural talent, appears unusual to Young:

The power of a great pianist and the power of a gifted violinist is seldom possessed by one and the same person; that is, the power to move, reaching the sublime and awakening the emotions of the listener. But members of that race, whose sorrow for ages had been appeased through the rhythmic chord of their soul, have inherited the principles of its beauty, and careful training makes them artists rare and of immeasurable scope (pp. 78-79).

Selene, thus, becomes a counterstereotype who, despite her penchant for the classics rather than for spirituals or jigs, indicates her creator's acceptance of a popular notion about his race. Despite Young's constant attempts to divorce Selene from limiting, degrading stereotypes, she has still "got rhythm." His primary concern is to suggest that African-Americans need only to have their banjos replaced by violins to demonstrate the race's potential for "culture."

Other examples of the early Black writers' difficulty in dealing with popular racial assumptions can be found in comments by William Wells Brown, J. McHenry Jones, and James H. W. Howard. In *Clotelle,* Brown contributes to the exoticism and mystery surrounding African-Americans in popular representations of them by observing that "few persons can arrive at anything approaching the real age of the Negro by mere observation, unless they are well acquainted with the race" (p. 11). Jones substantiates the white novelists' portraits of the contented slave by remarking in *Hearts of Gold* that "the Afro-American is proverbially cheerful. He banishes sorrow as an evanescent dream" (p. 17). And in *Bond and Free* (1886), James H. W. Howard does nothing to calm the widespread fear of miscegenation fanned by pro-slavery writers when he asserts that "there is an open secret which existed in the accursed days of slavery, and which exists among the race today. That secret is, that a real black man is generally extremely partial to very light women" (p. 40).

Elsewhere in his book, Howard uses the mulatto slave, Elva, to illustrate another degrading racial generality. Elva, he says, possessed an intelligence that

was remarkable, and she possessed all of those qualities peculiar to her sex. Perhaps the admixture of Indian and Anglo-Saxon blood in her veins answered for the possession of these qualities. But making such an admission as this strengthens a theory which was quite prevalent in the days of slavery and, perhaps, exists among a few Negro-haters today—that a Negro is incapable of any deep thought. Nevertheless, Elva was thinking and rolling out dough at the same time (p. 15).

Howard's conclusion about this racial theory of intelligence remains ambiguous. The reader wonders why he theorizes that Elva's intelligence is due to her Indian and Anglo-Saxon blood as some "Negro-haters" believed if he had no intention of soundly refuting this assumption. Perhaps he, like the audience whom he hoped to reach, had been so completely indoctrinated with such attitudes that he found it impossible to insist upon Black ability. Once again, the insidious power of a national attitude can be seen undermining the Black man's faith in his own intelligence.

In the preface to *Selene,* undoubtedly one of the most artificial of the early novels, Kennett Young insists, "Personal acquaintance with the leading characters of this story is had, and a just delineation of them, without equivocation, is attempted. Nothing is overdrawn, for personal knowledge of incidents herein recorded, is recorded as those incidents have recurred to the mind." Young reveals that he was at school with the prototype of Howard. It is unfortunate that another writer was not sufficiently impressed with the actual Howard so as to produce a biography of him, for a comparison of Young's schoolmate with the hero of his novel would reveal which attributes were considered necessary to add and which to subtract or change in order to transform him into the proper hero of a nineteenth-century novel. Despite his assertion of realistic intent, Young's story is filled with counterstereotypic characters and melodramatic episodes that destroy its force as art and must have weakened even its effectiveness as propaganda.

No doubt, all of the early Black authors intended to write moving tales peopled with believable characters. They also, however, wished to produce novels in the accepted mode of the time and to write propaganda powerful enough to sway their readers' minds and hearts in favor of the African-Americans and the alleviation of their condition. These mixed intents, in view of the literary techniques chosen, proved incompatible.

The white characters appearing in these novels fall into two broad classifications, the "poor white trash," all except one of whom are threats to the Blacks, and the more cultured and refined white men and women of means. Howard, in *Bond and Free,* paints a general picture of the poor whites, a people whom even the slaves despised. Howard's Silvers family belongs to this lower class, rejected by the wealthy plantation owners, mistrusted by the slaves, and treated with contempt by the freedmen. With the exception of Sallie Silvers, who is taught to read by the slave Purcey and later aids in her escape, all the poor whites depicted in the novels are enemies of Black freedom. Dreaded overseers were often selected from their ranks, as were "nigger-traders" and kidnappers. Whatever their social or economic status, however, the whites who are helpful to Blacks are generally portrayed as refined and the slave owners, slave catchers, and northern racists as repellent.

The description of Dick Jennings, a slave trader in *Clotelle,* is typical: "A more repulsive-looking person could scarcely be found in any community of bad looking men. Tall, lean and lank, with high cheek-bones, face much pitted with small-pox, gray eyes with red eyebrows, and sandy whiskers, he indeed stood alone without mate or fellow in looks" (p. 10). A similar description is given in *The Garies and Their Friends* of slaveholders in general. Revealing how northern Blacks working in hotels can immediately recognize transplanted southerners, Webb says:

When a gentleman presented himself at the bar wearing boots entirely too small for him, with his hat so far down upon his forehead as to obscure his eyes, and whose mouth was filled with oaths and tobacco, he was generally looked upon as a favorable specimen to operate upon; and if he cursed the waiters, addressed any old waiter among them as "boy" and was continually drinking cocktails and mint-juleps, they were sure of their man (p. 41).

Abraham Biggers, a wealthy slaveholder in *Bond and Free* was

short in stature, heavily built, stub-feet, stub-hands, and stub-nose. His head was round and his neck short and thick. He looked out of two very restless and small eyes, overhung with large shaggy eyebrows while all over his countenance could be discerned low cunning, cruelty, and utter meanness (p. 29).

Other upper-class whites range from the villainous Dr. Leighton, who frames Lotus Stone and attempts to murder the heroine of *Hearts of Gold,* to the sympathetic Mr. Garie, who marries a mulatto, one of his former slaves, and moves to the North to ease her fears concerning the future of their children. Thomas Stevens, the instigator of most of the evil in *The Garies and Their Friends,* is both comic and sinister:

He was rather above than below middle height, with round shoulders, and long, thin arms, finished off by disagreeable-looking hands. His head was bald on top, and the thin greyish-red hair, that grew more thickly about his ears, was coaxed up to that quarter, where an attempt had been made to effect such a union between the cords of the hair from each side as should cover the place in question. . . . His baldness might have given an air of benevolence to his face, but for the shaggy eyebrows that over-shadowed his cunning looking grey eyes. His cheek-bones were high, and the cadaverous skin was so tightly drawn across them as to give a very parchment-like appearance. Around his thin, compressed lips there was a continual, nervous twitching, that added greatly to the sinister aspect of his face (p. 124).

In contrast, William Wells Brown presents *Clotelle's* Reverend James Wilson, who defensively uses the Bible to justify his slaveholding, as "a good-looking man about fifty years of age, with a white neck-tie, and a pair of gold-rimmed glasses" (p. 56). His daughter, Georgiana, northern-educated with abolitionist sentiments, is "tall and graceful, her features regular and well-defined, and her complexion . . . illuminated by the freshness of youth, beauty, and health" (p. 73). Georgiana belongs to that class of white females, popular in abolitionist views of the South, who were constantly sickening and dying because of their proximity to the suffering of slaves. Although now and then she has some effect in softening her father's demeanor toward his bondsmen, she is, ultimately, ineffective. Georgiana faints and expires from a ruptured blood vessel when she discovers that her father has had Clotelle flogged for helping Jerome to escape. Made of sturdier stuff, Clotelle survives her beating and goes on for more harrowing adventures.

That not all northern-educated southerners returned with a new understanding of the humanity of Blacks is proved by Henry Linwood, a graduate of Harvard, who buys Isabella. He keeps her as his mistress even after he marries and then, weary of the discomforts of the relationship, weakly permits his mother-in-law, Mrs. Miller, to sell her and Clotelle, their daughter. Linwood is only sketchily drawn, as is his wife, who is sympathetic to Clotelle, but is also too weak-willed to oppose her mother.

Mrs. Miller, who sells Isabella to the disgusting slave trader Jennings and delights in degrading Clotelle, is a cruel harridan: "a woman of little or no feeling, proud, peevish, and passionate, thus making everybody miserable that came near her; and when she disliked any one, her hatred knew no bounds" (p. 33). She "thunders" commands at her slaves; her eyes "flash fire"; she stalks up and down her room "like a caged lioness." Perhaps the source of her rage at discovering her son-in-law's infidelity is the fact that her own husband fathered seven mulatto children.

The only virtuous white man developed to any degree in this book is the aristocratic Antoine Devenant, who marries Clotelle and rescues her from slavery. A French soldier on vacation in America when he spots the girl at a slave auction, Devenant is described as romantically as Jerome, Brown's Black protagonist: "Over his noble brow clustering locks of glossy hair were hanging in careless ringlets. His finely-cut classical features wore the aspect of one possessed with a large and noble heart" (p. 82). Brown's mention of Devenant's "noble heart" becomes unintentionally funny when, at the soldier's first glimpse of Clotelle, he suffers a reaction that outside the high-voltage atmosphere of sentimental fiction would be diagnosed as a coronary attack: "He felt shortness of breath, his heart palpitated, his head grew dizzy, and his limbs trembled; but he knew not its cause. This was the first stage of 'love at first sight' " (p. 75).

Like *Clotelle, The Garies and Their Friends* presents a rare instance of a relationship between a white man and a mulatto woman that is legitimized by marriage. Frank Webb avoids any physical description of Mr. Garie and permits him to speak naturally. Although some amount of description would have aided in his realization, the subdued way in which he is handled makes him and his marriage much more believable than the high-strung relationship between Devenant and Clotelle. He is presented as a good-intentioned man, saddened, but not despondent, about the social ostracism that he and his family must suffer in the South and naively unsuspecting of any further threats to their happiness once they move to the North. Webb's thesis, however, argues for the similarity of northern and southern racial oppression. Consequently, both Garies are killed during one of Lawyer Stevens's raids.

The most successful Black/white relationships depicted are the friendships of John Saunders and Seth Stanley in *Appointed* and that of Madison Washington and the appropriately named Mr. Listwell in *The Heroic Slave*. Saunders and Stanley were classmates at the University of Michigan. After graduation, because of racism, Saunders is unable to find a position in which he can use his training as a civil engineer and accepts the unrewarding post of a clerk in Stanley's father's office. Whenever Stanley, who belongs to an idle, rich set, needs someone to serve as valet on his yacht, it is Saunders who is temporarily relieved of his duties at the office to fulfill this menial function. Close companionship on the yacht, however, leads to a genuine friendship between the two, which is strengthened (in a prophetic pre-Hemingway touch) during a vacation in the Michigan woods. Saunders reveals to Stanley his career disappointments and growing hopelessness; Stanley, on his part, confides to his new friend particulars of his relationship with Margaret, the girl whom he wishes to marry, details that he has been careful to conceal even from his white friends. These details are not sexual, or even particularly romantic, but concern Stanley's worries about "deserving" someone as virtuous as Margaret.

It is through his acquaintance with John Saunders that Seth Stanley is drawn slowly out of a selfish, wasteful life and made aware of the sufferings of others. Toward the book's end, Stanley's Christian name is symbolically interpreted by Saunders and an important role for him in the future of his country predicted: "Stanley's Christian name, Seth, is from the Hebrew, and its meaning is Appointed. Who can tell but what he may be APPOINTED of God to help bring this fearful race question to a peaceful and successful solution" (p. 290). Despite this optimistic prophecy, the book ends shortly after Saunders's death; and Seth, shaken and certainly more aware of the dangers for Blacks, is, nevertheless, not developed to a point at which he might attempt to remedy the situation. Like Jerome in *Clotelle,* he seems an example of unfulfilled promise, due to a failure of authorial energy and imagination.

Listwell is more successful in aiding Douglass's protagonist, Madison Washington. A farmer from Ohio who becomes a staunch abolitionist, the white man, like the shrewd Quakers in *Clotelle,* befriends the hero during his flight to the North. Later, after Washington is recaptured and en route to the deep South, Listwell slips him the files that he uses to free himself and his fellow mutineers. Listwell's abolitionist feelings and compassion for the young slave are made believable by Douglass's probing of the farmer's thoughts and self-image. Nevertheless, his propitious appearance at critical moments in the hero's life is too contrived and patronizing to be completely effective.

The white characters in the early Black novels, in large degree, then, share the artificial portraiture of the Black protagonists. The white villains, in particular, are painted in the most lurid tints. In a switch on the popular tradition, however, the whites remain in the background for the most part and are frequently only sketchily drawn.

A much more realistically and imaginatively compelling group are the secondary Black characters. As both human beings and as Blacks living in nineteenth-century America, they are immensely more believable than the major protagonists. It is from the mouths of these minor figures, usually common slaves or emancipated "uncles" and "aunties," that the resonant chords of Black humor are sounded and the fancies of African-American folklore take flight. Such figures provide ballast for books otherwise riddled with the clichés and didacticism of romance and propaganda.

Nevertheless, it is among these minor figures that Black stereotypes from plantation and Reconstruction fiction can most easily be found. In *Iola Leroy,* for example, the reader is presented with loyal, old Uncle Daniel, who refuses to accompany the younger slaves in their attempt to run away and join the Yankees. Secretly entrusted with his master's family fortune, Uncle Daniel insists that he must remain on the plantation and care for the women and children until young "Marster Robert" comes back from battle:

> "Marster Robert has been mighty good to me. He stood by me in my troubles, and now his trouble's come, I'm a gwine to stan' by him. . . . I specs dem Yankees be all right, but I knows Marse Robert, an' I don't know them, an' I ain't a gwine ter throw away dirty water 'til I gits clean." [25]

Despite the degrading, postbellum insistence that all "good niggers" were faithful retainers, Uncle Daniel is not without historical validity, and his portrait does not strike the reader as completely false. There are known instances of slaves entrusted with the safety and fortunes of white families, the heads of which had gone off to fight for secession. More importantly, Harper's rendering of the imagery and rhythm of folk speech is sensitive enough to humanize Uncle Daniel simply through his manner of self-expression.

Closely related to the tradition of the contented, loyal slave is that distortion, the comic darky who is fond, like Uncle Remus, of spinning yarns or who continually and unconsciously demonstrates his inferiority by his absurd antics and ludicrous pride. To fit the image, *Clotelle* contains Sam, a self-satisfied house servant who

> seldom let a day pass without spending an hour or two in combing and brushing his "har." He had an idea that fresh butter was better for his hair than any other kind of grease, and therefore on churning days half a pound of butter had always to be taken out before it was salted. When he wished to appear to great advantage, he would grease his face to make it "shiny" (p. 22).

Sam is fond of entertaining the other servants with stories of his exploits. His tales all attest to his absurd pride, rationalization of his errors, blind luck, and particular good fortune in having a kind master. Exactly such qualities were attributed to scores of Sambos in the writings of the southern humorists. When Sam is a servant to a local doctor and fancies himself learned in his master's practice, he becomes known as the "Black Doctor" among the slaves. One of his patients has a toothache, and Sam sweats and struggles to pull the offending molar, only to discover that he has had his pliers around a perfectly healthy tooth all the while. His rationalization of this situation is to console himself "with the thought that as the wrong tooth was out of the way, there was more room to get at the right one" (p. 25).

There occurs an episode in which he mistakenly mixes a prescription for pills with one for ointment, then finally combines the two compounds, rolling them into pellets and deceptively labels them simply "pills." After the patient who takes them actually recovers, Sam

> immediately ran into the kitchen amongst his companions and commenced dancing.
>
> "What de matter wid you?" inquired the cook.
>
> "I is de greatest doctor in dis country," replied Sam. "Ef you ever get sick, call on me. No matter what ails you, I is de man dat can cure you in no time. If you do hab de backache, de rheumatics, de headache, de collar morbus, fits, any ting else, Sam is de gentleman dat can put you on your feet wid his pills" (p. 27).

This episode appears to be very loosely based on Brown's own experience as a doctor's helper before he escaped from the South.[26]

Not all of Sam's escapades turn out so happily. When the doctor discovers that while he was asleep, Sam had worn his best suit, boots, and gold watch to a "Negro ball" and had ridden there on his best saddle horse, Sam is unable to worm his way out of the situation:

> After breakfast, Sam was taken into the barn, tied up, and severely flogged with the cat, which brought from him the truth concerning his absence the previous night. This forever put an end to his fine appearance at the negro parties. Had not the doctor been one of the most indulgent masters, he would not have escaped with merely a severe whipping (p. 28).

This incident appears to be the only one in which an actual folk motif was utilized by Brown. In *Lay My Burden Down: A Folk History of Slavery,* Benjamin Botkin includes a tale called "The Boots That Couldn't Come Off," which concerns Abraham, a houseboy who ruins his master's boots and horse in an escapade similar to Sam's:

> His master was awful mad and said he was a good mind to take the hide off Abraham's back. . . . Then poor Abraham had to out and tell the whole story, and his master got to laughing so 'bout how he took all the gals away

from the other boys and how them boots hurt him that it looked like he never could stop. When he finally did stop laughing and shaking his sides, he said: "That's all right, Abraham. Don't never let nobody beat your time with the gals." And that's all he ever said to Abraham 'bout it.[27]

Sam, however, is "severely flogged with the cat" by his "indulgent" master. Abraham's ability to make his owner laugh at his adventures, a traditional slave method of avoiding punishment, literally saves his skin. Brown, however, ignores this self-preserving deception and shows his houseboy receiving the punishment that he "deserves." The entrenchment of the humorous darky stereotype in the popular imagination is attested to by the fact that Brown, who had escaped from slavery himself, could incorporate an instance of severe flogging with the cat into a novel about injustice to the Black man and cap it with no comment other than a completely nonironic reference to Sam's "indulgent" master. Since the book's other instances of cruelty against slaves are accompanied with expressions of outrage from Brown, Sam's activities can properly be seen as psychologically unreal matter, literary trappings to an accepted humorous portrayal.[28]

Although Sam's type of minstrel humor is usually confined to minor characters in the early African-American novels, and comic dialect most often distinguishes these lowly actors from the more serious protagonists, Brown places even his eloquent hero, Jerome, in a burlesque situation. In exile in England, the escaped slave, unaccustomed to horseback riding, finds himself invited to a fox hunt. Unable to make his mount jump the first fence and terrified of being thrown, he pleads a sudden illness and ignominiously trots back to the stables. The English family with whom he is staying calls the doctor, providing Brown with an opportunity for several passages of low comedy involving tepid baths and the application of leeches, all of which remedies, of course, leave Jerome a physical wreck. Since the fox-hunting episode is an isolated incident, having no bearing upon the plot, the reader can assume only that it is included because Brown wishes to introduce a little comic relief and realizes that such slapstick is customary in stories dealing with the activities of Blacks.

In addition to its influence on characterization, the popular tradition clearly affected the plots of these early works. Most of the novels are extremely episodic, sometimes moving from one violent conflict to the next with only character description in between. At their least successful, these incidents are highly charged, relying upon coincidence and sentimentality for their effect; at their best, they are dramatic, realistic depictions of the conditions of slavery and caste. In other words, at their weakest, these episodes are similar to those melodramatic and sentimental scenes that riddled popular white fiction; and in their most compelling moments, they approach the energy and realism present in the slave narratives of the earlier part of the century.

Sentimental scenes abound, scenes focusing upon unfortunate and heartrending events designed to arouse sadness and sympathy in the reader. Frequently, nature is shown reflecting the characters' emotions or the authors' judgments of the action. Closely related to these sentimental episodes are many melodramatic conflicts, usually clashes between Black characters representing Good and white characters representing Evil. Just as a romantic rendering of nature is used to reinforce the melancholy of the sentimental scenes, the melodramatic episodes are enhanced by gothic overtones of flickering candles, dark shadows, bloody stains, hints of the supernatural, and a general atmosphere of horror.

Carl Van Doren has observed that after the Civil War the conflict between romance and realism in fiction broke out in earnest:

> Granted, controversy finally ran, that real persons and events should of course be represented, ought they to be merely everyday persons and events . . . or ought they instead to be selected with a view of making more of heightened moments and superior men and women than could be made of the commonplace? [29]

The Black novelists of the period, like most of their white counterparts, clearly opted for "superior men and women" and "heightened moments."

One such moment occurs in *Selene* as a scene of bitter renunciation between Howard and Felicia, who has falsely accused him of reneging on a promise to marry her. "Felicia Randolph," Howard cries, "—for you are unworthy the name of another—you shall never again look upon my face" (p. 24). Crushed by this threat, Felicia shortly dies of a broken heart or, as Young puts it, is "ruthlessly torn from the role by Death's impartial hand" (p. 25).

Like this episode, the other sentimental scenes in these books almost always involve love and foreshadow death. In *Clotelle,* when Isabella discovers that Linwood has secretly married another, Brown provides her with an emotional setting, flooded with melancholy moonbeams that heighten her exotic beauty. She is also given an improbable, heart-tugging speech to deliver tremblingly, before falling to the ground in a swoon, a foreshadowing of her upcoming persecution and death at the hands of slave catchers.

Sentimental scenes, moreover, are not confined to earthly locales. After Isabella's death, Clotelle is sold into slavery with her father's silent consent. Many years later, when Linwood meets his daughter in a hotel in Europe, "tears rushed to his eyes, and turning upon his heel, he went back to his own room. It was then that Isabella was revenged; and she no doubt looked smilingly down from her home in the spiritland on the scene below" (p. 55). Both the enlargement of Brown's southern and European landscape to include a hovering heaven and the concept of Isabella as a vengeful saint are ridiculous, superfluous touches that distract the reader's attention from a potentially dramatic meeting between father and daughter and quickly dissipate any emotion aroused by the recognition scene.

Heart-tugging, deathbed scenes abound. While Dr. Lotus Stone in *Hearts of Gold* is unjustly imprisoned, a fellow convict is severely injured in a mine accident. Because of the inhuman conditions at the prison camp, the wounded man lies neglected until it is too late to save his life. Just as the moon was pulled in to increase Isabella's poignancy in the revelation scene in *Clotelle,* here, too, it is employed to indicate the convict's basic goodness and ultimate salvation. A gust of wind blows out the single, pine-knot torch that has been throwing flickering, eerie shadows on the walls of the dark, stagnant cell. As the light disappears, the convict dies. Clouds over the camp immediately roll back, and a flood of moonlight flows in through the broken roof of the building, shrouding the dead man in "a sheen of silver" (p. 251).

Similar incidents can be found in almost all of the early African-American novels. *Selene,* especially, is choked with melodramatic scenes involving madness and a deathbed episode rivaled only by Little Eva's flight to glory. Irene, Selene's mute daughter, a symbol of the lack of communication between her parents, floats off to join the innumerable orphans and afflicted children of popular romance whose lives and deaths were necessary to provide another catch in the throat to the "true feelers."

Improbable episodes of suspense and violence, usually occurring during slave escapes, appear in almost every one of these novels. Howard's *Bond and Free,* for instance, offers three different tales of escape; eight of the novel's nineteen chapters are directly involved with this subject. *Clotelle,* too, bases much of its interest upon its protagonists' flight from the South. The major difference between these fictional versions of escape and those recounted in the autobiographical slave narratives is that in the novels both the sufferings of slavery itself and the tedium and day-by-day ugliness of a life of running and hiding are heightened dramatically or sentimentalized. Moreover, psychological anguish is slighted in the fiction in favor of physical adventure. Emphasis is placed upon melodramatic or humorous encounters between runaways and slave catchers, breathtaking heroism on the part of escaped slaves, and suspenseful flights by beautiful, "tragic" mulattoes. The most successful of the narratives, on the other hand, achieve their compelling power by emphasizing not only the physical, but also the psychological, suffering of the slave that led him to attempt something as dangerous as an escape and his desperation in the face of the punishment of being sold deeper South to a less careless master, if he were caught.

In *The Garies and Their Friends,* even the genuine danger and excitement of escape are replaced by a scene of gothic horror involving the leading Black protagonist, Mr. Walters, and Lawyer Stevens, who has instigated the death of Mr. Garie, Walters's friend. The scene occurs when Stevens comes forward to identify himself falsely as Garie's heir:

". . . I am, as I said, Mr. Garie's first cousin."

"If you are that, you are more," said Walters fiercely—"You're his murderer!"

At this charge Mr. Stevens turned deathly pale.

"Yes," continued Walters; "you either murdered him, or instigated others to do so! It was you who directed the rioters against both him and me—I have proof of what I say and can produce it—Now your motive is clear as day—you wanted his money, and destroyed him to obtain it! His blood is on your hands!'' hissed Walters through his clenched teeth.

In the excitement consequent upon such a charge, Mr. Stevens, un-noticed by himself, had overturned a bottle of red ink, and its contents had slightly stained his hands. When Walters charged him with having Mr. Garie's blood upon them, he involuntarily looked down and saw his hands stained with red (p. 254).

Appropriately for moralistic fiction, the wages of Stevens's crime are guilt, fear, and misery. Toward the end of his unhappy life, he reveals that he never enjoyed his wealth and has been constantly haunted by visions of his victim:

''And haven't I suffered,'' said he, shaking his bald head mournfully; ''haven't I suffered—look at my gray hairs and half-palsied frame, decrepit before I'm old—sinking into the tomb with a weight of guilt and sin upon me that will crush me down to the lowest depths of hell. Think you,'' he continued, ''that because I am surrounded with all that money can buy, that I am happy; every piece of gold I count out, I see his hands outstretched over it, and hear him whisper 'Mine!' He gives me no peace night or day; he is always by me, I have no rest'' (p. 318).

Suspicious of the origins of her father's wealth, Stevens's daughter tracks down his accomplice, an Irish hoodlum named McClosky, in the paupers' ward of a large city hospital. With his last breath, he tells her of killing Mr. Garie and of her father's masterminding the mob raids upon Black homes. Just as he finishes his tale, McClosky dies of typhus. If this were not enough appeasement of the gods' poetic wrath, Miss Stevens, distraught and on the verge of collapse herself, returns home to find that her father has leaped to his death.

Similarly melodramatic episodes, although generally without Webb's gothic overtones, can be found throughout the other books. Most of the incidents rely heavily on chance revelations and improbable discoveries for their effect. Coincidence, it is fair to say, serves as the major technical device used to develop these narratives and ensure their emotional scenes.

In Jones's *Hearts of Gold,* one complicated example concerns Regina, who like Young's Selene has her correspondence intercepted by the villain. Consequently, she does not hear from Lotus Stone after she goes south. Unknown to either of them, however, the doctor has moved to the same small town where she is teaching school, and the two are unexpectedly reunited at the bedside of one of her favorite pupils. Further coincidences involve a long-lost and extremely important letter being propitiously discovered; a stranger arriving just in time to beat off Regina's attacker; and a train that rumbles onto the scene at the same moment that the villain conveniently falls onto the tracks.

Victoria Earle's *Aunt Lindy* (1893) is a slight sketch built almost entirely upon coincidence. The story involves an elderly couple who suffered the usual torments under slavery and, living out their last days in freedom after the war, are particularly saddened at the thought of their many children who were taken from them and sold. A fire devastates a nearby town, and one of the victims is brought to recuperate at Aunt Lindy's cottage. She immediately recognizes the burnt man as Marse Jeems, her former master. At first seized by a passion for vengeance, she hears the strains of a religious hymn drifting in through the window from a nearby Black church and subdues her hatred. When he is well, Marse Jeems, in an apparently spontaneous character reversal, aids Lindy and Joel financially and finds their first-born son, who just happens to be the new minister at the nearby church.[30]

This device of reuniting long-lost relatives is a favorite one with the Black novelists, growing out of the realities of the slave experience and providing them with opportunities for drama and sentiment. Occasionally, it is true, members of slave families that had been split up on the auction block or were separated when some of them struck out for freedom did find each other again. Most often, they did not. The anguish of losing mothers, husbands, wives, and children was, of course, a very real aspect of slave life, and the novelists recognized in such separations a potential narrative source. Clearly, they also recognized the emotional possibilities in scenes in which missing relatives are rediscovered.

In *Iola Leroy*, Frances Harper employs the situations of a field hospital and a country prayer meeting to make the reunions believable. Robert, a slave introduced early in the book before the heroine realizes that she is partly Black, turns out to be her uncle. They accidentally discover their relationship and set out to find others in the war-scattered family. Iola and Robert uncover his mother, her grandmother, at a country prayer meeting. One of the accepted forms of the religious service is a recounting of personal trials and tribulations by individual members, and through the old woman's revelations she is recognized. Iola and her brother, Harry, have also been separated from each other and from their mother. Harry meets their mother again in an army hospital, where he is recuperating and she is working as a nurse. Later, he finds Iola and the part of the family that she has assembled. Except for the two white fathers involved, the family is, once again, complete. Although the chance meeting of so many relatives strains the reader's credulity, Harper's colorful depiction of the emotional prayer meeting and her description of the crowded field hospital add detail and realism to her account.

William Wells Brown foregoes any such believable setting for the reunion of his main characters. Clotelle and Jerome's reunion could have been lifted unchanged from the pages of any particularly sentimental domestic romance of the period. Several years after his escape from slavery and refuge in England, Jerome becomes exhausted by his strict regime of hard work and study. He decides to vacation in France. While strolling through a French military cemetery one afternoon, he happens upon a valuable and unmistakable clue to the whereabouts of Clotelle, his long-lost love. Brown neglects to explain why Jerome would decide to spend his holiday in a cemetery and how he happens to choose this particular one. To fulfill the demands of romance, after all, his hero and heroine must be reunited by the close of the book. The picture of the lovelier-than-ever Clotelle, accompanied by her fatherless child and bereaved father-in-law, laying a tribute upon her noble husband's grave and, in her sorrow, forgetting a small Bible containing her name and address just where the weary Jerome will pause to rest, provides the author with another opportunity for a customary scene of sorrow and anticipation.

Clotelle also contains an equally improbable reunion scene between Brown's heroine and her father. While on their wedding trip to Germany, Jerome and Clotelle discover that the man in the next hotel room is Henry Linwood. In a scene surpassing Webb's for gothic machinery, Linwood is shown as ill, deranged with fever, and crying aloud that he did and, then, that he did not kill his daughter. All night long, he shrieks and hallucinates while a fierce storm rages outside. Clotelle nurses him through the night, and in the morning both his fever and the storm subside. He receives Clotelle's forgiveness for all past sins against her and her mother and, after a lecture on black-white equality, accepts the dark-skinned Jerome as his new son-in-law. If it is all quite unbelievable, it is also just the sort of tying up of loose ends and emotional distributing of poetic justice that the nineteenth-century reading public applauded.

Speaking of the sentimental novels of popular white authors of the 1850s, Carl Van Doren mentions that pietistic favorites such as Timothy Shay Arthur's *Ten Nights in a Bar-Room* (1854) and Susan Warner's *Wide, Wide World* (1850) emerged from

> a ruck of smaller undertakings which swarmed over literature, coloring the world with pink and white, scenting it with the dry perfume of pressed flowers, quieting it to whispers and gentle sobs, neglecting all the bitter and pungent tastes of life, softening every asperity, hiding every thorn and thought.[31]

Despite the continuing popularity of *Uncle Tom's Cabin,* the majority of readers after the middle of the nineteenth century did not go to fiction for the stark truths of social injustice. It was necessary, then, for the first Black novelists to adapt their racial militancy to an accepted form if they hoped to capture the attention of the American public. Unwilling or unable to experiment stylistically, they clothed their own protagonists in satins and sighs and ran them through a maze of improbable conflicts, urging all the while the acceptance of the Selenes and Jeromes as representative Blacks. As a result, these books often seem completely unlike customary novels, even those as artificial as early white popular fiction. They seem, rather, to be fantasies, embodying in symbolic characters the qualities deemed essential for the success and survival of the race. Nowhere does nineteenth-century America's fancies about itself appear more incongruous than in the novels in which they are adopted by its Black citizens.

Further complicating the expression of the early writers was the problem of their dual audience. The public to whom the novelists hoped to appeal was composed of Black and white readers with conflicting attitudes about African-Americans and race problems. The impact of both literary and nonliterary expectations of this mixed audience increased the tendency in the novels toward either flattering portraiture or condescending portrayals of Blacks and, thereby, reinforced their drift toward unreality. As James Weldon Johnson noted in 1928:

> the Aframerican author faces a special problem which the plain American author knows nothing about—the problem of the double audience. It is more than a double audience; it is a divided audience, an audience made up of two elements with differing and often opposite and antagonistic points of view. His audience is always both white America and black America.[32]

Attempting to explain the abundance of Black stereotypes and conventions of the plantation tradition in the short stories of Paul Laurence Dunbar, Benjamin Brawley attributes them to the literary climate of the times. Dunbar, he explains,

> was naturally influenced by the temper of his period, and by suggestions from editors as to what would make ready appeal. The country was still but thirty years from the Civil War, and there were many who looked back to the olden time with regret. The work of Thomas Nelson Page and Joel Chandler Harris was widely read, and Foster's "My Old Kentucky Home" was to be heard on every hand.[33]

The African-American was viewed as fundamentally different from the Anglo-Saxon, content to be a slave, loyal and docile, happiest when picking a banjo or spinning tales, superstitious and gullible, requiring the stern guidance of an understanding master. Once this ignorant, childlike being was tampered with by outsiders and was forced into the unnatural role of equality with whites, the myth continued, he lost the simple virtues of obedience and loyalty inculcated in him by his previous subservience and developed into an impudent nuisance, if not a depraved, vengeance-seeking beast, as Thomas Dixon, Jr., contended.

According to Saunders Redding, this paradoxical child/beast image of the African-American forced Black writers to choose one of three alternatives for their fiction: "It meant that he must create within the limitations of the concept, or that he must dissemble completely, or that he must ignore his racial kinship altogether and leave unsounded the profoundest depths of the peculiar experiences which were his by reason of that kinship."[34] Dunbar chose the last solution for his novels and presented Blacks as major characters in only one of them. The general Black reaction, however, was to reserve the demeaning plantation image for a few secondary characters and to idealize the main protagonists in their tales. Therefore, their major characters are meant to be counterstereotypes, drawn with the intent of demonstrating the race's beauty, nobility, intelligence, determination, and ambition and, thereby, appeasing the Black middle-class reading public.

In Sutton Griggs's case, a defense of Blacks through fictional demonstrations against the slanders of southern apologists was not sufficient. In the first and second editions of *The Hindered Hand* (1905), Ensal Ellwood and Mr. A. Hostility discuss and condemn the anti-Black position expounded by Thomas Dixon, Jr., in *The Leopard's Spots*. In "A Hindering Hand, Supplementary to *The Hindered Hand:* A Review of the Anti-Negro Crusade of Mr. Thomas Dixon, Jr.," an essay that concludes the third edition of the novel, Griggs removes this discussion from the story altogether and speaks out directly against Dixon's views. Unfortunately, although it follows the main body of the novel, this essay does not increase the artistic unity of the book, but adds yet another element of propaganda to a work already weakened by racial theorizing, political debate, and lengthy proposals for social action.

Furthermore, despite Griggs's resentment of the false picture of the Black proposed by Dixon, he himself fails to create a believable alternative. A reader unaware of Griggs's intentions might believe that he fell into the trap mentioned by Ralph Ellison in *Shadow and Act,* in which he warns Black writers to avoid aiming primarily for a white audience:

> Too many books by Negro writers are addressed to a white audience. By doing this the authors run the risk of limiting themselves to the audience's presumptions of what a Negro is or should be; the tendency is to become involved in polemics, to plead the Negro's humanity. . . . For us the question should be, what are the specific forms of that humanity, and what in our background is worth preserving or abandoning.[35]

Griggs, on the contrary, specifically intended his books as guides for Black readers. The presence of polemics and artificial characters in his novels indicates that writing for the Black audience in the early part of the century presented, in many ways, the same problems as writing for the white.

Both the African-American writer and the Black reading public had been trained to accept and to aspire to the standards of the white majority. This acculturation led to what Ellison, Langston Hughes, and other Black critics have long recognized as a serious problem of identity within the minority community. Ellison notes that

> all Negroes affirm certain feelings of identity, certain foods, certain types of dancing, music, religious experiences, certain tragic attitudes toward experience and toward our situation as Americans. You see, we do this all within the community, but when it is questioned from without—that's when things start going apart. Like most Americans we are not yet fully conscious of our identity either as Negroes or Americans.[36]

The same insecurity that prompted Blacks to purchase hair straighteners and bleaching creams also led them to look to the whites in America for approval of their art forms. As Wallace Thurman observes:

when it first became popular to sing spirituals for public delectation, the mass of Negroes objected vigorously. They did not wish to become identified again with what the spirituals connoted, and they certainly did not want to hear them sung in dialect. It was not until white music critics began pointing out the beauty of the spirituals, and identifying the genius that produced them, that Negroes joined the hallelujah chorus.[37]

Undoubtedly, this long-lasting cultural reliance, similar to a neocolonial mentality, was one of the major reasons that the earliest Black novelists so readily accepted the artificial heroes and heroines of popular fiction as models for their own protagonists. It also explains why so many of their female characters are mulattoes. Certainly, the slave narratives contain portraits of hundreds of individuals who would have been more suitable as models than those suggested by white popular fiction.

As late as 1930, Sterling Brown complained about the false way in which Black readers viewed fiction by Black writers:

> We look upon Negro books regardless of the author's intention, as representative of all Negroes, i.e. as sociological documents.
>
> We insist that Negro books must be idealistic, optimistic tracts for race advertisement.
>
> We are afraid of truth telling, of satire.
>
> We criticize from the point of view of bourgeois America, or racial apologists.[38]

The African-American novelists were restricted not only in characterization, but also in which aspects of their people's life they could treat. In 1928, James Weldon Johnson complained that "there are certain phases of life that he dare not touch, certain subjects that he dare not critically discuss, certain manners of treatment that he dare not use—except at the risk of rousing bitter resentment." [39] If the Black reading public as late as 1928 wished to censor any satire or criticism of members of the race in its authors' books and was cautious about which elements of Black life should be publicly presented, it is not unreasonable to suspect that a stronger feeling of racial propriety was present during the second half of the nineteenth century. A concern about their image was forced upon Blacks both during slavery and after the Civil War. In order to rally white support for the overthrow of bondage and the elimination of the injustices of caste, they needed to counter the degrading images insisted upon by southern apologists and did not wish their own writers to portray the race in any but the best of lights.

The distance between the middle-class writers and the masses of their people compounded the problem. After emancipation, the "house servant/field nigger" division widened within the Black community, one group striving to achieve economic success and social acceptance by acquiring the advantages of higher education and the other, by far the largest number of freedmen, struggling for day-by-day survival and, at best, literacy. Consequently, an emotional and psychological distance developed between the Black masses and the "talented tenth" who constituted the race's professional class. This class, which is satirized by Sutton Griggs throughout his books, has historically been more desirous of following white standards than the less well educated majority of their kinsmen. Many professionals were mulattoes whose parentage could be traced back to the master himself during slave times and who found it easier to escape to the North and, after the war, to work their way up the economic ladder than did their darker, more brutalized brothers and their descendants. Most of the nineteenth-century African-American writers appear to have belonged to this class or to have been free men and women in the North before the Civil War.

Black middle-class writers most often produced for middle-class readers of both races and not for the majority of their people, who did not naturally turn to fiction for artistic pleasure or moral guidance. It is noteworthy that, despite their artificial features, the works containing most of the realistic characters and folk themes are those of Sutton Griggs, who devoted himself to writing and publishing for the Black masses.[40] The differences between Griggs's Uncle Jack or Aunt Molly and William Wells Brown's Sam suggest the artistic result of writing for Blacks naturally acquainted with folk humor and traditions and that of attempting to influence sympathetic whites, generally unacquainted with ordinary Black people and trained to expect fictional stock characters, or of trying to reach Blacks who wished to forget their cultural heritage.

The economic need for publishers other than Griggs to be responsive to the desires of the general reading public contributed both to the artificiality in the Black novels and to their scarcity. The situation that Langston Hughes lamented in the 1950s must have been even more of a hindrance shortly after the Civil War. "Here are our problems," Hughes stated at that time:

> In the first place, Negro books are considered by editors and publishers as exotic. Negro material is placed, like Chinese material or Bali material or East Indian material, into a certain classification. Magazine editors will tell you, "We can use but so many Negro stories a year." (That "so many" meaning very few.) Publishers will say, "We already have one Negro novel in our list this fall." The market for Negro writers, then, is definitely limited as long as we write about ourselves. And the more truthfully we write about ourselves, the more limited our market becomes.[41]

This consideration, no doubt, led Paul Dunbar to compose his all-white novels and might also have been the impetus behind Amelia Johnson's *Hazeley Family* (1894) and Emma Dunham Kelley's *Megda* (1892), which, likewise, contain no Blacks.

Writing in 1931, Charles W. Chesnutt observed: "At the time when I first broke into print seriously, no American colored writer had ever secured critical recognition except Paul Laurence Dunbar, who had won his laurels as a poet." [42] Chesnutt added that the publication of a literary work by an African-

American was such a gamble during the first part of the twentieth century that when he submitted *The House Behind the Cedars* (1900), and several short stories on Black superstitions to Houghton Mifflin, the book was rejected with the suggestion "that perhaps a collection of the conjure stories might be undertaken by the firm with a better prospect of success."[43] Following this advice, Chesnutt resubmitted the stories that made up his first volume, *The Conjure Woman* (1899). His novel was, of course, soon published, but Chesnutt's racial identity was not disclosed for many years, since such a revelation would probably have hurt the sale of his books. Hugh Gloster notes:

> The publication of Chesnutt's folk stories in *The Atlantic Monthly,* representing the first time this periodical had accepted the contributions of a colored American, may be said to mark the coming-of-age of Negro literature in the United States. Before Chesnutt the fiction of Negro authors had been customarily received with the tacit understanding that it was inferior to that of white writers.[44]

Even after Chesnutt's success, subsequent African-American novels were almost invariably handled by small firms unable to promote the books nationally. Obviously, publishers catering to popular tastes reinforced the writers' tendency to accept the artificial traditions of the sentimental novel because it was the most financially successful mode of imaginative literature. It would have been difficult, indeed, if not impossible, for middle-class Black writers of the nineteenth century to have overcome their own cultural insecurities, those of their Black and white audiences, their collective literary training, and their publishers' pragmatism to produce works that would not betray the African-American experience. Only one force was available to counter the tendency toward fantasy: the Black tradition of realistic and satiric oratory, autobiography, and oral narrative.

2
Black Sources

"Miss Leroy, out of the race must come its own thinkers and writers. Authors belonging to the white race have written good racial books, for which I am deeply grateful, but it seems almost impossible for a white man to put himself completely in our place. No man can feel the iron which enters another man's soul."

Frances E. W. Harper, Iola Leroy

Four themes, reflecting historical realities, unite the action of the earliest African-American novels: the rise to prominence of a lowly slave, despite overwhelming obstacles; the dangers inherent to Blacks in both slavery and caste; the sudden reversal of the fortunes of mulattoes who thought themselves white or safe from society's discovery of their mixed blood; and, closely related to each of the others, an examination of miscegenation and its consequences for both races. These subjects are not unique, of course, to the first Black fiction. They were explored many times before the Civil War in the works of white abolitionists and, since they encompass the Black experience in this country, appear in one form or another in African-American writing down to the present day. Nevertheless, their handling in the early Black novels is historically and artistically significant because these books constitute the first fictional view of the African-American experience drawn by Blacks themselves.

To the extent that their picture is a delineation of the complexities of African-American life, it is successful; to the degree that it is indistinguishable from the artificial and racially degrading caricatures found in popular nineteenth-century fiction, it is a clear and powerful indication of the extent of the identity crisis faced by the earliest Black authors. Within the conventional and predictable structures of these novels appear moments of moving character portrayal and sharp evidence of clear understanding of the problems of being Black in nineteenth-century, white America. The writers' empathy with their race and their desire to express its sufferings and aspirations genuinely flash repeatedly through their books' sentimental and propagandist haze. The novels, therefore, are torn in two directions. Their authors' acceptance of prevailing, popular literary forms pulls them toward the empty flights of romantic fiction, while their urgency to continue the antebellum Black tradition of speaking the stark truth insistently tugs them back to their roots. In no other body of American writing are form and content so fiercely at war.

To complicate matters further, moreover, there are elements within the slave narratives and orations reinforcing some of the popular distortions. If the major movement of the novels' plots follows the story line insisted on by Horatio Alger's optimistic readers—for example, the rise to prominence of characters of low social and economic status—in the slave narratives, too, characters of the lowest possible social position succeed in leaving not only the social and economic condition that has trapped them but also the geographical locale of their bondage. The novels, unfortunately, move beyond the realities of the escaped slave's experience. In the most extreme version of the escape motif, Clotelle and Jerome do not rest in the refuge of Canada or a free state, but travel to Europe, where they are introduced to kings and entertained in all the Old World capitals. While not every protagonist in these tales achieves wealth and acclaim as extensive as Clotelle's and Jerome's, all of them, improbably, become financially independent when given a chance to strive on their own in the world. Only Jones, with his reference to Regina Underwood's poverty-stricken parents, suggests that escape did not guarantee success.

Despite their many setbacks, the characters either rise from lowly beginnings to social and economic success or maintain their solid, middle-class status. Poetic justice triumphs. Although some characters—Isabella of *Clotelle,* for example, and Washington Madison's wife in *The Heroic Slave*—suffer unjustly and die, in general the appropriate couples are married by the close of their tales and the villains banished. When one further weakens this conventional action with melodramatic clashes of handsome, noble Black heroes and repulsive, cruel white villains, the case for artistry in the early Black novels appears hopeless, indeed.

A look beyond the books' surface pieties, however, reveals themes linking them to the most deeply felt concerns of their people from their earliest expression down to the present. Despite its own vision of an ideal America, the tradition of anti-slavery oratory and narrative rooted the earliest African-American literature in the hard soil of the Black experience. The novelists' understanding of the difficulties for victims of miscegenation, their utilization of folk speech and folk motifs in their portrayals of minor characters, their satiric jabs at the country's political and religious hypocrisies, and their detailed descriptions of the conditions of racial oppression—all reflect the runaway slaves' revelations and infuse their books with power and truth.

Despite their didacticism, repetitious insistence on documentation, and instructive assertions of the validity of controversial interpretations or sensational scenes, the orations and narratives differ markedly from popular fiction in that they centered their appeal to action in the speaker's or writer's own experience of injustice and in personal, eyewitness instances of suffering. This distinction might, at first, seem small; but it is of immense significance. These works represented a heritage of Blacks speaking truly and imaginatively in their own voices about their people's predicament, thus providing later writers with a valid body of material on which to base their fictional versions of the African-American experience. Moreover, they demonstrated to the early writers the clarifying power of satire.

While their overall development under slavery followed similar lines, the individual narrators' lives were, naturally, different in their details. Moreover, although each writer frequently mentioned other slaves, cruel and kind masters, and especially members of his family, his primary focus was necessarily upon one life, his own. Perhaps because of the desire of later writers to diversify the picture of slavery—to increase, for instance, the different types of people who could be portrayed, and to show the effects of bondage in different geographical areas of the country—the step to an imaginative rendering of this material was a natural one. This desire for versatility might have been the artistic impetus that spurred William Wells Brown and Frederick Douglass to write novels dealing with the conditions of slavery after they had already composed personal narratives of their escapes from the South.

Sponsored and published by anti-slavery forces in the first part of the nineteenth century, these orations and narratives constituted, as J. Noel Heermance notes, "essentially the first major type of formal Negro literature in America."[1] Black oratory, which dates back to 1788,

> was social cause material, strongly polemical and dedicatedly attacking slavery and discrimination throughout the country. And, as such, it laid the directly didactic groundwork for all the early Negro prose, even as it inculcated in subsequent Negro generations its didactic tone towards the reader, its anti-slavery material, and its generally direct and argumentative approach to its material.[2]

Anti-slavery orations developed a definite form and content that were consistently followed by all of the speakers. In contrast, the narratives provided a more personal and individualistic quality to the same material. The underlying structure of the anti-slavery orations was that of repetition. Scenes of slavery followed by documentation proving the possibility of such occurrences, emotional appeals for justice, and satiric comments on American ideals and institutions provided the basic framework for most of these speeches. The orators repeatedly presented eyewitness accounts of beatings or other physical cruelties of slavery in order to impress such scenes on the consciousness and conscience of their audience. As Heermance notes:

> the blatant evils of slavery could not be over-emphasized in the eyes of the Abolitionists, and thus this constant citation and re-citation of these evils was deemed a necessary part of the orator's delivery. Furthermore, as

every good orator has always been aware, public delivery of events and ideas constantly needs repetition to account for the loss of attention and lapse of meaning which always accompanies oral communication between a speaker and a sizable, scattered, "large-hall" audience. . . .

In fact, in its ultimate sense, this use of repetition was the only "structure" which the anti-slavery orator was required to perfect. With each individual anecdote and concept... he needed repetition to drive the point home. And on a far more significant level, he indulged in this same didactic repetition throughout the whole address: for "variety" was simply "repetition" in a veiled and multi-colored dress. . . .[3]

The many similar accounts of the sufferings of the four mulatto heroines in *Clotelle;* the young protagonist's repeated, unsuccessful attempts to find a job in *The Garies and Their Friends;* the three separate, but essentially identical, escape attempts of the desperate slaves in *Bond and Free;* and the series of dangerous situations overcome by the persecuted hero and heroine of *Hearts of Gold*—all can be seen as instances of repetition deliberately employed to emphasize and reemphasize the oppressive racial conditions of nineteenth-century American society.

Slave narratives, unlike the orations, were structured upon a chronological progression from the time of the former slave's birth until his escape to a free state or to Canada. While several of the Black novels begin with or before the births of their protagonists—*Clotelle* and *Iola Leroy,* for example—others do not follow this birth-to-adulthood motif. Nevertheless, even those which begin at some moment of crisis in the middle of the lives of their main characters develop from that point in a straightforward, chronological fashion. Only Sutton Grigg's *Imperium in Imperio* (1899) employs the more sophisticated narrative device of a flashback at the novel's beginning, but even in this instance, the flashback begins with the protagonists' youth and continues to the time of one of their deaths. *Imperium in Imperio* is a frame story, then, which manipulates time only in this single, early movement out of the present.

The episodic nature of the autobiographies is also reflected in the later fiction. In the slave narratives, interest is achieved within the straightforward, chronological structure by the emphasis on exciting incidents demonstrating oppression and attempts to escape from it. Frequently featuring people other than the narrator himself, these episodes are very similar to each other in tone and detail. Scenes picturing the slave's burden of physical labor, for instance, or revealing the dangers inherent in his flight to freedom serve to reinforce the writer's assertion of continuous oppression and to arouse a sympathetic emotional response from his readers. Scenes of punishment and escape are also featured in the early Black novels by the same devices of repetition and moralizing. These episodes are frequently melodramatic, however, and must share the spotlight with moments of sentimental romance. Because the novelists had not found a consistent tone, either of outrage or of sentiment, these different scenes are juxtaposed and jarring, the transitions between the two moods being seldom effective.

Their inability—or refusal—to view their fiction primarily as storytelling, even if the story told would reveal their racial concerns through a subtle handling of its ironies, explains the early novelists' easy acceptance of these propaganda devices. Their books were envisioned as the next step in the Black literary tradition of vigorously battling slavery and racism. They were not composing belle lettres; they were manufacturing literary weapons. As Lloyd L. Brown has observed:

> For nearly all Negro writers throughout American history the question of what to write about was compellingly simple. The pen was an essential instrument in the fight for liberation. This concept was not arrived at through any wringing and twisting; nor through any high-flown debates about Art-For-Art's Sake *versus* Art-As-A-Weapon. Spontaneous and inevitable, it arose from the conditions of life—slavery and oppression. The very laws which made it a crime to teach a slave to read and write established the direction of Negro writing. If *learning* to write was an act against the slaveholders, then surely the *use* of writing would be a greater blow.[4]

The plantation owners had objected to reading and writing among their slaves on three basic grounds. First of all, African-Americans were considered such inferior creatures by those who accepted the most self-serving of the stereotypes that attempting to educate them, they convinced themselves, was a blasphemous attack upon the accepted hierarchical structure of human society. More to the point, time spent in schoolrooms was time not spent in cotton fields, and the economic system would have been damaged by such a shift of Black energies. The most potent argument against educating slaves, of course, was the white fear that such enlightenment would lead to a new understanding of themselves and their degradation and would result in insurrection. As Frederick Douglass proved, an introduction to books can provide images of freedom and yearnings for manhood that destroy one's complaisance in servility. These reasons, conscious or unconscious, lay behind the severe penalties inflicted in the antebellum South upon whites and Blacks alike who were caught instructing slaves.

Among free Blacks, then, and among those educated after the Civil War, the act of writing became itself symbolic of personal worth and was recognized as a powerful instrument for social change. With Black identity as well as Black progress in the balance, it is easy to understand why the earliest novelists seized upon the propagandist elements of their abolitionist oratory and narrative. This moralizing, reinforced by the same quality found in the domestic romances and "novels with a purpose," must have led them to accept an argumentative, preaching tone as legitimate to literature and especially effective for their own cause. Passages soberly reminding the reader of the true meaning of Christianity, the proper social function of the church, and the political ideals upon which America was founded or speculating about a future time in which slavery and racism would be abolished can be found in almost every one of the early novels. The works of Sutton Griggs, especially, with their utopian plans for racial harmony, abound with such sections.

The documentation of scenes of injustice proved one of the most reliable devices of Black oratory. Claims to eyewitness knowledge of conditions under slavery and the citing of written proof of the speaker's assertions were incorporated into the speeches in order to force the audience's acceptance of their validity. The speaker's claiming to have been present at the scenes described, his reading of newspaper accounts of slave auctions or advertisements for runaways, and his citing of actual laws promoting and sustaining slavery were all included in his discourse. The narratives, those written by escaped slaves rather than their white northern sympathizers, of course, were presented as true stories of the lives of their authors. To emphasize their veracity, even they, were frequently prefaced by pages of documentation testifying to the actual existence of the people and places mentioned in them. The first novelists attempted this same kind of verisimilitude by the inclusion of footnotes containing newspaper documentation of even nonpolitical incidents. Appended to the description of a steamboat explosion in *Appointed,* for example, is a footnote reading, "When the steamer Kate Adams was burned Dec. 23, 1888, the first alarm was given by a colored woman in the manner as described" (p. 276).

As has been noted, before the public could be expected to take political action against racism, it had to be educated about the evils of the system and, even more importantly, about the basic humanity of its victims. Harriet Beecher Stowe's understanding of the intent of Frank Webb to use his novel as just such a means of instruction is clearly indicated in the preface that she wrote for *The Garies and Their Friends.* "The book which now appears before the public," she states,

> may be of interest in relation to a question which the late agitation of the subject of slavery has raised in many thoughtful minds; viz.—Are the race at present held as slaves capable of freedom, self government and progress? . . . the incidents related are mostly true ones, woven together by a slight web of fiction.

An almost identical expression of historical content and political intent is found in Frances Harper's explanation of her reasons for writing *Iola Leroy:*

> From the threads of fact and fiction I have woven a story whose mission will not be in vain if it awakens in the hearts of our countrymen a stronger sense of justice and a more Christlike humanity in behalf of those whom the fortunes of war threw homeless, ignorant and poor upon the threshold of a new era. Nor will it be in vain if it inspire the children of those upon whose brows God has poured the chrism of that new era to determine that

they will embrace every opportunity, develop every faculty, and use every power God has given them to rise in the scale of character and condition, and to add their quota of good citizenship to the best welfare of the nation (notes following the text).

The 1853 edition of *Clotel* had been published in London in order to rally the support of British readers to the American anti-slavery cause, and the 1864 version was expressly intended to encourage the militance of the Union soldiers. There seems little doubt, even without the evidence of direct statements of purpose, that most of the early Black novels had some such extraliterary motive.

With an educative intent in mind, for example, Jones in *Hearts of Gold,* provides a forceful description of a small-town ghetto. After moving to the South, Regina, Jones's heroine, accepts a teaching position in a Black school. Jones uses Regina's growing understanding of her new surroundings to increase the reader's knowledge of conditions in the South:

> She stopped a moment in her reverie, and turning her thoughts from the school and its future, looked down the valley toward which the little stream was making its way toward the black smoke of the Steel Plant. Flanking it on all sides stood row after row of shacks, as they are called—one-story frame houses stripped on the outside, unplastered and forming a refinement of the old quarters famous in slavery days. Here lived the parents of the children she was to teach. The houses for the most part contained two rooms and a loft, where the children, by the help of a ladder, climbed to sleep. Some of these houses were occupied by two families and not infrequently contained a boarder or two besides. The workmen came from every part of the state, where colored men had opportunity to engage in skilled labor. It is useless to say that such environments and such a place, especially in its formative period, is a very hotbed of ignorance and vice. Hardly a night passed that forth from the low dives that were everywhere prevalent some human being was not ushered, shot or cut to death. Whiskey never more certainly performed the work of its fell master, the devil, than among these hardworking Negroes on the outskirts of Grandville (pp. 170–71).

This scene offers a decided contrast to the idealized portraits of luxurious antebellum plantations, happy darkies, and nostalgic freedmen prominent in so many novels set in the South. Moreover, it provides a look at the economic result for Blacks of the gradual change from an agrarian to a postwar industrial economy in this part of the country. Although no more than a brief glimpse, Jones's scene of southern ghetto life, with its naturalistic overtones, is one of the most effective touches in all the nineteenth-century Black novels.

With the voices of their orators echoing behind them, the novelists frequently resorted to such omniscient intrusion as Jones's in order to underscore a situation or scene. Other examples of such direct explanation are Brown's discussion of the social status of beautiful mulatto women supported by wealthy white men, his detailed description of the slave auction at which Isabella is sold to Henry Linwood, and Frank Webb's comments on the difficulty that northern Blacks face in finding jobs. The technique of authorial intrusion serves two functions in these books. It helps to ensure the desired response from readers by quickly indoctrinating them into the facts of the Black experience. Also, the author's voice, presenting some aspect of his peoples' lives and commenting on it, tends to counter the unreality caused by the books' many sentimental and melodramatic scenes.

This positive effect is diluted, of course, by the undramatic nature of this material and its consequent disruption of the fragile atmosphere established by the narrative. The reliance upon such moralistic and factual commentary, successfully employed in the orations and autobiographies, demonstrates the uneasy yoking of the early novelists' propaganda intent to their fictional form.

Another technique inherited from the Black tradition is the inclusion of sentimental verse to arouse or heighten the audience's emotional response. Heermance quotes an example of such verse from an anti-slavery lecture given by William Wells Brown in Salem, Massachusetts, in 1847:

> Shall every flap of England's flag
> Proclaim that all around are free,
> From furthest Ind to each blue crag
> That beetles o'er the western sea?
> And shall we scoff at Europe's kings,
> When Freedom's fire is dimmed with us;
> And round our country's altar clings
> The damning shade of Slavery's curse?[5]

The similarity is clear, both in content and intent, between this stanza and those eulogizing Canada as one of the refuges for the persecuted slave that appear throughout James H. W. Howard's *Bond and Free*. His gang of runaways, after overcoming numerous obstacles and finally reaching the Canadian border, bow "their heads in prayer" and sing "soul-inspired strains":

> Sing praise to Jehovah we are free,
> *Safe on the shores of Canada.*
> Let us unite in heart and hand,
> And shout for joy in the freedom's land (p. 144).

This tradition of impassioned speech and verse might also account, to a degree, for Clotelle's spontaneous rhyming and the high-flown rhetoric of Selene.

Occasionally, the early writers were able to harness their militancy and to utilize elements from the Black sources that do not preach or exhort, but compel solely by their imagination, honesty, and insight. Although awash with episodes of melodrama and sentiment, contrivances of coincidence, gothic exaggerations, and passages of propagandist rhetoric, these novels are buoyed up by their more vital and effective scenes dramatizing the precarious position of Blacks in nineteenth-century America. These more realistic episodes range from portrayals of discrimination in railroad facilities and housing, generally in the North, to grim pictures of southern mob violence and lynchings.

Employment discrimination in Philadelphia is the target of Webb's depiction of Charles Ellis's repeatedly thwarted efforts to find work. Ellis answers a newspaper ad for the position of an under clerk, and a telling conversation ensues between his two prospective employers, one a southerner:

> "Well, what do you say?" asked Western, after they had closed the door behind them. "Don't you think that we had better engage him?"
>
> "Engage him?" exclaimed Twining—"why you surprise me, Western—the thing's absurd; engage a colored boy as under clerk! I never heard of such a thing."
>
> "I have often," drawled Western; "there are the greatest number of them in New Orleans."
>
> "Ah, but New Orleans is a different place; such a thing never occurred in Philadelphia" (p. 291).

Needless to say, Charles Ellis does not get the job. Obviously, the most interesting aspect of this conversation is that it is the northerner, Twining, rather than his southern partner, who refuses to hire the boy. A northern free Black, Webb was clearly aware that racism existed in places outside the South during the nineteenth century; his story of murder, mob violence, theft, and political corruption ironically takes place in the "city of brotherly love," the "cradle of liberty."

In contrast, Jones's *Hearts of Gold* contains two vivid episodes starkly dramatizing racism in the South. One is the near drowning of Lotus Stone by a cruel prison guard. The other, less melodramatic, though considerably more violent and sensational, is the account of the lynching of Harvey Meeks. Meeks, a Black grocer, is arrested for defending a young Black boy from a white mob. The boy has had a fight with a gang of white boys, thereby provoking the wrath of a group of adult, white onlookers. Coincidentally, it is Meeks who also saves the book's heroine, Regina, when Dr. Leighton attempts to strangle her. It is his defiance of the whites on behalf of the boy, however, rather than his unknown attack upon the white Leighton, which leads to his death. Meeks is arrested and hurried to jail without a trial. Once night falls, an enraged mob drags him from his cell to a wooden bridge just outside of town. A rope is tied to the bridge railing, the noose tightened around Meeks's throat:

> They picked him up, lifted him upon the railing and then shoved him over.

As he fell he caught hold of the side of the bridge. "Let go," they cried. Harvey, like a drowning man clinging to a straw, tightened his grip.

"Here, I'll make him let go," someone said, and drawing out a long knife, he reached down and cutting off the victim's fingers one by one, passed them to the jeering crowd, as mementoes of the occasion.

At last the dying man, for want of fingers, loosed his hold and dropped with a dull thud over the side of the bridge. As his body writhed and twisted in the air, a hundred revolvers, more merciful to man's torture, filled the swaying body full of holes, putting the struggling soul beyond the reach of misery. . . .

Not satisfied with his bloody deeds, the man who cut off Harvey Meek's fingers, returned with some of his companions and drawing the body up, decapitated it. Attaching the rope under the arms of the corpse, he swung the ghastly, headless body over the bridge, to hang there over Sunday. Taking the head over to a neighboring saloon, the crowd pushed through the glazed doors in high glee. Two of the men staggered up to the bar and stood there, while one of them said, "Give us three whiskies; one for me, one for Jack, and one," he said, as he lifted by the ears the amputated head to the counter, "for old Harvey" (pp. 226–27).

Had Jones been able to resist passing judgment on Meeks's tormentors, this scene would have been a graphic dramatization of one of the horrifying and inescapable facts of southern life.[6] Instead, the force of the episode is diluted by the following sentimental observation in the middle of it:

The blood of that martyred Christian, spilt by the relentless cruelty of white heathen, ran red in the muddy waters of the eddying river. The evidences of guilt were carried on to the father of waters; the Mississippi bore them to the restless ocean and the accusing winds gathered them into their friendly arms and wafted them up to the courts of heaven (p. 227).

Perhaps his identification with Meeks lured Jones into sentiment and pathetic fallacy. More likely, however, he realized that the traditions of his genre encouraged a solid dose of "poetic" moralizing at this point, just in case his readers became too engrossed in the sensationalism of the scene to condemn Meeks's murderers properly.

Douglass's heroic slave receives a typical "cruel lashing" for his first escape attempt and is "tied up to the limb of a tree, with [his] feet chained together, and a heavy iron bar placed between [his] ankles" (p. 46). Like the unfortunate offender in the "Narrative of the Life of Moses Grady,"[7] Washington receives a "bleeding back, gashed by the cow-skin" and "washed by the overseer with old brine" (p. 46). And, like Henry Bibb, another escaped slave, Douglass's protagonist later returns from freedom to rescue his wife and is recaptured.

In addition to revealing physical violence as a commonplace in Black life, the

orations and narratives dramatized the social chaos sanctioned by slavery, particularly the separation of families and the confusion engendered by widespread
miscegenation. They painted in graphic detail the day-by-day brutalities suffered
by slaves, powerfully indicating not only their physical, but also their psychological and spiritual torment. Douglass's narrative is especially successful in con-
veying the dehumanizing effects of slavery's ruthless destruction of its victims'
identity and cultural heritage. Douglass himself did not know his own age or the
identity of his white father. Echoing his own experience, his protagonist in *The
Heroic Slave* attains psychological freedom the moment that he resolves to leave
slavery any way that he can: "for that moment he was free, at least in spirit. . . .
his fetters lay broken at his feet. His air was triumphant" (p. 40).

While Hugh Henry Brackenridge's *Modern Chivalry* (1792–1815) had established the tradition of satire in this country, and contemporary works such as
Twain and Warner's *Gilded Age* (1873) and DeForest's *Honest John Vane*
(1875) struggled to keep it alive, popular fiction refrained, for the most part,
from any sardonic view of American life. What satire existed in the popular
novel was generally directed against the foibles and egoism found in individuals,
rather than against those same qualities in the social structure. The escaped
slaves, however, added spice to their indictments of America by mocking the
hypocrisy and self-deception pervading the whole society. False religion and the
ineffectual, often immoral, functioning of the political system were particular
targets of their scorn.

The satire in nineteenth-century Black novels, too, moves beyond personal
attacks to the condemnation of an entire political and religious system. It is
likely, then, that these writers were following closely the lead of the earlier
spokesmen for their race in establishing a broad satiric target. As in the narratives, the aspects of nineteenth-century life condemned in the novels are slavery,
racist politics, and, most often, un-Christian Christianity. It is revealing that
genteel society, with its artificial standards of acceptance and rejection, is
mocked by some of the novelists, but aspired to by others.

Howard, in *Bond and Free,* uses cattle, valuable for their labor and breeding,
as a metaphor for the status of the slaves in the minds of their owners. Of Mr.
Maxwell, a wealthy plantation owner, Howard notes:

> His plantations were all in good condition, his human cattle fat and sleek.
> The latter, though worked hard, were well quartered and well fed. This, of
> course, made them prolific, and in fact, many of them were kept upon the
> estate on account of their breeding qualities (p. 9).

This apt animal imagery appears whenever Howard refers to slavery. The slave
on Maxwell's farm is simply another form of barnyard species. Abraham Biggers, "the owner of a plantation of over five hundred acres, upon which he had
fifty or a hundred human beings, besides other stock" (p. 15), wishes to sell
William to Mr. Maxwell, Purcey's owner. He sees a sexual alliance between the
two slaves as an added incentive for making the sale. "Ha! ha! Maxwell,"

Biggers proclaims, "that's it exactly! that's it! the gal takes to him, no trouble to make the match, two thousand dollars and he is yours; cheap, sir, cheap as bull beef at a penny a pound" (p. 33).

Brown devotes an entire chapter in *Clotelle* to detailing and satirizing the inhumanity that took place at a southern slave auction. At the sale at which Isabella and her mother and sister are torn away from each other, the bidding for Isabella begins at $500 and is raised each time that the auctioneer reveals another feature, such as piety or chastity, in her favor. She is finally bought for $2,000, and Brown notes sardonically:

> This was a Virginia slave-auction, at which the bones, sinews, blood, and nerves of a young girl of eighteen were sold for $500; her moral character for $200; her superior intellect for $100; the benefits supposed to accrue from her having been sprinkled and immersed, together with a warranty for her devoted Christianity, for $300; her ability to make a good prayer for $200; and her chastity for $700 more (p. 9).

Politics and politicians are also the objects of bitter humor. Perhaps the most understated example of political satire is Brown's brief mention that Henry Linwood, who allows Isabella and her daughter to be sold, is a respected and prospering member of Congress. Another ironic, if melodramatic, touch is Isabella's suicide within sight of the Capitol and the White House.

A more direct connection between politicians and injustice is made in *Hearts of Gold* in Jones's identification of the owner of the convict labor camp as "a millionaire senator, wined and dined as a social magnate in the capital of the nation" (p. 235). The official's guilt becomes clear as Jones depicts the degrading conditions within the prison and reveals that the free labor forced from the inmates has provided the politician with his millions. He has, moreover, never set foot in the camp and wishes to know nothing about its workings except its margin of profit.[8]

It is as if Frank Webb, in *The Garies and Their Friends,* found light touches with the satirist's brush unsatisfying and reached for the muckraker's hammer instead. He employs the dishonest lawyer, Mr. Stevens, to launch a prolonged attack upon the corruption rampant in nineteenth-century politics, journalism, and the legal profession.

Explaining the method by which he intends to acquire cheap property, Lawyer Stevens reveals his plan to use mobs of hoodlums to drive Blacks away from their homes and discloses that the entire plot depends upon cooperation from crooked public officials: "We will so control the elections in the district, through these men, as to place in office only such persons as will wink at the disturbances" (p. 166). Stevens is sure of the politicians' support because he helped to elect many of them. A bartender who had planned to testify against one of his henchmen, for example, is bribed with a small sum of money and the lucrative office of alderman.

Stevens is also extremely effective in controlling the press and its interpretation of the mob action. Following several riots, after which many Black families are forced to sell out and move, the newspapers inflame public prejudice and fear and hide or distort the truth about the dangerous situation, blaming the attacks in Black neighborhoods on the residents themselves. These accounts are completely puzzling until Webb reveals that many of them were actually written by Stevens and printed through political pressure upon the newspaper publishers and editors. It is only through collusion among the forces of law enforcement, who never arrest the criminals, and the controllers of public information that the mob and Stevens are successful.

Without a doubt, the institution that merits the most scorn is the church, especially in its role of piously championing slavery and racism. Many of the slave narratives tell of brutal, slave-owning ministers like *Clotelle's* Reverend Wilson, the "Slave-holding Parson," and mockingly record the sermons urging meekness and obedience that were faithfully delivered to the slaves. Two such churchmen are Francis Whitfield, a deacon in the Baptist church, who Henry Bibb says, "looked like a saint—talked like the best of slave holding Christians, and acted at home like the devil,"[9] and Peter Tanner, Bible-reading owner of Solomon Northup, who described him as

> an impressive commentator on the New Testament. The first Sunday after my coming to the plantation, he called [the slaves] . . . together, and began to read the twelfth chapter of Luke. When he came to the 47th verse, he looked deliberately around him, and continued—"And that servant which knew his lord's *will,*" here he paused, looking around more deliberately than before, and again proceeded—"which knew his lord's *will,* and *prepared* not himself"—here was another pause—"prepared not himself, neither did *according* to his will, shall be beaten with many *stripes.*"
>
> "D'ye hear that?" demanded Peter, emphatically. "Stripes," he repeated, slowly and distinctly, taking off his spectacles, preparatory to making a few remarks.
>
> "That nigger that don't take care—that don't obey his lord—that's his master—d'ye see?—that 'ere nigger shall be beaten with many stripes. Now, 'many' signifies a great many—forty, a hundred, a hundred and fifty lashes. *That's* Scripter!" and so Peter continued to elucidate the subject for a great length of time, much to the edification of his sable audience.[10]

While Bibb's and Northup's portrayals are of individuals, William Wells Brown in *Clotelle* broadens the indictment to include an entire slaveholding, churchgoing town. "The chiming of the bells," Brown remarks, "seemed to mock the sighs and deep groans of the forty human beings then incarcerated in the slave-pen. These imprisoned children of God were many of them Methodists, some Baptists, and others claiming to believe in the faith of the Presbyterians and Episcopalians" (p. 62). The value of the religion preached on Sunday is indicated by the activities of the churchgoers on Monday:

The clock on the calaboose had just struck nine on Monday morning when hundreds of persons were seen threading the gates and doors of the negro-pen. It was the same gang that had the day previous been stepping to the tune and keeping time with the musical church bell. Their Bibles were not with them, their prayer books were left at home, and even their long and solemn faces had been laid aside for the week. They had come to the man-market to make their purchases. Methodists were in search of their brethren. Baptists were looking for those that had been immersed, while Presbyterians were willing to buy fellow Christians, whether sprinkled or not (p. 73).

Unfortunately, the novelists neglect their most obvious opportunity for satire by never showing one of their ministers actually delivering a racist sermon and, like Peter Tanner, damning himself from his own sanctimonious mouth. The closest they come to portraying a clergyman expounding an ironic religious dogma is the self-righteous condemnation of intermarriage expressed by the minister in *The Garies and Their Friends.*

Webb also satirizes the segregation practiced during church services in the North. Aunt Comfort, respected throughout her integrated community as a talented and compassionate nurse, is welcome in any white home when illness strikes. Her welcome in the white church, however, is another matter:

Now, to Aunt Comfort (who was the only coloured person who regularly attended the church), a seat had been assigned beside the organ; which elevated position had been given her that the congregation might indulge in their devotions without having their prejudices shocked by a too close contemplation of her ebony countenance (pp. 250–51).

Unlike Aunt Comfort, of course, most Blacks, North and South, preferred their own religious groups, where they were not confronted by dogmas such as those of Frank Webb's clergyman, who "believe[s] the Negro race . . . to be marked out by the hand of God for servitude" (p. 137).

In addition to its religious practices, nineteenth-century America's social standards receive wry notice in these books. Social elitism, the ruling class's arbitrary and undeserved power, and the role of women in perpetuating its influence are the usual targets. The fear of social amalgamation, because it might result in intermarriage, is viewed by Frances Harper as the hidden motive for barring Blacks from white churches. The church "has its social as well as its spiritual side," explains a character in *Iola Leroy:*

"Society is woman's realm. The majority of church members are women, who are said to be the aristocratic elements of our country. I fear that one of the last strongholds of this racial prejudice will be found beneath the shadow of some of our churches. I think, on account of this social question, that large bodies of Christian temperance women and other reformers, in trying to reach the colored people even for their own good, will be quicker to form separate associations than our National Guard Army, whose ranks are open to black and white, liberals and conservatives, saints and agnostics'' (pp. 233–34).

This combination of false religiosity, social snobbery, and sexual fear, fostered by women, is attacked in *The Garies and Their Friends*. Lawyer Stevens's wife, who is as dedicated as her husband to the destruction of the Garies, approaches a friend to enlist her help in having the Garie children expelled from school. Mrs. Kinney agrees that the idea of Black children sitting alongside white is a shocking breach of social mores and urges Mrs. Stevens to do whatever she feels necessary to rectify the situation. She then hurries away so as not to be late for her meeting of the church missionary society, which is waiting to discuss their latest project for the salvation of the "poor Patagonian[s]" (p. 155). Mrs. Kinney, Webb implies, is typical of hypocritical churchgoers, espousing visionary causes in distant lands and remaining deliberately blind to the injustice in their own communities, much of which their apathy, racism, and hypocrisy support.

Not all of the early writers, however, view society and the artificial class distinctions upon which it insists as objects of satire. In *Hearts of Gold*, for example, Jones lauds the conventional tastes and "refinement" present in a group of middle-class Blacks gathered for a banquet. His evaluation of the well-dressed arrivals reveals his feeling that the socialites are justified in being proud of deriving their standards of taste from those of white aristocrats, the "bluest blood in the land":

> As carriage after carriage drove up and their occupants alighted and tripped into the hall, they looked, and without doubt were, the equals in appointments and bearings of any Americans. . . . Here was to be seen the Afro-American at his best. The absence of flashy dress and cheap showy jewelry, so often attributed to the Negro as a necessity on all public occasions, was nowhere to be seen [sic]. . . .
>
> The average Afro-American has little inclination to copy the pace of those of his own financial class, but at heart he is an aristocrat and imitates the bluest blood in the land. . . . The social standards adopted by these people and the link that holds together a race so varied in appearance and origin is character. The mind, not the man; the heart, not the features. Nor does this distinction argue that all social lines in Afro-Americans are obliterated. Among these people, as elsewhere, the marks of class difference are severely drawn; but worth, not complexion, forms the barrier of demarcation (pp. 66–67).

That self-righteous whites, like Webb's clergyman or Mrs. Stevens, would also claim "worth" as their standard for acceptance or exclusion appears not to have occurred to Jones. This passage is yet another example of a middle-class, African-American writer accepting misleading white distinctions, this time "marks of class . . . not complexion."

Despite the brief examples presented here, there is surprisingly little satire of a sustained sort in the early novels. The influence of the Black literary tradition in endowing the novelists with a sardonic point of view and a consistent mocking tone was limited, possibly because of the nineteenth-century African-American's cultural insecurity. Satire points out the incongruities and absurdities in individuals and societies. Affectation, egoism, hypocrisy, and self-deception are traditional targets for the satirist's bemused or outraged stare. Most of the features of the American dream were perfectly acceptable to the Black writers, however. White middle-class standards of education, industry, and financial success, as interpreted by a leader like Booker T. Washington, were most African-Americans' goals as well. As John Hope Franklin has pointed out, Washington "accepted uncritically the dominant philosophy of American business," its "doctrine of triumphant commercialism," and the "vast majority of the Negroes acclaimed him as their leader."[11]

"The early Negro novelist had the soul of a shopkeeper," Robert Bone has asserted; "his world view . . . equates wealth with virtue."[12] Education was esteemed as the surest way to wealth. As the authors of *Appointed* explain:

> Next to the promises contained in the Holy Writ, education was the hope of the Afro-American. The desire had descended as a fixed feature in the character of succeeding generations, and the burst of liberty, opening up new opportunities that hitherto had seemed but a dream, met with an unprecedented response by both parent and child (pp. 210–11).

Although Clement St. John in *Hearts of Gold* is shown heroically rescuing Lotus Stone and thwarting the evil Dr. Leighton, his most persistent claim to the reader's admiration is his success in becoming a respected journalist in the face of the overwhelming odds against him. For many months, he must bear the brutal remarks and practical jokes of his white coworkers before he is accepted on his own merits. Of course, Jones's "honest lad" never despairs of success; in time, he gains the confidence of his employers and, incredibly, the goodwill of the other workmen. Goodwill is not all he gains, however. Before long, he has worked his way up from errand boy to typesetter, then to reporter, and to editorial assistant. He caps his achievement by establishing his own newspaper dedicated to presenting the Blacks' point of view of the day's events and to publishing articles and essays submitted by African-American writers. His success is further enhanced by the series of articles that he writes exposing the conditions in the convict labor camp where he finds Lotus Stone. Ultimately, he even exerts pressure on the governor, which results in the doctor's release. Only an adventure out West, during which he exposed a dastardly plot to cheat orphans

of their inheritance and widows of their homesteads, would have established
Clement more securely in the Horatio Alger mode of striving and succeeding, to
rise, like Ben Franklin, from lowly beginnings to a postion of prominence and
power.

Except for Frank Webb's unfavorable portrayal of Lawyer Stevens and his
crooked real estate manipulations, there is no criticism and certainly no satire
directed against the aspirations of the business community, as there is in
twentieth-century Black novels. Prejudiced hiring practices are scorned, of
course, but the ultimate possibility of obtaining the jobs sought and the value of
advancing through the established economic system are never questioned. Almost all of the characters are shown to be struggling toward the "better" life,
and, besides freedom, this life consists of a well-paying job, a secure home, and
opportunities for education and further advancement. By viewing such aspects of
American life uncritically, as objects of unquestioning aspiration, the novelists
were clearly reflecting widely held contemporary attitudes.

Faith in the American dream was, of course, a basic tenet of nineteenth-
century popular dogma. For the African-American, this faith took the form of
trust in racial progress, particularly in the fields of education and business. Such
aspirations were echoes of the same general hopes and desires found in white
America and reflected in its popular literature. Fictional heroes were those who
developed industry and thrift, who showed initiative and responsibility, all qualities necessary for business success. In addition, the propaganda intent of the
novelists must be kept in mind. Only Blacks shown quietly "making it" through
the system, despite the odds against them, could serve as guides to the struggling, middle-class Black audience or could calm the racial fears of white readers.
The irony of achieving a professional status, at least in title, yet remaining
politically impotent and, therefore, second-class within the white system—an
incongruity obvious to W. E. B. DuBois—seemed unappreciated by any of these
writers except Stowers and Anderson in *Appointed* and Martin Delany in his
sharply critical *Blake; or, The Huts of America* (1862).

Except for John Saunders, the overeducated clerk in *Appointed,* the characters
in the other novels who are not slaves are successful businessmen, mechanics,
contractors, journalists, teachers, or doctors. Frank Webb's Mr. Walters, the real
estate magnate, is their greatest development. More than any of the others, he
demonstrates a wily businessman's pragmatism and an optimistic political
leader's racial ambitions. When Mr. and Mrs. Ellis ask his advice about putting
their son out in service, he strongly urges them against it, suggesting that they
follow the example of ambitious white parents who teach their boys to be sales-
men. He suggests that they do as white people do and give Charles "a stock of
matches, blacking, newspapers, or apples" and let him learn the fine points of
trade. The results, Mr. Walters suggests, will be a rags-to-riches story similar to
his own: "The boy that learns to sell matches soon learns to sell other things; he
learns to make bargains; he becomes a small trader, then a merchant, then a
millionaire. Did you ever hear of anyone who had made a fortune at service?"
(pp. 62–63).

Charles is so thoroughly indoctrinated with Mr. Walters's values that he admonishes his scruffy, boyhood pal Kinch to "cut marbles" because they make "one such a fright . . . with chalk-marks and dirt from head to foot" (p. 295) and urges him to dress better and look neater. When Kinch mocks his newfound gentility, Charles replies with an observation about the importance of appearance that could have been lifted whole out of Alger's *Bound to Rise* or *Strive and Succeed:* " 'Oh Kinch!' said Charlie gravely, 'I'm not joking—I mean what I say. You don't know how far rough looks and an untidy person go against one. I find that anyone who wants to get on must be particular in little things as well as great' " (p. 296). Webb obviously agrees with Charles and there is not even a hint of mockery at the boy's priggish and practical suggestions to his more easygoing friend. As a matter or fact, Kinch, of all people, turns into a gloved and top-hatted dandy by the end of the book.

Of course, if Charles is successful, he will, as hoped, become another Mr. Walters. Although Webb seems almost blind to the larger implications of his protagonist's situation, the fact is that despite Walters's enormous wealth, he is unable to escape the ravages of Stevens's white mob; his mansion is attacked along with the much more modest homes of his friends. Even great wealth, without political power, was clearly insufficient for the Black man in nineteenth-century Philadelphia. Yet, Charlie Ellis and even Kinch are being reared to fill Mr. Walters's expensive, if insubstantial, shoes. On the whole, then, the writers' espousal of the middle-class, Protestant work ethic and their expectation of sharing in the country's riches and being accepted as cultured and educated citizens severely limited the satire in their books. Even though Mark Twain and a few other scoffing commentators mocked the hypocrisy and artificiality of an industrial society devoted to a progress defined as profits, prestige, and power, Black middle-class readers and writers were too new to the opportunities offered by the economic system to spurn them.

Moreover, the white standards that Blacks found reprehensible, such as the antebellum buying and selling of human beings or the continuing belief in white superiority, were such painful reminders of oppression that they are most often dealt with in the novels with a rage and subjectivity irreconcilable with well-written satire. White attitudes so destructive of Black life could not be presented by its victims with a Swiftian detachment. They were cancerous evils to be rooted out by immediate exposure and condemnation. Such a decision led, inevitably, to melodrama, in which the forces of evil are portrayed as luridly as possible, and to propaganda and its lengthy passages of righteous moralizing. Even in the slave narratives and orations in which satire was a frequent feature, it was sandwiched between sections of militant rhetoric.

Without a doubt, the most important artistic influence of the Black literary tradition on its novelists was as a source of realistic folk characters. Without these believable minor figures, the early novels would bear only a tenuous relationship to the actual lives of Black people in this country. While the sections of moralizing and satire discussed earlier aptly apply to the African-American experience, attention is focused in a piece of fiction on character and action. For reasons already examined, however, the protagonists in these books and their adventures frequently fail to compel belief. Instead, it is with certain minor characters that the humanity of the Black person is salvaged from the fantasy world of popular fiction.

Theodore Gross has shown that both literarily and historically the African-American has been depicted as more of a formula than a human being.[13] It is clear that Blacks as well as whites fell victim to the urge to stereotype and idealize. Nevertheless, despite some holdovers noted earlier from plantation and Reconstruction images of loyal slaves and humorous darkies, many minor characters in the early Black novels strike a believable, complex stance of self-preservation against the white power structure.

Black folklore offered the early novelists a rich gallery of realistic and imaginative portrayals. As Ralph Ellison explains, folklore

> offers the first drawings of any group's character. It preserves mainly those situations which have repeated themselves again and again in the history of any given group. It describes those rites, manners, customs, and so forth, which insure the good life or destroy it; and it describes those boundaries of feeling, thought and action which that particular group has found to be the limitation of the human condition. It projects this wisdom in symbols which express the group's will to survive; it embodies those values by which the group lives and dies.[14]

Folklore, in other words, provides a group identity for members of a given culture. It reveals and inculcates the world view and the norms of behavior deemed successful in the collective wisdom of a people. And it reinforces this view and these norms through characters wise in the ways of the world because they carry the history of the struggles of their people in their bones. By accepting Black folklore as a source for their own imaginative understanding of their race, the early writers were rejecting, at least momentarily, the artificialities of popular, white myths about African-Americans and were trusting, instead, the Black experience and sensibility. They were asserting the validity of the slaves' understanding of slavery and rejecting their masters' distortion of their lives.

In *The Garies and Their Friends,* Webb presents a lengthy scene in a northern hotel which Black waiters, who are actually members of the Under-Ground Railroad Company, slyly trick southern visitors into helping their cause. These waiters

> would ... tell ... the most astonishing and distressing tales of their destitution, expressing, almost with tears in their eyes, their deep desire to return to their former masters; whilst perhaps the person from whose mouth this tale of woe proceeded had been born in a neighboring street, and had never been south of Mason's and Dixon's line. This flattering testimony in favor of the "peculiar institution" generally had the effect of extracting a

dollar or two from the purse of the sympathetic Southerner, which money went immediately into the coffers of the vigilance Committee (pp. 40–41).

Such trickery is reminiscent of the pranks played by Br'er Rabbit, and Webb may have had this character in mind when he described the waiters' secret relish at successfully duping white southerners. Hughes and Bontemps, in *The Book of Negro Folklore,* note that

> the American Negro slave, adopting Brer Rabbit as hero, represented him as the most frightened and helpless of creatures. No hero-animals in Africa or elsewhere were so completely lacking in strength. But the slave took pains to give Brer Rabbit other significant qualities. He became in their stories by turn a practical joker, a braggart, a wit, a glutton, a lady's man, and a trickster. But his essential characteristic was his ability to get the better of bigger and stronger animals. To the slave in his condition the theme of weakness overcoming strength through cunning proved endlessly fascinating.[15]

The slave's instinct for survival is recognized by Benjamin Botkin in the form of Old John, the folk figure who generally fools his master and delights his fellow slaves. According to Botkin, this motif was an expression of the bondsman's wish fulfillment:

> . . . in his folk stories and anecdotes he took a subtle revenge on his master by turning the tales on him. Just as Br'er Rabbit, in a politer form, for the entertainment of the whites, symbolizes the triumph of cunning over superior force, so among themselves the Negroes told more realistic and more caustic tales of Old John, the slave who outwits his master, even though he sometimes gets caught. . . . His hard-hitting lore reflects the way in which the Negro has adapted himself to a white man's world by "hitting a straight lick with a crooked stick."[16]

In *Iola Leroy* the slaves use codes, such as saying that the butter is fresh and the fish and eggs are in good condition in order to pass the news of a Yankee victory and that the butter is rancid and the produce stale to announce southern success. Harper's account of this special use of language works effectively because she dramatizes a group of slaves engaged in such deception and skillfully records their slang and dialect. An example is the following exchange between Linda and another slave:

> "Oh, sho, child," said Linda, "I can't read de newspapers, but ole Missus' face is newspaper nuff for me. I looks at her every mornin' wen she walks kine o' droopy den I thinks things is gwine wrong for dem. But ef she comes yere looking right pleased an' larffin all over her face, an'

steppin so frisky, den I knows de Secesh is gettin' de bes' ob de Yankees. . . .

"Ole Miss is in de parlor prayin' for de Secesh to gain de day, and we's prayin' in de cabins and kitchens for de Yankees to get de bes' of it. . . . While you was gone to market old Miss com'd out yere, her face looking as long as my arm, tellin' us all 'bout de war and a saying dem Yankees shipped our folks all to pieces. And she was 'fraid dey'd all be down yere soon. I thought they couldn't come too soon for we. But I didn't tell her so."

"No, I don't expect you did."

"No, I didn't; ef you buys me for a fool you loses your money shore. . . . An' when she war gone, we jes' broke loose. Jake turned somersets and said he warnt 'fraid ob dem Yankees; he know'd which side his brad was buttered on. . . . As to Jinny, she jis' capered and danced all ober de flore. An' I jis' had to put my han' ober her mouf to keep old Miss from yereing her. . . . Oh, honey, I war jus' ready to crack my sides larffin, jus' to see what a long face Jinny puts on when ole Miss is talkin' an' den to see dat face wen Missus' back is turned, why it's good as a circus. It's nuff to make a horse laff" (pp. 10–11).

In passages such as this one, Harper abandons the stereotypes and effectively draws her minor characters as completely believable human beings. This impression is reinforced in a later picture of Linda (now Aunt Linda) and her husband, Salters. Aunt Linda is posed as an amusing and realistic foil for the book's idealized heroine, Iola, who has dedicated her life to the education of former slaves. Despite Iola's fervent appeals, Aunt Linda stubbornly insists that she has too many chickens to feed and too many meals to cook to find the time to learn to read. Her playful relationship with Salters further humanizes her and makes her a convincing individual.

The reader's interest in another Aunt Lindy, the heroine of Victoria Earle's short sketch by that name, depends entirely upon a similar use of folk materials. Lindy's most interesting attribute is her knowledge of folk medicine, revealed in a charge to her old husband, Joel, to fetch her a "hole passel of mullein leaves . . . er han-ful ob mountaing mint, sweet balsam—an' cam'le" (p. 11).

While the Black novelists use many of the clichés employed by white writers, two popular Reconstruction characters—the ungrateful, wretched freedman and the vengeful, brutal Black—are understandably absent from their works. As one might also expect, because of their propagandist aims, there are no lazy, thieving freedmen in these writings as there were in popular white novels. Unlike the figures in pro-slavery fiction, evil Blacks are those who thwart the advancement of their race rather than those who attempt to exercise their newly acquired, postbellum rights. The closest the novelists come to portraying African-American villains is their picture of Blacks or mulattoes like Hawkins and Jefferson Coleman in *Bond and Free,* who are hired by whites to trap runaway slaves.

Very little time is spent describing them, however, and none in explaining their reasons for betraying members of their own race.

A more complete picture is of slaves selected to be dreaded overseers. Uncle Dick of *Bond and Free* accepts such a position. Howard says that whenever Black was set over Black,

> the slaves were made to suffer, if possible, greater persecution than under a white man. The authority given them over their brethren, and their great anxiety to retain it by pleasing their masters, led them to extremes in their treatment. . . . White men were hard drivers and cruel overseers, but black men exceeded them, besides being very deceptive and treacherous. They would pry into the secrets of the poor slaves and then expose them to their masters.[17]

One of the sources of the Black drivers' cruelty, which led to the destruction of Blacks by Blacks, was that depicted in Ralph Ellison's *Invisible Man:* the acceptance of many of the norms of the white power structure and the desire to achieve a successful position within it. For the Black slave driver, as well as for Bledsoe, the president of Ellison's Negro college, this complex motivation results in the maintenance of Black powerlessness and the reinforcement of the minority's derogatory self-image. Neither in Uncle Dick's fields, in Howard's novel, nor in Bledsoe's classrooms was there the slightest suggestion of equality. It was precisely the maintenance of inequality, both between Black and white and within Black society, that kept Uncle Dick and Dr. Bledsoe in power.

An equally complex group are the servants in *Clotelle* who delight in the mistreatment suffered by Brown's mulatto heroine. Ordered to cut the curls from the head of the newly enslaved child, Dinah the cook relishes the punishment and, afterwards, rejoices that the light-skinned Clotelle "'gins to look like a nigger now" (p. 40). Dinah's unnatural cruelty toward both a child and a member of her own race is not left a mystery for long. Brown reveals that Dinah was the mother of thirteen children, all of whom had been taken from her when they were small. Her hatred for the white masters who mistreated her and her children is transferred not only to all whites but also to mulattoes, whom she feels deserve her contempt because they deliberately try to look and act like whites: "I don't like dese merlatter niggers, no how. Dey always want to set dey seff up for sumfin' big" (p. 41).

Dinah is incapable of looking at Clotelle and seeing a suffering child. All she sees is a nearly white face, an abstraction of those who took away her babies, and a creature previously pampered and doted upon, while her own children have known only privation because they were born Black. Such probings of the cook's motivations raises Brown's portrayal of Dinah above the common picture of a "sooty-browed" mammy of the kitchen to that of a complicated human being, moved by old wounds and animosities to a cruelty completely out of keeping with the tradition of the white-kerchiefed, broad-bosomed, grinning Aunt

Jemima, of which she could so easily have been an example. It is impossible to forget, however, that the complex Dinah appears right alongside Sam, the buffoon. This fact is an indication of the almost schizophrenic tensions in the sources, aims, and choices of the earliest Black novelists.

Another intriguing secondary character is the Reverend Ananias Fogg in Jones's *Hearts of Gold*. His "black trousers ornamented with tobacco juice and bulging slightly at the knees" (p. 159), Fogg appears at first as simply a ridiculous burlesque of the Black preacher. Black ministers, as noted, were commonplace in southern humor, in which they were shown to be ridiculous, proud, ignorant, and superstitious; they conducted emotional church services on Sunday and fell into all of the sins of the flesh during the rest of the week. Jones's preacher, whose "sermons were a combination of bluff, bluster, and crocodile enthusiasm" (p. 159), also stands guilty of these charges, but he is not simply a repetition of the common stereotype.

Fogg's comic air is dissipated by his later portrayal as both a kind-hearted cleric and, perversely, a threat to the heroine's safety. Despite his bluster and hypocrisy, Fogg devotes himself to his parishioners and undergoes any self-sacrifice to minister to their needs, even to the extent of compromising his own religious convictions to assure widows and orphans that their deceased husbands and fathers, riotous lives notwithstanding, are surely saved. In spite of this sympathetic aspect of his character, Fogg's personality has its darker side. He is a frequenter of a rooming house run by Mrs. Landers, with whom he enjoys long, brandy-soaked conversations into the late hours of the night. Although Jones carefully avoids being explicit, he hints several times that Mrs. Landers's rooming house is actually a brothel and that she is something other than fit company for his married minister. Sexual transgressions were frequently attributed to Black clergymen by southern humorists. Fogg's sins, however, are not merely the traditional ones of concupiscence. Drunk on Mrs. Landers's brandy, he attempts to seduce Regina and, when she repulses him, retaliates by slandering her. Although his vengeance causes short-term embarrassment rather than long-term harm, Fogg's vindictiveness is more than enough to remove his clown's makeup. Jones misses the opportunity to draw a picture of a convincing human being, torn by contradictory desires and prone to destructive as well as helpful action, by failing to explain or demonstrate fully Fogg's understanding of himself and his motivations. He remains an ultimately unsatisfactory, if fascinating, character, with one foot dancing along the minstrel stage and the other groping for ground among the more complex villains of Western literature.

In general, then, the early novelists reject commonplace white views by portraying evil Blacks as those who hurt their own people. Blacks are considered to be villainous in direct proportion to their betrayal of the race's cause or their harm of their fellows and not, as in Reconstruction novels, on account of brutality or vengefulness against whites. In the best of these depictions—Aunt Dinah's, for instance—social and psychological reasons for their cruelty and betrayal are suggested, and thus some depth of characterization is achieved.

Mulatto characters receive the most interesting handling. While the Black writers, it is true, follow popular white conventions in portraying the beauty, intelligence, and pathos of the person of mixed blood, they nevertheless inject the lives of these characters with realism by demonstrating the social intricacies that miscegenation created. Clotelle is a typical heroine of the tragic octoroon variety in that she is pictured as living a secure, even luxurious, childhood until her mother's racial mixture is revealed and they are both sold into slavery. After that, she suffers at the hands of both vengeful whites and jealous Blacks until she is rescued by Devenant. Despite the artificiality and idealization in her portrayal, Brown suggests some of the actual complexity of the life of the person of mixed blood, especially in his portrayal of Clotelle's relationships with other Blacks, such as Dinah the cook.

As mentioned earlier, the mulatto was generally considered a pathetic creature because he or she was part white. Whatever they thought of Black bondage, the idea of whites suffering the hardships and indignities of slavery was repulsive to most nineteenth-century Americans. Brown was well aware of this basically racist soft spot in the national heart, and through his presentation of Lizzie, a blue-eyed, fair-skinned mulatto "with an expressive and intellectual forehead and a countenance full of dignity and heroism," and of her child of "alabaster whiteness," through whose veins "the blood of some proud Southerner, no doubt, flowed" (p. 15), he exposes the public horror of slavery's victimizing those considered white.

Like the other early Black novelists (Charles Chestnutt, of course, being in a category of his own in dealing with this theme), Brown accepts only partially the literary tradition of the mulatto who must suffer throughout the story and then die. Because of the propagandist intent of these books, traditional romantic pathos could not be an end in itself. Even the characters who meet unhappy fates do not run the well-trod, melancholy course but are victims of the same murderous circumstances as their darker brothers and sisters. Moreover, the problems of the main characters who are mulattoes demonstrate a more complete understanding of the social problems relating to miscegenation than the stereotype of the tragic octoroon permits.

Clotelle provides further examples. Marion and her children suffer the traditional fate of being sold into slavery after the death of her white husband. Her sister Isabella is pursued and forced to jump from a bridge into the Potomac in a suicidal effort to avoid recapture. Clotelle, however, successfully breaks the pattern by escaping slavery to live a life of luxury in France as a lawfully married woman and is even united, by the end of the book, with Jerome, her first love. More believably, Brown suggests through the glee of the cook, Dinah, and the other darker servants who witness the young Clotelle's humiliation that much of the mulattoes' suffering stems from their alienation from both Blacks and whites. The complete and cruel isolation of the mulatto, of course, has become à popular theme in twentieth-century American fiction, finding its most forceful embodiment in the person of Joe Christmas in William Faulkner's *Light in August*.

James H. W. Howard makes this same theme explicit in *Bond and Free*. Purcey, whose father was white, has two half-sisters, Emiline and Eloise, who react to her in surprisingly different ways. Emiline "was of a brown-skin hue, with thick lips, stubborn hair, and very coarse features. . . . With that feeling born of slavery, Emiline cordially hated Purcey; first, because, as she termed it, 'she was half white and stuck up,' second, because of the natural animosity borne by all field hands toward all house servants" (p. 12). Eloise, however, has a completely different opinion: "There was but one person on earth that she seemed to care for, and that was Purcey. She loved Purcey with a devotion that her nature in no way betrayed, and when asked why she loved her so, she would say, 'Cause she's white and ain't like us common niggers' " (p. 119). The two reactions, as superficially different as they appear, are in essence the same, since both sisters judge Purcey by the accidents of her skin and rank. Such an attitude among Blacks themselves, who of all people should realize the dehumanizing blindness of such standards, indicates the destructive pervasiveness of racism in American culture.[18]

There are, it is true, characters of mixed blood suffering their expected literary fate in these novels. In every case, however, factors are presented that qualify the standard tragic mulatto plot. Regina Underwood's parents in *Hearts of Gold,* a white abolitionist's daughter and a runaway mulatto, flee to Canada and live and die in poverty. Regina herself, however, never suffers directly because of her mixed blood. She lives a useful life teaching school in the South and marries the man of her choice by the book's end. Clement St. John of the same book experiences the identical pressures and prejudices as other African-Americans, however light or dark their skin, and eventually achieves resounding professional success.

In Harper's book, Iola Leroy and her brother, reared in luxury and educated in the North, were unaware throughout their childhood that their mother was part Black. When their father dies, their parents' wedding contract is declared illegal, and the family is separated and sold. Frances Harper spends little time, however, emphasizing the pathos of her heroine's situation; she is much more concerned with showing Iola's slowly increasing knowledge about the degradation of the slaves and her decision to alleviate their sufferings after the Civil War. Iola is, nevertheless, acutely aware of the problems in a racially mixed alliance and refuses to wed the white Dr. Gresham, believing that their union could not stand the strain of social ostracism likely to occur once her race were revealed. She is never shown to suffer greatly from this decision and eventually marries another mulatto, Dr. Latimer, who shares her dedication to the uplift of the newly freed slaves. John Saunders in *Appointed* is discriminated against in his attempts to find a suitable job in Michigan and is murdered by a racist mob during a visit to the South. His misfortunes, however, are those likely to happen to any Black man, not specifically a mulatto.

Of all these protagonists, only Clarence Garie leads a disastrous life that can be directly linked to his mixed blood; even in this case, his misfortune is not foreordained, but results from his futile attempt to pass for white. Mr. Walters in *The Garies and Their Friends* presents what may be taken as Webb's attitude toward "passing":

> "An undetected forger, who is in constant fear of being apprehended, is happy in comparison with that coloured man who attempts, in this country, to hold a place in the society of whites by concealing his origin. He must live in constant fear of exposure; this dread will embitter every enjoyment, and make him the most miserable of men" (p. 275).[19]

Clarence Garie's relationship with his sister, Emily, who has opted to ignore her white complexion to remain with the Blacks who have befriended her, is almost completely destroyed by his decision to pass. His downfall comes when a malicious former acquaintance, Lawyer Stevens's son, reveals his secret. His engagement to Birdie, a white, New York society girl, is broken by her father, and the full weight of a life of useless deception crushes him. He is literally destroyed by this misfortune, after which both he and Birdie die of broken hearts. Unfortunately succumbing to the lure of romantic fiction, thus diluting the realistic point of what has occurred, Webb paints a sentimental scene of Clarence's reunion with his sister. Emily, because of her acceptance of her identity, suffers no such catastrophe and, like most of the other mulatto heroines, is happily married in the end.

Of course, a world in which all the right people eventually meet and marry is hardly the real one. The Black novelists can be seen, in this instance, as substituting the popular allegiance to the power of romantic love for the much more degrading stereotype of the self-destructive tragic mulatto. Moreover, the understanding shown by all of these writers that it is alienation from both Blacks and whites that causes the genuine suffering of the person of mixed blood provides a realistic and compelling basis for their treatment of such characters.

Without a doubt, the nineteenth-century novel that flows most surely from the Black literary tradition and, therefore, deserves special attention is *Blake; or, The Huts of America* by the abolitionist and Black nationalist Martin R. Delany.[20] The plot of this novel, which was serialized in the *Weekly Anglo-African* from November 1861 until late May 1862, is divided into two parts, the first dealing with American slavery, the second with bondage in Cuba. It is unified by the themes of oppression and responses to it, Black family life and religion, and, in particular, the figure of Henry Blake, the West Indian slave.

Delany's plot serves a twofold purpose similar to those of the slave narratives. It offers a Black interpretation of bondage and emphasizes the exploits of an individual slave who is daring and clever enough to thwart the system. Floyd J. Miller notes, "the complete novel contains perhaps six chapters that have not yet been uncovered," no doubt dealing with the Cuban slave uprising and Henry's return to his wife, Maggie.[21] After the excitement of the early episodes of American bondage and escape and the gripping mutiny on the slave ship *Vulture*, the last part of the book, which should be the most compelling, is limp. Revolutionary action is repeatedly promised, but unfulfilled, and Delany disastrously slows his narrative by including a number of unnecessarily lengthy prayers and speeches. Presumably, the lost chapters provide a resolution of both the slaves' eagerness for change and the fulfillment of Blake's role as a revolutionary leader.

Blake is vaster in scope than the other nineteenth-century Black novels, encompassing the slavery experience in Cuba as well as in America. Several of the other works, however, also expand the scene of the slave narratives, *Clotelle* taking its readers to Europe, *The Heroic Slave* leading them onto the high seas. *Blake*'s primary contribution, then, does not rest with the broad scope of its action, but with Delany's revelations about the complex relationships of Black to Black and the similarity of racial and economic exploitation, wherever slavery occurs.

Three motifs are developed in Delany's examination of Black interaction: the status of the mulatto, the generation gap, and the role of religion. Besides educating his white readers in the realities of slave life, the writer illuminates the gradual development of Blake from an individual, rebellious slave to the leader and spokesman of his people. In the beginning, he is solitary and questioning; by the end, he is united with others of the oppressed and has become the lawgiver.

Despite occasional aid, such as that offered by the mulatto gentleman of Detroit to Blake and his band of runaways, the usual relationship between the novel's fair-skinned Blacks and their darker brothers is every bit as cruel and exploitative as that between the white masters and their slaves. In his role of naive questioner, Henry uncovers the practices of a wealthy, mulatto planter family, the Metoyers. "You seem to understand these people very well, aunty," Blake remarks to his aged informant; "Now please tell me what kind of masters there are generally in the Red River country." "Haud 'nough, chile," she replies, "haud 'nough, God on'ly knows!" "Do the colored masters treat theirs generally worse than the whites?" "No, hunny, 'bout da same" (p. 72). When Blake asks why Blacks would treat other Blacks so cruelly, old Aunt Dolly explains that they accept the white ways of conducting business. The imitation of such self-destructive values is one of Delany's major ironic thrusts and is directly related to the widespread antebellum miscegenation. As he explains,

> Like those of Charleston, some of the light mixed bloods of Richmond hold against the blacks and pure-blooded Negroes the strongest prejudice and hatred, all engendered by the teachings of their Negro-fearing master-fathers. All of the terms and epithets of disparagement commonly used by the whites toward the blacks are as readily applied to them by this class of mixed bloods (p. 116).

One such family, the Lateurs, forces its dark-skinned, old mother to be a nanny for all the children and to wait for her meals until everyone else has finished eating (p. 71).

An interesting fact of southern racial legalisms is revealed by Blake's questioning:

> According to an old-existing custom said to have originated by law, a mulatto or quadroon who proved a white mother were themselves regarded as white: and many availing themselves of the fact, took advantage of it by leaving their connections with the blacks and turning entirely over to the whites. Their children take further advantage of this by inter-marrying with the whites, by which their identity becomes extinct, and they enter every position in society both social and political (p. 116).

The mulattoes unable to pass, whether because of a Black mother or pigmentation too dark to be disguised, are outcasts, accepted by neither segment of society: "Shy of the blacks and fearful of the whites, they go sneaking about with the countenance of a criminal, of one conscious of having done wrong to his fellows. Spurned by the one and despised by the other, they are the least happy of all the classes" (p. 116). Evidence of their insecurity is the "Brown Society" of South Carolina, "an organized association of mulattos, created by the influence of the whites, for the purpose of preventing pure-blooded Negroes from entering the social circle, or holding intercourse with them" (p. 109).

Two elderly couples are employed in the novel to demonstrate the gulf in attitudes between older slaves and younger ones like Henry and his associates. Daddy Joe, Mammy Judy, Uncle Jerry, and Aunt Rachel have silently suffered injustice all of their lives and are fearful of taking any steps to change their situation. When Henry urges them to come along with him to Canada, they protest, "we ole folks too ole fah gwine headlong out yandah an' do'o whah we gwine. . . . We ole folks ain' politishon an' undestan' de graumma uh dese places, an' w'en we git dah den maybe do'n like it an cahn' git back" (p. 30). Although they are persuaded to attempt an escape once their daughter Maggie is sold to Cuba and most of their friends on the Franks's plantation have run away, their real trust is not in Henry, the revolutionary leader, but in the Lord. After an angry outburst by Blake, Mammy Judy cautions, "Come, come, Henry, yeh mus'n talk so; we is po' weak and bline cretehs, an' cahn' see de way uh de Laud. He move' in a mystus way, his wundahs to puhfaum" (p. 16). Blake recognizes the limitations of this advice and observes that it is useless for him to listen to the same gospel from her that he has heard all his life from the slaveholders.

Delany's attitude toward religion is a complex, but logical, one, similar to Frederick Douglass's. Although the Blacks in the novel are not allowed to attend the same churches as their masters, religion serves two vital, yet contradictory, functions for them. It is both a comforter in their trials under slavery and, as Henry Bibb and Solomon Northup have shown, an aid in enforcing and maintaining the system of bondage.

With both Maggie taken away from them and Henry in imminent danger of being sold, Mammy Judy and Daddy Joe fall on their knees together: " 'Look to de Laud ole umin, 'e's able t' bah us out mo' neh conkeh. Keep de monin stah in sight!' advised Daddy Joe. 'Yes, ole man, yes, dat I done dis many long day, an' ah ain' gwine lose sight uh it now! No, God bein' my helpeh, I is gwine keep my eyes right on it, dat I is!' " (p. 25). Later in the novel, when Henry reveals to another old couple his plan to unite the slaves for a general uprising, their response is a spontaneous religious litany: " 'Blessed be God's eternal name!' concluded the man himself. 'I've long been praying and looking, but God has answered me at last.' 'None could answer it, but a prayer-hearing God!' replied the wife. 'None would answer it but a prayer-hearing God!' responded the husband. 'None did answer it, but a prayer-hearing God!' exclaimed the woman. 'Glory to God! Glory to God! 'Tis none but He can deliver!' " (p. 117). The genuine religious fervor of Delany's slaves cannot be questioned.

While the faith of the Blacks is a powerful source of their strength and endurance, it is also a factor in maintaining their bondage. Madame Montego wonders aloud to Placido, "Why so many more of our people than the whites attend church?" The poet conventionally replies, "Because . . . we are really more religiously inclined than they." "I have also often wondered why it was that we are so much more submissive than they," she continues significantly (p. 282). At one point, Daddy Joe attempts to pacify Henry by reminding him, "De wud say 'stan' still and see de salbation,' " to which the determined slave replies, "I've been 'standing still' long enough—I'll 'stand still' no longer" (p. 21). When the old folks voice their fear that Henry has lost his religion, he explains, "You're mistaken, Mammy; I do trust the Lord as much as ever, but I now understand him better than I use to, that's all. I don't intend to be made a fool of any longer by false preaching" (p. 20). Like the slave narrators, he sees the whites' interpretation of religion as only a reflection of their designs for power: "I have altogether lost my faith in the religion of my oppressors. As they are our religious teachers, my estimate of the thing they give is no greater than it is for those who give it" (p. 21).

That Henry has not rejected his belief in a personal, more meaningful God is clear when he fervently prays for the faith, hope, and love necessary to effect his own escape and to remedy the situation of his people (p. 69). Whenever he gathers a group of slaves together to instruct them in ways of obtaining freedom, he opens the discussion with a prayer or asks someone he considers more worthy to do so. As he progresses on his journey, instructing others in the tactics of escape and unifying them in a determination to resist oppression, he repeats Daddy Joe's old biblical admonition, "Stan' still children, and see da salvation of da Lawd" (p. 79), transforming its meaning, however, from one cautioning patience, long suffering, and visionary hope for a better world after death to a completely secular, militant code, advising secret preparation for either personal or collective overthrow of bondage. Salvation now means political freedom. Blake turns the very language of the whites' self-serving religious dictums against them.

At the end of the book, when he and the Cuban Blacks are forming their secret organization, he reveals that he has accepted the concept of a pragmatic use of religion. "The whites accept of nothing but that which promotes their interests and happiness, socially, politically and religiously," he observes. "They would discard a religion, tear down a church, overthrow a government, or desert a country, which did not enhance their freedom. In God's great and righteous name, are we not willing to do the same?" (p. 258). Blake's God is not the master slaveholder that the whites believe in, but a spiritual force enflaming the hearts of all individuals with an understanding of their human dignity and overturning the works of those seeking to oppress others. When Placido says, "God wills what's best, Henry," he is not cautioning patient acceptance of suffering in the manner of the slaveholder, Mammy Judy, and Daddy Joe, but is establishing a divine basis for revolutionary action. "Then we would what God wills," replies Blake (p. 241).

Delany's attitude toward Black superstition and conjuring is no less involved. Henry makes it his special mission to debunk the widespread reliance on charms whenever he has a chance, judging that the only obvious effect of such "foolishness and stupidity" is to put "money into the pockets of the pretended conjurer," giving "him power over others by making them afraid of him" (p. 136).

His interpretation is reinforced when he ventures into North Carolina's Dismal Swamp, where a number of the old confederates of the insurrectionist Nat Turner are still hiding. Among them is old Gamby Gholar, a noted conjurer, who attempts to frighten the runaway with an assortment of charms. When Henry stands his ground, Gamby Gholar accepts him as the leader for whom he and the other inhabitants of the swamp have been waiting and offers him the breastbone of a small bird, which he calls the "charm bone of a tree frog" (p. 113). Blake accepts the charm and also allows himself to be anointed "a priest of the order of High Conjurors" (p. 114).

While Delany explains that Henry agrees to this ceremony because "amusing enough it was to him" to consent "to satisfy the aged devotees of a time-honored superstition among them," he also recognizes a significance in their belief that transcends Gamby Gholar's inept rattling of worthless trinkets in a hollow gourd. In all of his travels, it is only in the Dismal Swamp that he discovers any semblance of a Black organization united to overthrow oppression. Gamby Gholar, Maudy Ghamus, and others reveal that there were enough Blacks hiding in the swamp to rise up effectively against the whites, but they needed the cooperation of the slaves on the outside and, despite repeated attempts to gain their trust and support, had been unsuccessful in doing so: "Take plenty goomba an' fongosa 'long wid us, an' plant mocasa all along, an' da got nuffin' fah do but come, an' da 'ooden come!" (p. 114). Blake recognizes that these renegades view him as the spiritual descendant of Nat Turner, and as their hope, therefore, for organizing all the Blacks and fulfilling the dreams of their slain leader. They create him a conjurer of the highest degree, a "seven finger High-glister": "With this qualification he was licensed with unlimited power—a power before given no one—to go forth and do wonders" (p. 115). These wonders will involve instilling a sense of worth and power in a previously helpless people.

Ronald Takaki, in *Violence in the Black Imagination,* notes that despite Blake's "judgment [that] black redemption requires not only economic enterprise and African nationalism but also violence against the white oppressor," he "seems to be ambivalent toward anti-white violence."[22] Takaki ascribes this ambivalence to Delany's and his wife's divided racial allegiance as mulattoes and to the writer's acceptance of the idealistic premises of the Constitution. In the absence of the novel's concluding chapters, it is impossible to make a final judgment about the extent of Delany's militancy. It is true, however, that his hero is careful to shed no blood, and in spite of their superior numbers and the confusion of the whites, no violent rebellion occurs when the *Vulture's* slaves are loosed. The violence in the book, as in the narratives and orations for the most part, is directed against the Black dependency, fear, and degrading self-images that exploitation fosters.

Clearly, even though popular stereotypes and the pressure of contemporary literary tastes had considerable influence, the Black novelists followed in significant ways the tradition of their slave orators and autobiographers. The presence of imaginative and believable folk characters, whether lowly like their various wise "aunties" or heroic like Henry Blake; the realistic depictions of the horrors of slavery; and the satiric jabs at the church and the political system—all reveal their indebtedness. The early twentieth-century author who utilized this tradition most fully and who was most obviously the forerunner of militant modern writers was the prolific Baptist minister Sutton Elbert Griggs.

Part 2
THE MAJOR WRITERS: GRIGGS, DUNBAR, and CHESNUTT

3

Sutton Griggs: the Dilemma of the Black Bourgeoisie

> Observe that all of the races of mankind that have achieved greatness have developed a literature. Not a single race that has no literature is classified as great in the eyes of the world. . . .
>
> Where people have not the habit of reading there will not be much writing. The future progress of the Negro race calls for an awakening on the part of the people to the necessity of cultivating the habit of reading and a stimulation of the art of making literature as indispensable aids to the development of the spirit of patriotism.
>
> *Sutton Griggs,* Life's Demands; or, According to Law

As these remarks indicate, Sutton Elbert Griggs approached the writing of fiction with the same utilitarian view as his predecessors. The result, however, was vastly different. Griggs's five novels move away from the earlier diffuse rendering of white society's racist attitudes and behavior to center, for the first time in Black fiction, directly on the tensions and ironies within the emerging African-American community.[1] His portrait is one of conflicting generations and warring classes, of trustworthy leaders and deceitful demagogues. In sharper focus, it is a picture of the turn-of-the-century African-Americans simultaneously stung by bitterness, self-deception, and insecurity, but strengthened by their people's traditional determination, perception, and hope. Griggs's picture is a fast-action photograph of a race in transition, a group portrait of a family whose features were not yet clear.

Sutton Griggs's novels are literary collages, part propagandist blueprint for political action, part gothic romance of the maze and morass of miscegenation, and part symbolic description of the conditions threatening the internal and external life of the "New Negro" of the turn of the century.[2] Griggs yokes together these disparate elements to focus upon the profound dilemma of the middle-class African-American who daily experienced the murderous rebuffs of white society. Griggs's uneasy solution is Black psychological, economic, and social independence, pragmatically tempered by political cooperation with enlightened whites.

His books, therefore, provide a decided contrast to the simpler styles and visions of his predecessors. More importantly, they dramatize the agonizing birth of a new Black consciousness. Nineteenth-century America provided a difficult confinement for the laboring Black race; therefore, its emerging professional class was weakened by insecurity and contradictions, some of which are reflected in Griggs's own political philosophy.

His espousal of Black activism and self-determination clearly establish him, like Martin Delany, as a middle-class forerunner of today's revolutionary Black artists. Nevertheless, his flashes of Emersonian optimism and trust in racial cooperation blunt the edge of his protest against American institutions and limit the thrust of his radicalism. There are in his works, of course, no naive assurances that African-Americans can "make it" in the United States simply by following the prevailing code of hard work, education, and ambition. Nor is there much hope of escape to some more congenial country. Rather, his books cry out for Black independence and self-reliance on American soil, but also insist that progress will depend upon "conservative" leaders in both races. He strongly rejects violence, a possibility that he explores fully and often, as a means of righting wrongs, yet just as strongly urges full political participation by Blacks and peaceful, but militant, social action.

His insistence upon self-help stems from his own pride in his people's accomplishments despite oppressive social and economic conditions. In a tribute to John L. Webb, a southern Black businessman and philanthropist, Griggs asserts: "The Negroes are strong enough numerically to provide much for their own welfare that is not being provided, and the results of this neglect constitute a very dark chapter in the life of the race."[3] This theme of racial ability and consequent responsibility forms the backbone of his novels.

Sutton Griggs's career was nurtured in the Southern Baptist church, to which, throughout his life, he devoted whatever energies were not directed toward specifically racial concerns. Born in Chatfield, Texas, on June 19, 1872, the son of Reverend Allen R. Griggs, a pioneer Baptist preacher in Texas, Griggs was educated in the public schools of Dallas and graduated from Bishop College in Marshall, Texas, in 1890. He completed his education at the Richmond Theological Seminary and accepted pastorates at the First Baptist Church, Berkley, Virginia, and later at the Edgefield Baptist Church and the First Baptist Church, East Nashville, Tennessee.

It was during this period that he produced the novels and many of the pamphlets and collections of essays urging racial pride and self-help upon which his literary fame rests. Providing an example in his own career of the self-reliance and professionalism that he preached, Griggs managed the Orion Publishing Company, which produced all but the first of his novels, from 1908 to 1911. This period was Griggs's most militant, one which projected him, within the relative safety of the church, as an outspoken racial leader: "With a brilliant mind and a ready pen, Doctor Griggs went to the fray in such militant fashion that he was almost termed a radical on racial matters. He was acclaimed as a champion in all sections and his appearances before the sessions of other religious groups were occasions of wild demonstrations of enthusiastic approval."[4] Ruth Marie Powell, in her history of the American Baptist Theological Seminary, suggests that Griggs's oratory, even within the confines of ecclesiastical issues, adopted racial goals. One of his speeches, she says, "stirred the great body of Southern Baptists to the idea of ministerial preparation for the Negro in the South."[5]

About 1920 however, when Griggs moved to Memphis and took up the pastorate of the Tabernacle Baptist Church, he began to step back from his earlier fiery rhetoric and insistence upon African-American self-determination. The author of the article about Griggs in *Negro Baptists of Tennessee* speculates that the cost of maintaining the Orion press and other financial problems "served to cool his enthusiasm and sober his thought on racial attitudes." Whatever the cause, to the puzzlement of many of his friends, Griggs at this time "became the champion of inter-racial good-will and cooperation and the many books written during his life in Memphis were conciliatory and he soon became known as the 'Negro Apostle to the White Race.'"[6] It should be noted, however, that the theme of racial cooperation was always present in his works, muting his call for Black self-determination.

During this period Griggs's identification as a part of the American establishment as well as an African-American spokesman is testified to by his work during World War I as a speaker, presumably in Black communities, in support of the purchase of Liberty Bonds and for other similar campaigns. More and more, during the last decade of his life, he devoted his energies to such fund-raising on behalf of the church. He served as president of the American Baptist Theological Seminary from April 8, 1925, to October 1, 1926, resigning to accept his father's former pastorate in Texas, where he died on January 3, 1933.[7]

Like his predecessors, Griggs succumbed to the dangerous allure of popular fiction. His females, too, are "queenly" and "beautifully formed"; they have noses "of the prettiest possible size and shape," chins "that tapered with the most exquisite beauty," lips that "seemed arranged by nature in such a manner as to be incomplete without a kiss," heads "of perfect shape," "tender brown eyes so full of soul," hair "glistening as if in pride of its extreme blackness," eyebrows "that were ideally beautiful," necks, "which with infinite regard for the requirements of perfect art, descended and expanded so as to form part of a faultless bust," arms that "tapered so exquisitely at the wrists," and figures composed of "a series of divinely fashioned curves." His typical hero is "tall and exceedingly handsome," possessing a form that conveyed "an impression of nobility and strength," with "smooth" skin, a "frank, open" face, "intellectual" brows, and a head "of splendid shape." Moreover, like the earlier fictional representatives of their race, Griggs's protagonists, male and female, are cultured, talented, and virtuous, having great intellectual potential. Because their primary function, however, is to embody conflicting political positions, rather than merely to serve as idealized models of Black potential or as traditional heroes and heroines of popular romance, these characters are different in an essential way from those of his predecessors.[8] Although they, too, fall in love and marry and are victims of lynching attempts and other threats upon their lives, Griggs's focus is not on romance or adventure, but on the political realizations, theories, and solutions that they represent through their actions.

Furthermore, his complex plots of miscegenation and intrigue are more than an obedient nod to the entertainment demands of a popular audience. His narratives are invested with a symbolic import that transforms them into compelling metaphors for Black and white life in the turn-of-the-century South. His books contain more deaths and disasters than those of his predecessors combined. Within the five plots appear two sudden insanities, three deathbed scenes, two deaths in a fire, five supposed deaths in a fire, two fatal heart attacks, two killings in self-defense, one attempted murder, two slayings with sexual overtones, four shootings, four suicides, one attempted suicide, one legal hanging, one tarring and feathering, four lynchings, one attempted lynching, and two political executions! An examination of these scenes reveals, however, that Griggs generally abandons sentimental or melodramatic depictions as irrelevant to his purpose. The deaths in his books most often dramatize the irresponsible and widespread destructiveness of a racist climate and the dangers of Black political involvement.[9] More importantly, coming as they do with such unrelieved frequency, they establish an atmosphere of constant external tension that corresponds to the violence and frustration burning within his Black characters. America's social and psychological climate is, in Griggs's view, one and the same.

The most fully developed of these violent scenes are those of lynchings. His inclusion of the gruesome details of such killings almost entirely precludes a sentimental rendering, and his focus upon the social causes permitting them minimizes their sensationalism. Through his skillful handling, the lynchings become metaphors for Black/white existence. This symbolic intent is clear in the treatment of one such murder in *Overshadowed* (1901).

Griggs tells his story through the eyes of the white man responsible for the lynching and concentrates upon the psychological effects of his guilt. The repentant politician reveals that at one time in his career he manufactured a rape charge against an innocent Black in order to arouse the electorate and ensure his reelection on a strongly racist platform. As he expected, the accused man was dragged from his home, tortured, and killed. Appalled by the sight of what he had caused, the congressman screwed up sufficient courage to venture close to the body after the mob had dispersed:

> "The murdered Negro was yet hanging there, and by the light of the moon struggling through the treetops and falling in spangles over his form, I saw a horrible sight. The face was ploughed up with bullets, his eyes were bulging out, his stomach was ripped open and his entrails were visible. . . . My strength failed me, and I fell forward, and clutching at anything to keep me from striking the ground, caught hold of the dead Negro.

My weight, added to his, broke the rope, and we fell down together, my
head getting caught under his mangled form'' (pp. 133–34).

Black life was as cheap after Reconstruction's decline, when the Ku Klux Klan
was rising, as it had been in slavery. Just as human bondage debased master and
slave alike, the postwar South mired itself in its "nigger problem" by blinking at
violent expedients such as lynching. The fortunes of white America, Griggs
contends, are inextricably entwined with those of the race that it captured and
exploited; like the politician in *Overshadowed,* his South traps itself under the
African-American's "mangled form.'' This lynch scene establishes the givens of
Griggs's psychological landscape, the tangled jungle of Black and white suffering and guilt that his protagonists will attempt to clear.

Griggs's despair of changing traditional race hatreds is suggested by his treatment of the murders of Bud and Foresta Harper in *The Hindered Hand* (1905).
This horrible episode is made more terrible by being static. It is enclosed within a
narrative frame depicting a small, white boy, Melville Brant, who begs permis-
sion from his mother to watch the lynching from his porch, then slips away for a
closer look. He returns home a few hours later with a piece of charred flesh, the
grisly souvenir of his afternoon's entertainment. The scene is sensational because the torture of the victims before their deaths is rendered in graphic detail.
Griggs's interest, however, is at least equally divided among Bud's and Foresta's
sufferings, the irrationality of the mob, and the degrading influence of the entire
experience upon Melville Brant, the next generation of southern white.

It is a scene not only of physical horror but also of political pessimism. The
Melville Brants of the South are neither shielded from such atrocities nor instructed to repudiate them. Lynching is, instead, an initiation rite into the tribal
customs of white society. Enclosed within its narrative frame, the double murder
suggests not only the debasement of Black and white life, but the unchanging
repetition of self-destructive rituals. Melville Brant returns home no longer innocent, but armed with a token of the insecurity of his race and prepared to venture
from his porch at a later date—not to observe, but to participate.

It is in the psychology and rituals of Black society, however, that Griggs is
most interested. Time flows in layers in his books to provide an image of
simultaneous racial identity and development. The past, with its inheritance of
slavery, is ever present to his protagonists; and the future, with its promise of
either racial equality or genocide, seems already disturbingly in view.

Griggs's first novel, *Imperium in Imperio* (1899), is a visionary work positing
the establishment of a secret, nationwide organization of educated Blacks bent on
either a complete redress of grievances or the formation of a separate Black state.
This Black underground, the Imperium, functions in the same way as the turn-
of-the-century United States government, except that its movement is revolutionary, not reactionary. Griggs recognized that there were a growing number of
frustrated, young African-Americans whose energy either would explode in a
suicidal attack upon the racist system that daily diminished them or would be

channeled into constructive methods of helping themselves and their people. As Mr. King, the white editor of the *Temps* in *Imperium* realizes, this new generation would not be content to wait and pray for justice as their fathers and grandfathers had been:

> He reasoned that the Negro who had endured the hardships of slavery might spend his time looking back and thanking God for that from which he had made his escape; but the young Negro, knowing nothing of physical slavery, would be peering into the future, measuring the distance that he had yet to go before he was truly free, and would be asking God and his own right arm for the power to secure whatever rights were still withheld. . . .
>
> So, his ear was to the ground, expecting every moment to hear the far off sounds of awakened Negroes coming to ask for liberty and if refused, to slay or be slain (pp. 42–43).

The Imperium is composed of just such dissatisfied members, angry enough to combine into a dangerous underground, highly disciplined, and determined to make their grievances known to the society at large.

Elsewhere, Griggs comments upon the political potential of the Black schoolteacher, the profession for which most college-educated Blacks were trained: "The Negro school teacher has perhaps been the greatest conservator of peace in the South, laboring *for* the Negro by the appointment of the whites, being thus placed in a position where it was to his interest to keep on good terms with both races" (*Unfettered* [1902] p. 56). In *Imperium*, however, the powerful, tradition-bound whites who control the school system fail to recognize any such peace-keeping function among educated Blacks and provide them with few opportunities. Their own people, moreover, sensitive to class restrictions and judging manual labor by the educated to be degrading, cut them off from any other means of making a living: "And instead of the matter growing better, it was growing worse year by year. Colleges were rushing class after class forth . . . and there was no employment for them" (p. 130).

Despite his acute awareness of America's failures, Sutton Griggs proves to be as intensely patriotic as any of his predecessors. He accepts the promises of America and condemns both Black and white failure to fulfill the country's professed ideals. Since he recognizes the threat to national allegiance that the severe economic dilemma of his people represents, he depicts their plight as a warning to the nation as a whole:

> They grew to hate a flag that would float in an undisturbed manner over such a condition of affairs. They began to abuse and execrate a national government that would not protect them against color prejudice, but on the contrary actually practiced it itself. Beginning with passively hating the flag, they began to think of rebelling against it and would wish for some

foreign power to come in and bury it in the dirt. They signified their willingness to participate in such a proceeding (p. 131).

Fearful of this explosive bitterness, Griggs insists that racial success or failure depends upon the quality of leadership that his people develop. Throughout the novel he warns against demagogues who would sacrifice the African-American cause for personal political gain. When the reader is introduced to the Imperium, it is in the hands of just such a leader. Stung by the racism that has frustrated his own professional and personal life, Bernard Belgrade, a mulatto and the first president of the organization, directs it to take up arms immediately against the white oppressors.

Bernard has been pampered and catered to all of his life and enters politics not through any deep concern for his race, but essentially out of personal ambition: "He decided to become the obedient servant of the people that he might thus make all the people his servants" (p. 95). Bernard's vehemence against whites is spurred by the suicide of Viola Martin, the young woman whom he wished to marry. Viola intended her death to be a political statement. While she loved Bernard, she considered it a treasonous act against her race for a person of pure African extraction to marry someone of mixed blood. As she explains in her suicide note, she had read a book entitled *White Supremacy and Negro Subordination*, which

"proved to me that the intermingling of the races in sexual relationship was sapping the vitality of the Negro race and, in fact, was slowly but surely exterminating the race. It demonstrated that the fourth generation of the children born of intermarrying mulattoes were invariably sterile or woefully lacking in vital force. It asserted that only in the most rare instances were children born of this fourth generation and in no case did such children reach maturity" (p. 173).

Her suicide, then, is her solution to the conflict between ideals and supposed reality. To Bernard it is the mandate for political militancy. "By the eternal heavens," he pledges, "these abominable horrors shall cease. The races whose union has been fraught with every curse known to earth and hell, must separate. Viola demands it and Bernard obeys" (p. 176).

Under his guidance, the Imperium forms the following resolve:

Whereas, the history of our treatment by the Anglo-Saxon race is but the history of oppression, and, whereas, our patient endurance of evil has not served to decrease this cruelty, but seems rather to increase it; and, whereas, the ballot box, the means of peaceful revolution is denied us, therefore:

Be it resolved: That the hour for wreaking vengeance for our multiplied wrongs has come.

Resolved secondly: That we at once proceed to war for the purpose of accomplishing the end just named, and for the further purpose of obtaining all our rights due us as men.

Resolved thirdly: That no soldier of the Imperium leave the field of battle until the ends for which this war was inaugurated are fully achieved (p. 226).

Bernard is opposed immediately by Belton Piedmont, a childhood rival and, ironically, the man whose life Bernard saved at one time and who introduced him to the secret workings of the organization. Belton rejects Bernard's plot for all-out war against white society not only because he recognizes the ultimate futility of such a course but also because he, unlike Bernard, does not hate all whites.

From the beginning of the novel, Griggs develops Belton, who is, no doubt, modeled upon Booker T. Washington, as a conciliator rather than an avenger. His high school graduation address was entitled "The Contribution of the Anglo-Saxon to the Cause of Human Liberty." When Mr. King of the *Temps* paid his way through college, he asked in return that Belton remember that not all white men are racists and that even the racists have some good qualities. Belton, Griggs emphasizes, "decided from that moment to never class all white men together, whatever might be the provocation, and to never regard any class as totally depraved. This is one of the keys to his future life. Remember it" (p. 47). Later, the white president of Belton's college deeply affected him when, in his baccalaureate address, he warned the graduating members of the class to resist the lure of political demagoguery that could dangerously enflame the passions of their people.

Predictably then, Belton counters Bernard's declaration of war with a more conservative proposal. First, in a speech appearing to echo Griggs's own convictions, he seeks to persuade the angry Blacks that advantages have accrued to the African-Americans from their acquaintance with the Anglo-Saxons: Christianity, "civilization," and, particularly, the English language. Like B. T. Washington, Belton seems to see a bright side to every wrong that the Blacks had to suffer. He exhorts the assembly to forego seeking revenge. American whites he asserts, are simply ignorant of the new militancy in the race and, instead of being attacked, need to be educated. He urges that the Imperium reveal its existence and extent and attempt to impress the nation with this new generation's resolve to die if it cannot achieve justice. He proposes further to give the national government four years to respond to the demands for a redress of grievances and a change in white attitudes. If, after four years, however, a positive response is not forthcoming, Belton urges a radical solution—the takeover of Texas and establishment there of the Imperium as a separate and distinct government with every intention of retaining its autonomy and of fighting off invasions from foreign powers, notably the United States. Griggs's own allegiance to Texas, no doubt, accounts for Belton's selection of this state as a new Black homeland.[10]

Belton's proposal defeats Bernard's declaration of war, but the ambitious, young mulatto is not content to lose influence over the organization so easily to his childhood rival. Bernard secretly rallies support for an alternate plan to penetrate the United States Navy with spies, thereby eventually sabotaging it, and then to inform America's enemies of the group's intent to capture Texas, promising them the state of Louisiana in return for their help in the struggle. Belton, of course, representative of "the spirit of conservatism in the Negro race" (p. 262), quickly rejects Bernard's treasonous proposal. Thereupon, Bernard wastes no time in declaring him a traitor to the Imperium and ordering him executed.

Confident once more of his power, Bernard prepares to put his plan into effect, but is thwarted at last by the defection of Berl Trout, another more conservative, nationally patriotic Black. Knowing full well that he too will be executed, Trout informs the government of the existence of the Imperium and of its plot to combine with foreign powers. Clearly speaking for Griggs, he characterizes Belton as representative of a necessary spirit of conciliation in the race, an attitude rapidly being replaced by the treasonous, suicidal ideas of demagogues like Bernard. With no sense of sarcasm, Trout lauds Belton as "the last of that peculiar type of Negro heroes that could so fondly kiss the smiting hand" (p. 262). In the tradition of the Black Baptist minister, Griggs urges Christian forbearance, sacrifice, and hope.

Imperium in Imperio is Griggs's own political statement, in thinly disguised narrative form, intended to arouse in his readers an awareness of the two vastly different directions in which African-Americans might move. In addition to being a study in types of political leaders, the novel is a blueprint for possible racial action. As the book ends, the Black organization is about to be crushed. The trustworthy leader, Belton Piedmont, who has escaped the determination of a racist teacher to humiliate him, the desire of a white doctor to murder him, and the intent of the legal system to unjustly execute him, is, ironically, killed by one of his own racial kinsmen in a raw power play for political control. The hope for racial unity and progress seems, therefore, farther away then ever because of the Blacks' own blindness in allowing hatred of whites to dupe them into following a self-serving, untrustworthy leader.

In his second novel, *Overshadowed,* Griggs lowers his sights from vast plans for racial organization to focus upon the emerging Black middle class. His tone is satiric, ridiculing in particular the group's insecurity, which causes it to sacrifice its own members on the altar of white acceptance. Erma Wysong announces this theme, the problem of identity, which unifies all of the novel's disparate action:

"Because our race has borrowed the white man's language, manner of dress, religion, ideas of home, philosophy of life, we have apparently decided that everything that the white man does is good for us to imitate. We do not stop to think that the white race has deep, ingrained faults as a race; and thus we proceed to imitate faults and virtues alike, indiscriminately and instinctively" (p. 42).

The irony of freed Blacks and their children imitating the group that enslaved them testifies once again to the race's slavery-born questioning of self-worth. Unlike his predecessors, Griggs perceives this weak spot in his people's psyche and refuses to ignore its consequences.

Throughout his works there appear white characters who are not limited to the traditional romantic hero/repulsive villain portrayal, but who are present primarily to enunciate white racial views.[11] Surprisingly, the author frequently agrees with their derogatory conclusions about Blacks—for example, the white politician in *Overshadowed* who reinforces Erma's observation that African-Americans are unable to move away from the plantation tradition of seeking white approval. The congressman observes,

> "You know . . . the Negro's weak point is gratitude to the white . . . a merchant can keep a Negro's trade forever by merely speaking to him kindly. The Negro seems to feel that he owes the white man his trade for that friendly greeting, and he will not quit trading with him to trade with a member of his own race. A smile from a white man will go farther toward getting a Negro's trade than a day's pleasant conversation from another Negro" (p. 131).

This subservience not only keeps Blacks economically dependent upon whites but also leads to their rejection of their own culture.

The Black church with its stirring music and emotional rituals was, where it could survive, an antebellum source of African-American expression and strength. As Imamu Baraka has observed, "the kind of church Black people belonged to usually connected them with society as a whole . . . identified them, their aspirations, their culture: because the church was one of the few places complete fulness of expression by the Black was not constantly censored by the white man."[12] Griggs sees this life-giving force being dissipated in the early years of the twentieth century by Black middle-class embarrassment in the face of a supercilious white society ignorant of their worship's meaning and unmoved by its vitality. Aunt Molly, a representative of the older generation, keenly regrets the changes in her church. "We is lettin dese white folks teach us too much," she complains to Erma:

> "Our church hez dun away wid dem good soul-stirrin' himes in which my soul jes' 'peared ter float right up ter God, and now we hez god a choir whut sings de himes which gibs de feelin's of white people's souls which ain't allus lack ourn. An' our elder is done quit preachin' an gwine ter readin' de Gospil ter us, an' de Speerit hez fersaken him. An' dey hez been tellin' us ter do lack white folks an' let our feelin's stay dammed up, wen it do feel so good ter let um out. An' child, bless yer soul, dey doa'n let me shout at church fir fear white folks would laugh at 'um an' fir fear dey would lose de name ub' 'Ristocrats.' But, bless yer soul, hunny, I shouts at home" (p. 59).

The diluted, imitative, new worship spawns such creatures as the Reverend Josiah Nerve, a character reminiscent of Reverend Fogg in J. McHenry Jones's *Hearts of Gold*. While Reverend Nerve derives a measure of his characterization from traditional southern humor, he is essentially representative of the middle-class dilemma.[13] His status-conscious congregation rejects him and sends him out to earn a Doctor of Divinity degree. Nerve, to his credit, realizes the mistake that his congregation is making:

"They have got me out now hunting for a D.D. just like white folks when neither me nor them knows any more about what D.D. means than Sam Smith's old mule. . . . The whites regulate all of our tastes even to telling us who are our greatest men among us. We won't acknowledge a man is great until the whites have done so" (pp. 69–71).

One preacher whom he knows was so desperate for a D.D. that he offered a theological seminary a barrel of pickled herring in exchange for it and threatened to camp atop the barrel on the school's front lawn until the coveted degree was conferred. In an attempt to pacify his own congregation, Reverend Nerve calls himself D.D.S., Doctor of Divinity Sum—Doctor of Divinity To-Be. In a gesture right out of the minstrel tradition, one which, nevertheless, fits Griggs's concept of Black self-destruction, Nerve sets fire to his church in order to collect the insurance money and build a fine brick edifice in its place. He is discovered, of course, and is last seen fleeing town on a northbound train.

As has been seen, the earlier Black writers, both slave narrators and novelists, directed their satire against Christianity's apologia of slavery and exposed the hypocritical white church members' racist dealings. Griggs, instead, focuses his criticism upon the results of the slavery mentality in the Black church. Frank Webb's Aunt Comfort was good enough to nurse sick white people, but not good enough to worship in the same pews with them. A similar snobbery, based upon a feeling of inferiority, motivates Reverend Nerve's congregation and the cruel members of Erma's church who force her to leave when she accepts a job as a maid. While the chains and whips of slavery have disappeared, Griggs's middle-class Black is still trapped by its psychological shackles.

Before his ignominious departure, Reverend Nerve mentions another borrowed pretension, marriage restrictions based upon skin color. Viola Martin's preoccupation with this subject in *Imperium* is indicative not only of the widespread Black acceptance of marriage as a tool for political and social change but also, ironically, of skin color as a determinant of human worth. "Nowadays you never hear of two coal black persons marrying each other," Nerve contends:

"The black man is pushing the black woman aside to grab the yellow woman; and the black woman is pushing the black man aside to grab the yellow man. I know a number of black mothers with black daughters that have sworn they will poison their daughters if they attempt to marry black

men. Besides don't black women with short hair rob horses' tails, billy
goats and graveyards to get hair like that of white folks'' (p. 69).

Color and class prejudices within the race lead to a number of contradictory
opinions when Erma's engagement to Astral Herndon is announced. Some insist
that Erma is making a serious mistake because Astral's complexion is darker than
hers; others severely criticize Astral for choosing a wife of mixed blood when
there are many available girls of pure African extraction. A large group disagrees
with this opinion, reasoning that "each succeeding generation should be as far
removed as possible from the original color which had so many ills chargeable to
it" (p. 184). And still another faction opposes the marriage because Astral is an
intellectual and, although educated, Erma works as a common domestic.

The class snobbishness of the newly educated Blacks is dramatized repeatedly
in *Overshadowed*. When, because of financial distress, Erma advertises in the
local paper for the position of washerwoman, cook, or nurse, she is ostracized by
her former friends. Margaret and Ellen, who consider themselves part of a
growing Black aristocracy, explain their action in terms of the class's self-
interest: " 'Why it will have a tendency to stop parents from educating their
children, if they are to act like that,' remarked Margaret. 'Yes,' joined in Ellen,
'and it might make some of our weak-minded parents think that we educated girls
ought to cook and wash clothes and scrub floors at home' '' (p. 36).

Ironically, Margaret's mother, Aunt Molly, put her through school and continues to support her by taking in washing. At one point, Aunt Molly confesses to
Erma: "I was tinking powerful hard ub 'doptin you fir my own gal ter hab wid
me. My Margie ain't so steddy as she mont be, and you would be sich good
soshasun fir her. But more'n one 'siety gal on my hans just now 'ud be more'n I
could stan' up ter" (p. 47). Although Griggs understands her motivation, Aunt
Molly and her generation must bear some of the blame for Margaret's misguided
self-image. "Heroic soul!" Griggs calls her:

> Perhaps no monument will ever be reared to those noble Negro women
> who, emerging from slavery, were at once enslaved again by their children
> and bore their heavy burdens uncomplainingly, in a vain attempt to build
> up upon their poor bruised shoulders an aristocracy such as they had left
> behind, their educated children to be the aristocrats (p. 39).

When Erma attends church, she is barred from her customary seat, and when
she takes another place in the only pew available, certain members of the congregation insist that the ushers remove her from the building. An indignant doctor
who insists upon Erma being expelled complains: "Do you think that white folks
would allow a white servant girl to sit on the front pew in their church? We shall
never amount to anything as a race until we learn to do as white people" (p. 58).
Objecting to the idea of supporting themselves as Erma is doing, Ellen and
Margaret agree:

"White girls occupying the social station in their race that we do in our race would suffer themselves to be carried out of their homes dead before they would perform such menial tasks. Why, just think if we educated girls go to work, it can be truthfully said that our race has no first-class society" (pp. 36–37).

Griggs understands that this class snobbishness and insistence that physical labor is degrading are the direct result of the slavery experience. In a frantic and self-deceptive effort to move their race as far away as possible from its heritage of subservience, the new middle class has adopted the worst qualities of white antibellum society. Erma comments: "The Southern white people are the parents of the idea that physical labor is disgraceful, and being such an imitative· people, we have accepted without question, their standard of what is honorable . . . . you know how hard a Negro will throw a stone at another if he feels that he has the sanction of the white people" (pp. 42–45).

The futility of their desire to establish an aristocratic, Black leisure class is brought forcefully home with Margaret's downfall. Introduced to Horace Christian, a young, white congressman, Margaret is soon seduced. Finding herself pregnant, she has no choice but to leave town and face beginning her life over again someplace else. That someone as spoiled and indolent as she will succeed in salvaging her life seems unlikely. Margaret's fate foretells the consequences to a race that plans to rely upon an idle, complacent, superficially educated, and white-worshipping class for its self-esteem. Such dependence will result, Griggs foresees, in a continuance of racial exploitation, an ironic return to the conditions before Emancipation, when the use of Black women like Margaret by the white master was commonplace. Instead of signaling a genuine level of culture and hope in the race, Margaret and her kind are, instead, symbolic of a psychological dependence that, unless recognized and eliminated, could easily lead to a return of the oldest forms of exploitation.[14]

Griggs employs a white labor leader to criticize another hindrance to racial progress, the reluctance of turn-of-the-century African-Americans to insist upon their own rights. Unlike his rejection of elitism, in this case, Griggs extols a valuable quality, militancy, one of several white attributes that he considers worthy of imitation.[15] The labor leader explains the rejection of Blacks from unions for the following reason:

"The greatest objection we have to the Negro is that his nature does not seem to have in it the seditious element to any appreciable degree. He will move along patiently, enduring evils and debating his right—actually his right to rebel against oppression. He has an abnormal respect for constituted authority. He does not admit to himself the inherent right to throw off the hand of an oppressor. He stands and looks pleadingly at him, waiting for the time to come when the better sense of the oppressor will assert itself. . . . The Anglo-Saxon has never gotten anything for which he did not fight, or impress the party concerned that he was ready to fight for it. . . . The Negro, lacking this spirit, has no place in our ranks'' (pp. 101–2).

It is the whites' insistence on their lawful rights, their willingness to unite with others to ensure those rights, and, as important, their recognition of the value of their labor that Griggs considers worthy of imitation. It is impossible for an idle Black class to succeed; therefore, it is essential for Blacks to join the labor force with the same determination and pride as white workers.

Like Margaret, Erma is in danger of becoming a white man's mistress, although she does not even realize it. She is the unwitting victim in a bizarre revenge plot devised by her aunt, Dolly Smith, against a former governor of the state who, in reality, is Erma's father. He repudiated her mother and drove her away when he learned of Erma's conception, and the child never knew of his existence. To effect her revenge, Dolly tricks the governor's son, who lusts after Erma and is unaware that she is his half-sister, into forging a $10,000 check to establish the girl as his mistress. Erma is ignorant of the entire scheme and learns of it only when the forged check is detected and the governor's son must stand trial. The point of this complicated subplot seems that of indicating the long-range consequences of miscegenation as well as demonstrating that there are some Blacks, like Dolly Smith, who for reasons of profit or revenge will callously endanger others of their race. Erma is embarrassed and discomfited by her aunt's scheme, but, because of her independence, is not destroyed.

Her brother, John, however, embittered by conditions that prevent him from joining a union and unable to find work without being a member, kills a labor official and spends the rest of his life in prison. Her brother's fate is the major blight on Erma's happiness with Astral. Seven years after their marriage, John escapes from prison and makes his way to their home for one of those improbable reunion scenes of which the early novelists were inordinately fond. He dies of the results of prison privations, and Erma dies of the shock of seeing him so unexpectedly and losing him so quickly.[16]

Although Erma has not suffered greatly solely because of her race, an embittered Astral refuses to allow her or her brother to be buried in the South because no one in power can promise that his son will not be discriminated against later in his life. Astral believes racism to be the reason for Erma's and John's untimely deaths. He refuses all well-meaning advice to accept the gradual changes taking place and, in a gesture of defiance, takes the coffins aboard a ship bound from New York to Europe and orders them interred at sea.

His last speech in the book is a dramatic oration in which he invests himself with the role of an outsider from all nations of men:

> "And now, I, Astral Herndon, hereby and forever renounce all citizenship
> in all lands whatsoever, and constitute myself CITIZEN OF THE OCEAN, and
> ordain that this title shall be entailed upon my progeny unto all generations,

until such time as the shadows which now envelop the darker races in all lands shall have passed away, away and away'' (p. 217).

Astral's passion does not evoke a sympathetic response in the reader because Griggs fails to prepare adequately for his dramatic renunciation. The interest in *Overshadowed* is essentially in Erma; and while Dolly Smith's use of her dramatizes the problem of traditional sexual exploitation, Griggs's handling of this subject is so mysterious and the incidents, as they are slowly revealed, so bizarre that any criticism of actual racial conditions is diluted. John's frustration is more obviously a matter of discrimination, but once again Griggs pulls his punches by giving a top official a speech partially explaining labor's reluctance to admit Blacks. Moreover, he saves John from hanging through an ironic and incredible switch with a dead-drunk Horace Christian that necessitates the use of a secret solution to darken Christian's skin, poison to puff out his lips, a frizzy wig, and old clothes. Although Griggs suggests that the plot is successful because to the white prison guard all men with black skin look the same, any more general racial meaning is as disguised as Horace. The switch is distracting and unbelievable and does nothing to add to the theme of white oppression since one of its perpetrators is Congressman Lanier, a white friend of Astral.

Nevertheless, taking Astral's declaration as a valid reaction to the social conditions of early twentieth-century America, as Griggs appears to have wished; such a hopeless, isolating gesture at the book's end makes *Overshadowed* a much more despairing novel than *Imperium in Imperio*. At the end of the first work, the revolutionary forces are in disarray, and the future is uncertain, but at least there has been an attempt at a unified stance against a common foe. Belton's proposal, however visionary, presents a possible political alternative to remaining in a racist society. The book's abrupt ending generates the feeling that although the Imperium showed bad judgment in selecting leaders and, consequently, is about to be crushed, the seething spirit of frustration in its members will not disappear, and the new generation's desire for justice and self-government will manifest itself again with the formation of other organizations and the formulation of other political proposals.

Overshadowed, however, moves to no such logical resolution of its action. Its picture of the Black middle class suggests that Bernard's view of the African-American's struggle as one of Black *versus* white is an oversimplification. The real cancer eating away at the soul of the Black community is not contemporary white injustice, as destructive as that might be, but its own debilitating feeling of inferiority. The symptoms of this disease are a slavish, irrational imitation of white standards and rejection of those who, for reasons of skin color or occupation, do not fit those standards. Racial insecurity, Griggs suggests, is every bit as suicidal as a headlong plunge into violence.

This analysis of African-American problems seems a valuable advance over the intrigues of *Imperium in Imperio*. Unfortunately, Griggs's insights are forgotten in Astral's complaint about white racism. His dramatic declaration, therefore, seems a throwback to earlier, simpler concepts that the book has shown to be inadequate. Astral appears finally as a pathetic figure unwilling or unable to appreciate what Erma understood about the identity problem of the Black community and, therefore, incapable of formulating any plan for revitalization. His final speech diminishes the book's insights to the proportions of personal grief and rebellion.

In *Unfettered* (1902), Griggs reasserts his interest in positive political solutions. He shifts his attention in this book from the failures of middle-class Blacks to the needs of their lower-class brothers. The major themes of the novel are embodied in the paradox of the necessity of superior cultures "uplifting" inferior and the Black need for self-reliance. The paradox is resolved when it becomes clear that Griggs views the race's lower class as so different from the middle class that it practically constitutes a separate and impoverished culture within the race. By working toward the alleviation of its misery, more fortunate Blacks would also be ensuring a lessening of bias against themselves; cultural "uplift" and self-reliance, then, are one and the same.

When the novel begins, Dorlan Warthell has been a secret speechwriter for the Republican party in the South for a number of years. He breaks with the organization, however, over the question of America's expansionist policies in the Philippines. Concerned about the political and social status of the Filipino, he debates this issue with Morlene, a staunch defender of the party. "The Negro women of the South are, perhaps," Griggs observes, "the most ardent and unyielding Republicans in the whole length and breadth of the land" (p. 126).

Morlene proudly proclaims herself an "expansionist" because she feels that the acquaintance of backward nations with other countries, even one coming as a conquering force, will ultimately lead to a unified world: "The classification of mankind into groups called nations affords a feeling of estrangement which destroys or modifies the thought of universal brotherhood and gives rise to needless bickerings which result in wars" (pp. 86–87).

Her arguments convince Dorlan to rethink his rejection of the Republicans. His ultimate solution to the problem of political allegiance complements Morlene's view and introduces Griggs's concept of the obligation of the fortunate to help others:

> He now saw in the verdict of the North the high resolve to begin at the very foundation and actually lift the Filipinos to such a plane that they would not only have freedom, but the power to properly exercise and preserve the same. . . . So nobly, so thoroughly was it to do its work of leading the Filipinos into all the blessings of higher civilization, that other nations in contact with weaker peoples might find here a guide for their statesmen to follow (pp. 155–56).

It is a short step from this concept of international "uplift" to its application to the divisions within his own race.

Unlike the protagonists in *Overshadowed,* Dorlan and Morlene are not persecuted by other middle-class Blacks, but they are deeply troubled by the condition
of the race as a whole. Educated and hard-working African-Americans are discriminated against, Griggs indicates, because whites see the race as a monolith
and judge the accomplishments of the able by the failures of the frail. This
growing realization takes concrete form when Dorlan observes a parade of
lower-class Blacks cavorting in the city streets:

> He was in the act of going out of the gate as the procession got opposite to
> him, and he paused to allow it to pass. There was a great concourse of
> Negro boys and girls, men and women, following the band of musicians.
> Their clothes were unclean, ragged and ill-fitting. Their faces and hands
> were soiled and seemed not to have been washed for many a day. The
> motley throng seemed to be utterly oblivious of its gruesome appearance,
> and all were walking along in boldness with good cheer.
>   "Now those Negroes are moulding resentment against the entire race,"
> thought Dorlan, as his eyes scanned the unsightly mass. "Be the require-
> ment just or unjust the polished Negro is told to return and bring his people
> with him, before coming into possession of that to which his attainments
> would seem to entitle him. It is my opinion that there must be developed
> within the race a stronger altruistic tie before it can push forward at a
> proper gait. The classes must love the masses, in spite of the bad name the
> race is given by the indolent, the sloven and the criminal element." Taking
> another survey of the throng, he said, "Ah! the squalor and misery of my
> poor voiceless race! What we see here is but a bird's-eye view. The heart
> grows sick when it contemplates the plight of the negroes of the cities"
> (pp. 160–61).

It is to the development of the masses that Griggs feels the Black professional
class should devote itself. Instead of bickering among themselves, more fortunate members of the race should attempt to raise those less fortunate, if not out of
brotherhood, then out of pragmatic self-interest.

While Dorlan is watching the parade, there occurs an incident that adds another
possibility to his political alternatives. He spots a huge, very black man in the
middle of the throng, carrying a banner and being pulled along in a dogcart. The
stranger, it turns out, is an African touring the southern states in search of the
descendants of his tribe's former chief, who was captured and brought to
America as a slave. Dorlan recognizes the African writing on the banner as an old
family motto and discovers that he is the descendant for whom the African is
searching. Griggs uses this improbable encounter to confront his protagonist with
a political dilemma. As a representative of the educated, yet oppressed,
African-American minority, Dorlan can choose to reject America and his heritage of slavery and return to the land where his ancestors were princes, or he can
accept his American identity and work to upgrade other American Blacks. Both

the African and the dirty, boisterous crowd are alien to him, however. While the African represents the Blacks' rich past, the ragged throng represents their debased present. As a middle-class African-American, Dorlan has been trained away from Africa by the slavery experience and away from the masses of his people by formal schooling. In none of his other books does Griggs so clearly present the isolation of the Black bourgeoisie. Dorlan is not African despite his recognition of the motto and his distant kinship to the tribesman; nor is he one of the Black masses despite his lifelong presence in America. Ultimately, he rejects returning to Africa as a self-deceptive attempt at escape and turns again to face his responsibilities to his fellow African-Americans.

He does not return, however, to a reliance upon the Republicans. Instead, he searches American tradition and settles upon the Emersonian concept of self-reliance as the philosophy most suited to his personal and racial plight. This decision seems a significant clarification of Griggs's ideas about Black social activism. While Belton and Bernard in *Imperium* espoused very definite ideas of Black power, their plans were based upon separatism. By refusing to go to Africa and grounding his political theories in Emersonian principles, Dorlan very clearly roots himself in the American experience and relates his people's development to its expressed traditions. Even by 1902, Griggs seems to have moved closer to racial cooperation and amelioration than Belton, his "conservative racial leader."

If Dorlan's decisions typify the political and cultural dilemma of his class, Morlene specifically gives voice to the plight of the Black woman. When both she and Dorlan are free to marry, she refuses to do so, explaining that a wife traditionally serves to inspire ambition and hope in her husband, but with racist conditions as oppressive as they are, a Black wife cannot hope to fulfill this role. The position of the Black woman in a white society has long intrigued African-American writers. In the nineteenth century, this theme was handled in such disparate forms as Isabella's suicide and Clotelle's flight in William Wells Brown's novel and Iola Leroy's resourceful attack on the freedmen's problems in Frances Harper's account.

Morlene knows that the Black woman's situation is dependent upon the Black man's. He is unable to fulfill the traditional husband's role of protector and provider in a hostile white society that insists, out of its own insecurity, on limiting his powers to those of a "boy." She promises to marry Dorlan as soon as he develops a solution to the race's dilemma; and, since Griggs is still writing in the sentimental tradition, this request, like Viola Martin's, reinforces his protagonist's zeal. He develops "Dorlan's Plan, a Dissertation on the Race Problem," which the author includes as a sequel to the novel. The plan is based upon an Emersonian insistence upon self-worth:

> The hour has come when the race must take the matter of its salvation into
> its own hands. In times past, when the battles of the race were to be fought,
> others led and the trusting Negro followed. In this new era the Negroes

must lead, must bear the main brunt of the battle. Thus, while estranging
no friends of the past, and fully appreciating the continued necessity of the
outside assistance wherever attainable, the foreword of our new propaganda shall be Self-Reliance (p. 232).

Specifically, Dorlan calls for unity between the upper and lower classes,
cooperation with friendly whites, and, most importantly, dedication to the progress of the masses of unfortunate Blacks whose degradation will ultimately
undermine the fragile foundation of the middle class. Anyone expecting a call to
arms would be disappointed, however, as he grounds his plans in an extremely
conventional, middle-class framework. His platform calls for character building,
religious instruction, financial responsibility, and, basic to the rest, increased
education. He even suggests the widespread establishment of "penny savings
banks"!

In 1916, Griggs felt called upon to present a similar, but much more extensive,
plan in an essay entitled *Life's Demands; or According to Law*. In it, he clearly
indicates the nonviolent, nonseparatist nature of his scheme for his race's progress. "Success," he advises, "will come in proportion to the number and kind of
people a man can inspire to lend him their aid" (p. 12). This "art of winning and
holding co-operation" (p. 12) is dependent upon the development of self-
reliance, honesty, reliability, thoroughness in work, politeness, cheerfulness,
self-control, humility, industry, intellectual development, and perseverance. He
continually cites Booker T. Washington as a model for emulation, but Ben
Franklin, with his list of practical virtues, would serve almost as well.

Sounding very much like Frank Webb's Mr. Walters, Griggs assures his
reader that "the individual who will take himself in hand and cultivate and
steadily practice the things which have been set forth herein is sure to rise in life"
(pp. 26–27). Griggs's eagerness for Blacks to push themselves intellectually and
economically rests in large measure upon his awareness of contemporary political reality: "The lot of the race seems to be growing harder and harder. That
which alarms the race is but the coming of a condition long overdue. American
slavery and the Civil War caused a temporary suspension of the operation of the
law of the survival of the fittest, both in the North and in the South" (p. 112).
Revealing a surprisingly charitable view of slavery, he continues:

> The fact that the Negroes began life in America as slaves brought to their
> aid the knowledge and skill of their white owners, who helped them to
> adjust themselves to the new climate and stood guard over them, protecting
> them from many possible vices and injurious habits. Thus slavery served as
> a sort of shelter beneath which the Negro rested, temporarily exempt from
> some forms of the struggle for existence raging all around (p. 113).

Griggs ignores the fact that if slavery were indeed a shelter, it was of the flimsiest
construction, destined to crumble at the master's decision to send its inhabitants

to the auction block and—at its sturdiest—housing hunger, exhaustion, fear, and hopelessness. Nevertheless, he recognizes accurately the degenerating habit of psychological dependence that questionable white paternalism frequently fostered, and it is against this flaw that he preaches: "slavery has been abolished, the shelter is gone, and the Negroes have been summoned to the open field of struggle on their own merits, where they must compete and win, or go down in the great battle of life" (p. 113).

In his fourth novel, *The Hindered Hand* (1905), he again introduces two Black leaders who hold opposing views of the nature of this "great battle": "Ensal and Earl represented two types in the Negro race, the conservative and the radical. They both stood for the ultimate recognition of the rights of the Negro as an American citizen but their methods were opposite" (p. 48).

Like Bernard, Earl is a mulatto who is deeply stung by the discrimination that he receives from whites. Explaining his hatred of American society, he says: "Conditions have made me an outlaw among my kind. Rubbish aside, am I not as much of an Anglo-Saxon as any of them? Does not my soul respond to those things and to those things only to which their souls respond?" (p. 52). Toward his Black heritage Earl experiences "neither dejection nor elation" (p. 49).

Ensal, on the other hand, of unmixed African descent, feels pride in his enslaved ancestors for their ability to adapt to oppressive conditions and survive. Such adaptability, he judges, "assured the presence of the Negro on the earth in the final wind up of things, in full possession of all the advantages that time and progress promise" (p. 49). Earl feels no pride in this aspect of Black history; he admires the warring stance of the American Indians, feeling "that the dead Indian refusing to be enslaved was a richer heritage to the world than the yielding and thriving Negro" (p. 49).

When their friends Bud and Foresta are lynched in Mississippi, Ensal and Earl completely disagree about the proper response. Their violent and nonviolent approaches to racial oppression lead to conflicting plans and a literal struggle for mastery. Earl intends to take over the state capitol and the United States Government Building in Almaville in order to force national attention to the problems of southern Blacks. "I have picked a band of five hundred men who are not afraid to die," he reveals. "When called upon to surrender, we shall issue a proclamation setting forth our grievances as a race and demanding that they be righted. . . . We shall not surrender. Each one of us has solemnly sworn not to come out of the affair alive, even if we have to commit suicide" (p. 144). Like his idols, the American Indians, Earl's five hundred intend to stand and fight. Naively, in view of the fate of the Indians, Earl trusts to the basic fairness of the national conscience.

Ensal immediately rejects Earl's scheme as impractical and shows him a lengthy analysis of Black and white relationships that he has written. His essay reviews the injustices suffered by Blacks and the failure of white institutions to eliminate them. Trusting white patriotism, which he feels is of sufficient strength to revolutionize existing conditions, he urges Earl to forego his violent plan and, instead, to help print and distribute copies of his treatise. The essay concludes optimistically: "There is a vein of idealism running through our country that would hold the American people to the thought that the United States has a worldwide mission. It is the dream of this class that shackles, whether physical, political, or spiritual, shall fall from every man the world around" (p. 147). Needless to say, Earl scoffs at Ensal's hope of arousing justice from Americans who have for so long either perpetrated or acquiesced in injustice. He asserts the absolute necessity for militant action. He and Ensal struggle; he attempts to shoot the minister and is wounded himself.

For all of Earl's militancy, he is much less desperate and bitter than his friend Gus Martin. Gus "questioned the existence of God, and . . . asserted that the Gospel was the Negro's greatest curse in that it unmanned the race. As for the United States government, he said, 'The flag ain't any more to me than any other dirty rag. I fit fur it. My blood ran out o' three holes in the groun' to keep it floatin', and whut will it do fur me? Now jus' tell me whut?' " (p. 38). Gus, who is proud of his Indian ancestry, believing that it gives him courage to withstand oppression, considers futile any group action such as that which Earl recommends. He, and many like him, plan to rely on individual retaliation:

Word was being . . . passed down the line that every man was to act for himself, that each individual was himself to resent the injustices and indignities perpetrated upon him, and that each man whose life was threatened in a lawless way could help the cause of the race by killing as many as possible of the lawless band, it being contended that the adding of the element of danger to mob life would make many less inclined to lawlessness (pp. 192–93).

Observing Tiara, Griggs's heroine, embracing the Reverend Percy Marshall, whom he takes for white, Gus feels racially insulted and vows revenge. He kills Marshall, who is actually Tiara's light-skinned brother, and takes over a nearby house that he intends to use as a fortress to withstand the gathering mob of angry whites. To his surprise, he discovers that the tower of the house is already lined with armor plate and contains an arsenal. This oddity is never explained, although Griggs, no doubt, intended it to relate in some way to the fact that the house belongs to the Seabrights, the parents of Percy and Tiara, who are mulattoes passing as white and attempting to infiltrate white social and political circles.

Martin calls the local sheriff, the governor, the secretary to the president of the United States, and, most improbably, the British legation to ask for protection from the lynch mob. When his plea is repeatedly refused, he prepares, like his Indian ancestors, to stand and fight. Tiara, however, hears of what has happened, rushes to the house, and persuades the sheriff to let her go in and talk with Gus. When she reveals her identity as Marshall's sister, Gus surrenders. Upon leaving the fortified house, he is shot to death.

Understandably, Ensal judges plans such as Earl's and Gus's to be suicidal. In their many debates about America's racism, he frequently finds himself defending democracy and attempting to convince his friends that the Blacks' ills are due to local, rather than national, abuse of law. In one such discussion, he prophesies that "in the course of time the national government would mould the inner circles of government to its way of thinking" (p. 38). This assertion draws the following response from Gus: "Excuse me, Elder; but that kind o' talk makes me sick. You are a good Christian man, I really think; but like most cullud people you are too jam full of patience and hope. I'll be blessed if I don't believe Job was a cullud man" (p. 38). No doubt, Ensal derives his own patriotism and patience from his mother, who represents older-generation views. She listens apprehensively to his conversations with his friends: "She believed firmly in God and her only remedies for all the ills of earth were prayer and time. Therefore it ruffled her beyond measure to have a new spirit appearing in the race" (p. 38).

Shaken by his fight with Earl and believing Gus's mistaken report that Tiara has betrayed him with a white man, Ensal abandons his political efforts in America and travels to Africa. Before he leaves Almaville, however, he urges his fellow Blacks to reject plans like the Seabrights' to infiltrate white ranks by intermarriage. Unlike Earl, he is proud of his blackness and argues for the political expediency of racial purity:

> "May it continue your ambition to abide Negroes, to force the American
> civilization to accord you your place in your own right, to the end that the
> world may have an example of alien races living side by side administering
> the general government together and meting out justice and fair play to all.
> If through the process of being made white you attain your rights, the battle
> of the dark man will remain to be fought" (p. 198).

While Ensal is in Africa, the Seabright plan to infiltrate white ranks, a mysterious and complicated subplot of the novel, comes to the fore and is linked to Griggs's racial message. Earl's wife, Eunice, is in reality Tiara's sister, but, like her brother, she is fair enough to pass for white. Before Eunice's marriage to Earl, her mother had arranged a union for her with a prominent white politician, Mr. Volrees, from whom she ran away on their wedding trip. Volrees searches for her for several years and finally discovers that she is living in a suburb of Almaville under the assumed name of Mrs. Johnson. Still unaware that she is part Black, he hauls her into court on a bigamy charge. Eunice arrives at the trial leading a small boy by the hand, and many in the courtroom remark on the child's close resemblance to the complainant. He is not, however, Volrees's son; he is his grandson. It turns out that the boy is Earl Bluefield's child, and Earl is actually Volrees's illegitimate son by an unnamed Black woman. These family entanglements are not made clear until Tiara testifies about the Seabright plot, leaving Eunice hysterically denying the entire story because she does not wish to be considered Black. Volrees originally brought her to court to have her found guilty of bigamy, but after her mixed blood is revealed, the all-white jury is ironically trapped by the South's traditional use of the law to reinforce its racial double standard. The foreman of the jury explains:

> "One drop of Negro blood makes its possessor a Negro. Our great race stands in juxtaposition with overwhelming millions of darker people throughout the earth, and we must cling to the caste idea if we would prevent a lapse that would taint our blood and eventually undermine our greatness. It is hard, but it is civilization. We cannot find this girl guilty. It would be declaring that marriage between a white man and a Negro woman is a possibility" (p. 244).

The jury is put in the position of denying its own laws in order to maintain the myth of white superiority. What happens in the courtroom is a microcosm of the absurdity and horror of Black and white relationships in general. The jury's denial of the validity of Eunice's legally performed marriage ceremony appears ridiculous. It is worse than that. There were also on the books southern laws against murder, yet the lynchers of Bud and Foresta Harper were set free. Griggs recognizes that a legal system that ignores its own statutes when dealing with one segment of the population is not simply ridiculous, but absurd and terrible. In his classic study of southern psychology, *The Mind of the South,* Wilbur J. Cash has examined in detail the forces resulting in white southern society's "naive capacity for unreality." Sutton Griggs gave this "social schizophrenia" fictional form thirty-six years earlier.[17]

Eunice's violent rejection of Tiara's friendship, once their true relationship becomes public, and her breakdown under the pressure of public ridicule indicate the consequences of disclosure to one who expected to pass as white in American society. Griggs uses her downfall, however, to spur Earl to reinvolvement in the political scene. Like Bernard's responding to Viola Martin's suicide, Earl establishes Eunice in a northern sanatorium and fiercely pledges revenge upon the South.

This time, however, his scheme relies upon cunning, not violence. His assumption of an alias, John Blue, and his success in convincing southern politicians mistakenly to turn their election campaign into a rabid anti-Black crusade satisfies Griggs's obvious love of disguise. Clearly, the episode reemphasizes the writer's commitment to Blacks' returning to their roots for guides to action—in this instance, to the slave's role as trickster. Earl successfully stirs up hatred of northern liberals among the southern politicians whom he visits and plants the seeds of mistrust of southern demagogues among the northerners. In a significant departure from Bernard's and Belton's mulatto *versus* Black conflict in *Imperium,* after the election results soundly repudiate southern philosophy, Earl does not grab the spotlight for himself, but writes Ensal to come home and seize the opportunity to lead his people.

Surprisingly, it is Earl, then, who at the book's end is most responsible for the changes in the southern racial climate. Ensal is still abroad, working for the "uplift" of Africa, and is peculiarly indecisive about his future role. He refuses to return to America despite Earl's political success because he does not wish to be near Tiara, who he still believes has betrayed him. Once he hears of Tiara's testimony that Percy Seabright was her brother, however, he returns immediately. "Now all of you who believe in altruism," Griggs comments cynically, "who believe in the giving of one's self for others; who believe in fixedness of purpose; who have in any wise pinned your faith to that man Ensal—let all such prepare yourselves for evidence of the utter frailty of man" (p. 278). Once he discovers Tiara's identity, Ensal abandons Africa, explaining to his bewildered landlady that the only "race" in which he is interested is the race to be on board the first steamer returning to America. Unfortunately, in paying tribute once again to the conventional power of romantic love, Griggs confuses and weakens his protagonist's characterization.

Back in the South, after reuniting with Tiara, he goes to see a young, white attorney who, at the definite risk of his entire career, had attempted unsuccessfully to prosecute the lynchers of the Harpers. Ensal persuades him to enter politics as a spokesman for the enlightened South. "Nothing," Ensal assures him, "would give the Negroes greater joy than to see the right kind of a white man from the South made President of the nation" (p. 285). Ensal assures him that the participation of liberal southerners would eliminate the development of violent Black leaders. He leaves their conversation convinced that white politicians would henceforth come from the ranks of men like Attorney Maul. His next plan is to organize Blacks into the Eclectic party to break the hold that the Republicans have over them.

Ensal wires Earl the news of Maul's agreement with their plans. When Earl conveys the news to Eunice, however, she falls into a fit of despondency and vehemently denies that anything will ever change. Significantly, in spite of all Ensal's brave plans and words, on the day after his marriage to Tiara the couple "set out for Africa to provide a home for the American Negro should the demented Eunice prove to be a wiser prophet than the hopeful, irrepressible Earl" (p. 298).

Early in the story, Ensal is approached by a mysterious white man, going under the pseudonym of Mr. A. Hostility, who insists upon speaking privately with him. The "A." in his assumed name stands for Anglo-Saxon, he reveals, "the God-commissioned or self-appointed world conqueror. I am the incarnation of hostility to that race or to that branch of the human family claiming the dominance of that strain of blood" (p. 202). Mr. Hostility believes that the world will be conquered by either the Anglo-Saxons or the Slavs. For unrevealed reasons, he is pro-Slav and wishes Ensal to lead his race in such a way that the Anglo-Saxon will be weakened. Griggs uses the dialogue between Ensal and Mr. Hostility to repudiate, among other racist doctrines, the writings of Thomas Dixon, Jr.

Warning that "when the Anglo-Saxon feels the need of it, he is going to exterminate you folks," Mr. Hostility sets a sealed vial of yellow fever germs upon the table and urges the minister to organize his friends to empty the germs into the reservoirs of the South. Blacks, he assures Ensal, will not be harmed, as "the pigment which abides in your skin and gives you your color and the peculiar Negro odor renders you immune from yellow fever" (p. 216). Ensal, as might be expected, rejects this pseudoscientific plan to wage germ warfare and reaffirms the self-sacrificial faith of his mother: "Let the Anglo-Saxon crush us if he will and if there is no God! But I say to you, the Negro can never be provoked to stoop to the perfidy and infamy which you suggest" (p. 218).

By the book's end, however, Ensal is obviously seeking alternatives to life in America. No longer does he look upon Africa as only an inferior culture in need of help from American Blacks; rather, he considers it as a place of refuge, a homeland to which a desperate people can return if every other political plan fails. When he and Earl quarreled about the mulatto's scheme to take over key government buildings in Almaville, Earl "departed, determined upon making his offering in blood. True American that he was, Ensal was determined that the offering should be the output of brains rather than veins" (p. 161). However, his reliance upon faith in God and the Constitution is shaken by Bud's and Foresta's lynchings, the complexities of miscegenation, and the Seabright scheme to turn this fact of southern life to Black advantage, as well as by Earl's call to militancy and Gus's violent death. Despite Earl's successful political manipulations and Maul's cooperation, Ensal is no longer completely trustful, it appears, of a rational, nonviolent solution to racial problems. Consequently, he leaves America for Africa, not as a cultural missionary, but as an expatriate eager to escape a country that never accepted him.

While *The Hindered Hand* ends with the feeling that there probably will be little improvement in race relations in the United States, despite liberal white willingness, and that, therefore, the Blacks had better find alternatives, Griggs's last novel, *Pointing the Way* (1908), reaffirms his faith in the importance of middle-class Blacks working with responsive whites to effect change through the political system. Seth Molair, like Maul and Lanier, is the type of young white politician who Earl Bluefield hoped would come to power once the southern demagogues were eliminated.

Seth actually serves two functions in the book. As indicated, he fits the pattern of other responsible white leaders. In addition, to a degree found in none of the earlier novels, Griggs uses him, to explain the southern white's view. He is the embodiment of the new generation of whites in the South who, although steeped in the tradition of white superiority, are the only realistic hope for peaceful change.[18]

He explains the white view of southern society to Eina, Griggs's northern-born heroine. Generally, white characters in these novels are limited to criticizing Black behavior, in some cases supporting conclusions already reached by the author. Molair, however, dissects white attitudes and explains to Eina, who is of

English, Spanish, and Native American descent, that she will have to choose whether to align herself with the whites or the Blacks and warns her that once that decision is made, there can be no switching back. His description of southern society as a battleground reinforces Griggs's image of lynching as a metaphor for Black and white relationships:

> ". . . the white people in the South are not individualists. With the possibility of racial antagonisms on the one hand and social commingling on the other always confronting us, we are more or less in a chronic state of spiritual war, and, just as in the time of war you do not allow individual soldiers personal liberty, we withhold a great measure of personal liberty from all Southern people, whites and colored, and maintain certain well-defined customs. . . . In the South, social freedom is not permitted for reasons I need not discuss here. Whoever affiliates socially with the one race in the South is denied the social life of the other. . . ."
>
> "You mean to say that there is no such thing as being allowed to treat all upon the score of individual merit?" remarked Eina.
>
> "Exactly. Choice in the South lies not between individuals but between races. Moreover, if you have once passed as a white person, you will not be allowed to drop into the colored race. On the other hand, if you are once classed as a colored person, you can never change to the white race where the fact is known," replied Molair (p. 25).

Molair also announces Griggs's theme of racial coexistence: "The thing needed in the South is political cooperation between the better elements of whites and the Negro" (p. 41). He admits, however, that the two groups have become more polarized after Reconstruction than they were during slavery and sees no forces working toward uniting their political interests. He himself is as sympathetic to the plight of the poor whites as he is to that of the Blacks and explains the attitudes of this segment of the population to Eina:

> "In the days of slavery we kept them back by making use of slave labor. In those days there sprang up an animosity between the sleek, well-fed Negro slave and the poor whites who accused the Negroes of keeping them poor by working for nothing. . . . Now there came over from slavery . . . the inherited feeling of the poor white toward the Negro, which feeling is accentuated by the fact that the Negro is yet his industrial rival" (pp. 195–96).

Molair is dedicated to the "racial integrity" of both whites and Blacks and is shown accepting many of the myths of African-American peculiarity and white superiority. Nevertheless, fully aware that racial rivalry is "a veritable gold mine for the demagogue" (p. 196), he accepts the challenge to run for office. A vicious white leader, he realizes, would do nothing but exacerbate racial fears that are constantly simmering beneath the surface in poor white communities: "In return for office he tosses to this element the Negro, hobbled, gagged or quartered according as he thinks this will most please this element" (p. 196).

In a repetition of Ensal's action in *The Hindered Hand,* Molair is urged to run for mayor by Baug Peppers, Griggs's mulatto protagonist. Once elected, he is true to his promises and does what he can to improve the lot of Black citizens, including establishing the town's first Black fire company. That such isolated gestures alone will not solve the race's economic problems is suggested in an improbable interview between Molair and the president of the United States. The president voices a belief that Griggs shared with many of his turn-of-the-century contemporaries, the contention that society was properly advanced by the survival of the fittest. "I am no special friend of the Negroes," the president informs Molair, announcing his support of laissez-faire economic policies,

> "and if the necessity ever arises I will show you that I am not. I do not believe that the colored people should have special favors because they are colored, nor on the other hand, should they have special burdens because of their color.
> "America is a great Darwinian field, dedicated by fate to the cause of genuine democracy, the rule of united judgment of men. Here we are to have the wild grand play of universally and absolutely unfettered forces, and out of the strenuous struggle the fittest are to survive, and the final man is to be evolved. I believe simply in giving the colored man the same chance in this great Darwinian field that other men are given, no more, no less" (p. 191).

There are no rival Black leaders in *Pointing the Way*. Instead, Griggs establishes a Black counterpart to Molair in the person of old Uncle Jack, who gives Eina the freedman's viewpoint on the southern system. Uncle Jack and Molair do not disagree about the strict barriers to racial mingling that exist in the South, nor do they differ in their understanding of the need for white leaders who are dedicated to calming racial hatreds. Aside from their race and their different social and economic levels, their most obvious distinction from each other is a stylistic one. Just as Seth Molair is the culmination of Griggs's concept of the cooperative white politician, Uncle Jack is his most fully developed Black folk character.

There are several other significant folk characters in the earlier novels who are given only minor roles to play. Nevertheless, they are consistently employed as spokesmen for divergent racial and political views and as participants in scenes of satiric commentary. While many of these secondary characters could easily have been drawn as one-dimensional, comic darkies, Griggs invests them, instead, with racial awareness, important conclusions about political action, and activity within the stories that directly affects the plot. Most importantly, as folk characters—that is, characters espousing certain traditions and viewpoints held by the masses of their people and participating in ritualistic action that enriches their lives—these secondary figures provide the same kind of earthy humor, pathos, and realism as the portraits of the cunning slaves in Frances Harper's *Iola Leroy*.

In *The Hindered Hand,* Griggs introduces Uncle Silas, who responds to a family tragedy in the only way that his tradition-bound outlook permits. Informed by his wife, Dilsey, that their son has been lynched for murdering a white girl, he disclaims any blood relationship to Bud and accuses his wife of having had a lover who must be the boy's father. "I aint gwine ter say nothin' 'bout yer ter skanderlize yer," he promises; "I am gwine ter nail up de doh' 'twixt you an' me" (p. 115). This ritualistic act, symbolizing the spiritual barrier that Silas believes he had discovered between them, is also an outlet in physical activity for the sorrow and pain caused by the news of Bud's lynching.[19] Although Silas's accusation and consequent separation from Dilsey are cruel and self-deceptive, the old man is depicted as a suffering human being, lashing out in his pain at the person nearest to him. If Silas's action is misguided, it is also heartrending. As he hammers the nails into the door, Dilsey sits in their bedroom, silently sewing, unwilling to attempt to refute his charges, and sorrowing for their lost child: "And every lick that he struck was like unto driving a nail into his own heart, for he loved Dilsey, the love of his youth, the companion of his earlier struggles after slavery, the joint purchaser of their four-room cottage, and the mother of the two boys whom he had hitherto regarded as his sons" (p. 115).

Aunt Catherine in *Unfettered* is another old woman for whom freedom has been neither sweet nor easy. Broken by hard work, she is only faintly hopeful of a better future for her children and grandchildren. When she realizes that she is dying, she reverts to a superstition that she learned as a young girl back on the plantation. Calling for Morlene, she presents her with a small box:

> "Do yer see dis tin box? W'en yer wuz er gal, Lenie, did yer ebber heah dat our fust juty jedgment day would be to git up from whar ever we wuz burrit and hunt fur de diff'runt pieces ub our fingernails dat we had cut off all through life?"
>
> "Yes, Aunt Catherine," responded Morlene.
>
> "Wal, dis box hez got all my finger nails dat I cut off since I wuz er gal. Bury dis box at de foot ub Maury and Missus, Lenie. W'en jedgment day comes I want ter git up wid dem. Ef my nails is burrit by dem, I'll have ter go dar whar they is. See?" (p. 193).

Her desire to be buried with her former master and "missus" indicates the distance of many older Blacks from the hopes and plans of the new generation. Earlier, she had revealed that she actually longs for the days before Emancipation: "De Yankees was mighty anxious to set us poor darkeys free, but it ain't done me no good. Fack ub de mattah, Lenie, freedum mebbie good fur you young uns who wuzzunt use ter de old time. Fur your sakes I is glad its come. But I'se hed a hard time" (p. 138). Griggs understands and sympathizes with her, just as he does with Aunt Molly in *Overshadowed*. All of these characters could have been drawn as humorous old darkies, one-dimensional foils for Griggs's militant protagonists. Instead, they are portrayed with sympathy. Their ritual and superstition not only are interesting in themselves but also serve as effective means by which to establish their characters and to lend dignity and poignancy to their situations.

Uncle Jack of *Pointing the Way* is Griggs's most fully developed folk character. He is presented early in the novel as the traditional, loyal, former slave who stayed behind and cared for his master's family during the Civil War. Despite his loyalty, his own wife and children were subsequently killed by the Ku Klux Klan, but he did not allow this tragedy to embitter him against all whites. Nevertheless, he is no William Gilmore Simms stereotype.

Uncle Jack has been successful in his lifelong relationship with whites because he views them humorously and, like Old John, the conquering slave, has developed his humor as a tactic of self-preservation. As he explains to Eina when she turns to him for the Black point of view,

> "Ez er boy, I notussed dat dare warn't nevah no harm in er white man ef you could jes' git him ter laf right good and hard. . . . An' w'en yer come ter think uv it, de powah uv de cullud man ter start er laf hez kep' down er worl' uv trouble in dis Souf lan'. De elluphant pertecks hisself wid his snoot, de dog makes his gitby wid his teef, de bee makes yer 'speck hisself wid er sting, an' de cullud man hez been takin' keer uv hisself wid er joke, at leas' dats de way I got er long mos'ly" (pp. 61–64).

Like Frances Harper, Griggs is a skillful reproducer of the rhythm and imagery of Black folk speech.

Despite his intelligent and tactical use of humor, Uncle Jack could still have been fashioned in the image of Uncle Remus. He delights in narrating humorous stories of his success in outwitting whites and will continue to do so for hours, as long as he can sit back and have "er extry big chaw uf terbacky" (p. 88) while he spins his tales. Griggs, however, gives him a much more meaningful role in the novel. Uncle Jack is, of course, another representative of the generation of Blacks who grew up under slavery and developed from that experience an almost ennervating caution and reluctance to assert themselves. Nevertheless, he is able to put aside a lifelong habit of humorous and subtle appeasement of whites to become, in his old age, a political activist.

Espousing what Griggs feels to be a fatal dependence upon whites, Uncle Jack comments early in the book that "good white people kin lead cullud folks ef dey will jes' 'gree ter do so" (p. 99). Following political discussions with Eina that lead him to do much soul-searching, he decides to join with the more militant African-Americans to try to win Black voting rights. He agrees to cast a ballot in an upcoming local election, an illegal act that would allow the question of Black disfranchisement to be brought before the courts.

Before he agrees to go along with this dangerous plan, however, he makes a symbolic pilgrimage back to the plantation where he was a slave. He asks his relatives who live nearby for an all-night 'possum hunt, a 'possum dinner the next day, and, to the astonishment of everyone, a funeral service to be preached for him in the country church. All of his old acquaintances, Black and white, attend the service and deliver admiring eulogies about the old man while he sits in the back of the church, enjoying their praise. Unfortunately, Griggs passes up a chance to add more local color to his story by failing to present details of the 'possum hunt and dinner and by not dwelling on the people who attend the premature funeral. Uncle Jack explains his action in terms of symbolic death and rebirth:

> "For I 'gin my life uv buckin' ergin er law uv de white folks I jes' wanted ter close up de life I *had* been livin' squar' an' even. Ef I had waited till I bucked de law de white folks mout not 'uv been willin' ter say all dis dey done said ovah me ter day.
>
> "Yer see, dey ain't lak us. W'en massa rode erway ter de war and fit ter keep me in slav'ry I didun't make it er pussonal mattah. I didn't lak whut he did, but I kep' on lakin' *him* jes' de same. I hopes de white folks won't git mad at me fur tryin' ter git er ekal show in life fur a cullud an' er white boy. But ef dey does get mad, dey done 'spressed deyself 'bout my charackter'' (p. 150).

The funeral, then, is both a last joke played by the old freedman on the whites who unwittingly go along with it and the first revolutionary step in his new life of militancy. The trip back to the plantation, the scene of his youth, is Uncle Jack's recognition of the values of the earlier existence and a closing out of that life. Like Uncle Silas's nailing of the door, it is ritualistic action meaningful on one level for Uncle Jack himself and on another for the reader, whose understanding of the old man is sharpened and deepened.

In summary, Griggs uses folk material, such as Aunt Catherine's superstition about her fingernails and Uncle Silas's and Uncle Jack's consciously symbolic actions, as a major element of personal and racial characterization. While he is primarily concerned with the future of the new generation, he obviously feels great loyalty and respect for the older members of the race and views them as sources of cultural richness rather than as objects of ridicule.

Except for the symbolic interpretation of Uncle Jack's pilgrimage, *Pointing the Way* essentially repeats themes and character types found in the previous novels. Marriage as a way of solving racial problems appears again in the schemes of Miss Letitia, a middle-aged Black woman who attempts to manipulate not only the members of her family but also the political events in her town in order to combat prejudice: "Miss Letitia . . . had become a convert to the theory that the only hope of the American Negro lay in finally losing himself in the white race, in being utterly absorbed" (p. 31). Unlike Mrs. Seabright, however, Miss Letitia "had no sympathy . . . for such Negroes of light complexion as illegally affiliated with the white race or surreptitiously entered that race, holding that all persons with the blood of the colored race in their veins should remain within the ranks of the Negroes until the race as a whole was whitened'' (pp. 31–32). Clearly akin to those imitative Blacks satirized in *Overshadowed,* she ''viewed in the light of a shocking crime for two dark persons to marry each other, holding that every newly born dark child but prolonged the agony. . . . She was a believer in the white man's temperament, tradition, character, and civilization, and did not care to see these altered by a sudden infusion of Negro blood'' (p. 32). Like similar characters in the other novels, Miss Letitia is a prime mover of the plot. As a matter of fact, *Pointing the Way* is an annoyingly unsatisfying book, primarily because its political and economic concerns are so consistently subordinated to the demands of the love story.

The love story, moreover, is completely dependent upon Miss Letitia's insistence that her young cousin, Clotille, marry the fair-skinned Baug Peppers and upon Clotille's desire to please her cousin in order to inherit her fortune. The ''proper'' marriage is itself, of course, a political tactic here. Nevertheless, Miss Letitia's and Clotille's domination of the action diminishes it to the lineaments of an already discredited plan for racial amelioration and a slight tale of greed and deceit.

Despite her cousin's entreaties and threats, Clotille prefers Conroe, a college classmate who, unfortunately, is dark. She spends most of her time attempting to interest Baug in Eina in order to get him out of the way. The sad dependence of Griggs's political plot upon this kind of romantic intrigue is indicated by the climax of the book, when Baug Peppers appears before the United States Supreme Court to argue the case against Black disfranchisement. The focus is not on the racial and political tensions of such an event, or on the consequences envisioned by both Blacks and whites if Peppers is successful, or even on the personal fulfillment of a political career that the young lawyer must experience at such a moment, but, instead, on Peppers's decision to press the case so far in order to attract the attention of Eina. Several years earlier, when Eina discovered Clotille's plot to interest her in Baug, she resented being used and moved away, leaving no word of her plans or destination. Baug is primarily thrilled at appearing before the Supreme Court not because of the precedent-setting proceedings for his people, but because he is sure that Eina will hear about it and give him a chance to explain that he loves her. Since the sentimental tradition is always an insistent voice in Griggs's novels, *Pointing the Way* ends with Baug and Eina agreeing to marry; the Supreme Court's decision about Black voting rights, however, is not revealed.

Despite their different and frequently extremely complicated plots, Sutton Griggs's five novels develop consistent character types, political philosophy, and symbolic patterns of action that distinguish them from the earlier Black novels. Their most obvious distinction is in terms of their setting, which transcends the southern geographical locale to symbolize the psychological terrain of its people. All five stories take place in the urban, turn-of-the-century South with which

Griggs was familiar; it is a place and time of great transitions, a period in which old ways are being threatened and new directions are not yet clear.[20] Griggs's South is a place of self-deception and violence corresponding to the tensions within the psyche of the new Black generation. He does not take his characters to Canada or Europe in hope of freedom. He occasionally takes them to Africa, a spot appealing paradoxically to both his Baptist missionary zeal and his African-American longing for a homeland.[21] Ensal's movement from wishing to "uplift" Africa to turning to it as a welcome refuge seems a reflection not only of Griggs's personal ambivalence but also of the warring traditions of paganism and Christianity, African and European cultures, Black values and white, in the mind of the early twentieth-century African-American. The very term *African-American* suggests this tension.

Such a dilemma is not present in the works of the earlier Black writers because their focus is on Europe and the West, and their energy is directed toward developing a Black model who not only accepts most of white America's standards, but expects, as well, to profit by those standards. The early Black protagonists expected acceptance once white America realized that they were ideological brothers under the skin. Griggs's protagonists, on the other hand, are both more appreciative of Black values than their predecessors and more suspicious of white.

While as dependent in many ways as the earlier writers upon popular literary traditions, Griggs employs every element of his tales, even their sentimental descriptions and gothic plots to indicate the stifling entanglement of southern race relations and the consequent need for Black political strength. Nowhere is his difference from his predecessors more obvious than in his satiric examination of the African-American middle class, particularly its slavish and self-destructive dependence on white definitions of culture. This shift of focus indicates an important change in the Black artist's confidence in his race as subject matter and in his acceptance of his kinsmen as a proper audience for his work.

The fact that he centers his attention on Black foibles suggests that his books were primarily intended for Black readers who might recognize their own weaknesses in his pages and attempt to free themselves from psychological slavery. His satire, then, is not an artistic exercise, but continues within the tradition established by the slave orators and narrators, ridiculing the ridiculous in hope of reform. By Griggs's time, it is the Blacks as well as the whites who need reforming. Unlike J. McHenry Jones, who boasts in *Hearts of Gold* of his people's white-inspired tastes and standards of caste, Griggs sees the dangers of pretensions that comfort idle girls like Margaret and praises instead the traditional strength of hard-working, unlettered Aunt Molly. A Black leisure class is inconceivable to him, for the active involvement of the self-proclaimed aristocracy with the masses is one of the tenets of his program for racial progress.

Unlike the earlier writers, Griggs perceives and publicly admits that every Black man who announces himself a racial leader is not, therefore, trustworthy. Bernard Belgrade, Gus Martin, and Earl Bluefield, before his apparent conversion to nonviolent deception, are every bit as dangerous as James H. W. Howard's Black informers who thwart the runaways in *Bond and Free*. The rival protagonists in two of his novels, Bernard and Belton, Ensal and Earl, have names beginning with the same letters because Griggs conceives of them not so much as individuals but as alter egos, symbols of the opposing impulses within the new generation of Blacks. This new generation could choose suicide or salvation, depending upon the extent of its self-awareness and its perception of political realities. The fact that Griggs can so clearly analyze the problems confronting his race and so courageously satirize its self-destructive tendencies testifies to a maturity developing in the early Black novel that links it to the criticisms of modern artists like Ralph Ellison and John A. Williams.

Part of Griggs's rejection of violence and violent men is due, no doubt, to his theological training, but it also depends heavily upon his admiration of Booker T. Washington and the latter's reliance upon racial cooperation. Griggs spends almost as much time delineating a type of enlightened southern white as he does in developing his Black protagonists. Seth Stanley in Stowers's and Anderson's *Appointed* is one of only two characters in the earlier novels who are presented as possible forces for racial justice; and, as though the authors did not trust their own conception, the story about Stanley ends after he is unable to prevent John Saunders's murder and before he actively commits himself to Saunders's dreams. Douglass's Listwell experiences a moral and political conversion after overhearing Madison Washington's anguished protest against his condition. He is unable effectively to change the racist attitudes of others, however, and like J. McHenry Jones's Sallie Silvers, he is able to render only personal services to the Black protagonist. Lanier, Molair, and Maul, essentially the same character, represent a much more vital, effective force toward white political and moral responsibility.

Griggs was clearly in agreement with W. E. B. DuBois's contention that economic success without political power is an illusory hope upon which to rest racial progress. Among his minor characters, there are many spokesmen for types of political action that Griggs rejects. It is never clear whether he takes seriously Viola Martin's concern that intermarriage between Blacks and whites or mulattoes produces sterility and "devitalization" in the race. But he obviously views racial purity as essential to the Blacks' struggle. When Ensal leaves for Africa, his primary concern is to impress the importance of this view upon his brothers: "Fellow Negroes, for the sake of world interests, it is my hope that you will maintain your ambition for racial purity. So long as your blood relationship to Africa is apparent to you the world has a redeeming source specially equipped for the work of the uplift of that continent" (p. 198). The view that dark-skinned Blacks must marry those fairer than themselves is clearly scored in *Overshadowed* in the satiric condemnation of the self-destructive foibles of the middle class. Mrs. Seabright's secretive corollary to this plan, her desire to infiltrate the ranks of unsuspecting whites, thereby eventually taking over southern institutions, leads to much of the violence of *The Hindered Hand*—her son's murder, one daughter's madness, another's disinheritance, her husband's disappearance, and her own suicide. Miss Letitia in *Pointing the Way* is scarcely more successful.

Griggs places his hopes for progress in representatives of the new Black bourgeoisie, African-Americans proud of their race's strengths and dedicated to the success of all its members. *Imperium in Imperio* introduces this new spokesman: Belton Piedmont develops from his youthful, violent attack on prejudice, represented by his dunking a biased teacher, to an awareness of the power of militant, nonviolent protest while at Stowe University. His experiences after leaving college, particularly the nearly successful attempt on his life by Dr. Zackland, serve to confirm his understanding of the insecurity of the educated Black in the South. Because of his early encounters with concerned whites, however, he never abandons his faith in the presence of good individuals of both races and his hope for a peaceful solution to racial problems. This philosophy, nevertheless, leads to his death as a "traitor" to the Black cause.

Astral Herndon of *Overshadowed* reflects the pessimism of the book's title. Although educated, unlike Belton, he never actually assumes racial leadership. By the book's end, in a gesture that seems as futile as Viola Martin's suicide, he rejects all countries, declaring himself a "citizen of the Ocean." This is the most pessimistic of Griggs's novels, and Astral is the most pitiful of his protagonists. He is merely a representative of the personal frustrations of the new generation, with none of the necessary ambition, dedication, and perception.

Dorlan Warthell in *Unfettered* is a clear contrast to Astral. He severs his ties with the Republican party over the issue of imperialism, but, when convinced that America's presence in the Philippines will lead to unity and cultural uplift, accepts the decisions of the national administration. Choosing to work with the Black masses, he rejects the opportunity to travel to Africa as the long-sought descendant of an African prince and develops "Dorlan's Plan" for racial cooperation based upon Black self-determination.

The Hindered Hand offers Ensal Ellwood who, like Dorlan, publishes an essay offering practical methods of racial betterment. Griggs lauds him as a "true American" for refusing Gus's, Earl's, and Mr. A. Hostility's fiery schemes. His vacillation between feeling superior to Africa and dependent upon it reflects the ambivalence present in the minds of many turn-of-the-century African-Americans. Marcus Garvey and his nationalistic followers were still twenty years away.

Baug Peppers of *Pointing the Way* is Griggs's final development of this type. The author suggests that by successfully introducing Seth Molair to the South's political crucible, Baug ensures a catalyst for Black success on the president's "Darwinian field." Baug is professionally more successful than any of the other Black leaders, representing his race before the Supreme Court to argue for their rights as American citizens. Griggs's final fictional view, then, is optimistic. He has moved from a representative of his new professional who is killed by his own racial kinsmen for his "treasonous" refusal to participate in a violent attack on the government to one who is so honored by his fellows that he is allowed to represent their case for full citizenship before the country's highest court.

Despite this hope for a peaceful resolution of the conflicts that he has revealed in his five novels, Griggs offers no sure solution to the overwhelming problems of the Black in American society. The concept of Black leadership leads inevitably to a question of political allegiance. Griggs posits as valid two kinds of patriotism: national and racial. When a choice must be made between the two, it is the racial that frequently comes first, ironically, because the nation has failed to provide African-Americans with an acceptable alternative. Black self-reliance depends upon a sense of personal and racial worth that is essential for any group's survival. Whatever benefits accrue to the rest of the nation from Black self-development are important, but incidental.

Griggs's political narratives, then, set the stage for modern racial analysis and symbolic interpretations of the African-American experience. Moreover, they provide Black literature's first portrait of independent Blacks who are neither traditional figures nor counterstereotypes. Despite his pieties, Belton Piedmont is closer in temperament and fate to the hero of John Williams's *Man Who Cried I Am* (1967) than he is to William Wells Brown's Jerome or Frank Webb's Mr. Walters. Like the characters he portrays, Sutton Griggs is a transitional figure, one almost entirely unknown by contemporary white readers. In contrast, the most widely read Black author of the turn of the century was Paul Laurence Dunbar, a poet whose fiction is almost entirely apolitical.

4

Paul Laurence Dunbar: The Triumph of the Tradition

> My all absorbing desire is to be a worthy singer of the songs of God and of nature. To be able to interpret my own people through song and story, and to prove to the many that we are more human than African.
>
> *Paul Laurence Dunbar, letter to his patron,*
> *Dr. Henry A. Toby, July 13, 1895*

By the time Paul Laurence Dunbar died at the age of thirty-three on February 9, 1906, in Dayton, Ohio, he was so well known that the newspapers had run daily reports of his condition and his room was crowded with cards and flowers from well-wishers, most of whom had never seen the young Black writer. His short life was a rags-to-riches story dear to the heart of the nineteenth-century American public. Despite many handicaps—his birth as the son of former slaves, his childhood poverty, and his well-publicized failure after high school to find a job better than that of an elevator operator at four dollars a week—Dunbar had, in his brief lifetime, lectured and read his poetry in England and in cities across America and had published four novels, four collections of short stories, and eleven collections of verse, as well as assorted pieces in the leading journals and newspapers of the day. He had been championed by William Dean Howells, the most influential American literary critic of the time, had been awarded an honorary degree by Atlanta University, had served as guest speaker at a banquet honoring a North Carolina congressman, was on friendly terms with Theodore Roosevelt, and had been invited by a special envoy from President McKinley to participate in his inaugural parade. Like Benjamin Franklin, the prototype of America's cherished Horatio Alger self-image, Paul Dunbar had, figuratively at least, come to "stand before kings."

Yet this celebrated poet, who was acclaimed the "Orpheus of His Race" by the *Washington Post,* is rejected as a symbol of Black accomplishment by many modern readers and is seen as an artist thwarted in his personal and artistic development by "the tension between being a poet and an entertainer," which "formed the major conflict of his life."[1] He himself complained to James Weldon Johnson, "I have not grown. I am writing the same things I wrote ten years ago, and am writing them no better."[2] The portrait offered by Dunbar's biographers is that of a young man impaled on the horns of the same dilemma that threatened all the early African-American writers—whether to work within the cherished traditions of the vast white audience or to risk having no audience at all. Sutton Griggs, for example, remained virtually unknown because he appealed almost exclusively to Black readers; Martin Delany did not see *Blake* published in book form during his lifetime. To Paul Dunbar, fame was too sweet and poverty too pressing to make Griggs's choice, even when fame's honey turned to ashes in his mouth.

Dunbar was always appreciated as much for the rich, melodious voice with which he read his poems and the lively facial expressions and gestures that he used to interpret them from the lecture stage as for the poems themselves. In an age that stressed elocution, Paul Dunbar was a natural master. In 1896, Major Pond, his manager, and the guiding hand behind the lecture tours of W. D. Howells, Mark Twain, Frederick Douglass, and B. T. Washington, claimed, "[I had Dunbar] come over to my house a few evenings ago, and there give a reading to about thirty invited guests. The 'white' readers are not in it with him when it comes to delighting an audience. I want to make a contract to place him on the road for a period of two years."[3] Although Dunbar enjoyed reading his verse, he never wished to be an entertainer; although he was interested in rural Blacks, he never wished to be known exclusively for his dialect poems, in which Howells found "a finely ironical perception of the negro's limitation."[4] Yet, the public "demanded an image," and the young writer conformed, because he "had to get a hearing."[5] In order to judge accurately Dunbar's contribution to early African-American fiction, it is necessary to keep in mind these literary, economic, and social forces that were so influential in shaping his writing and, also, to try to determine his own idea of what he was attempting to do. His statement that forms the epigraph to this chapter provides clues to both of these influences.

Since Paul Dunbar earns his place in literary history as the first internationally accepted, fully professional, American Black writer, his understanding of what he was about is doubly significant. First, his success and his concept of that success reveal a great many things about the country in which he lived, particularly about the attitudes of the reading public, that segment of society which shaped the course of popular fiction. Second, Dunbar's own artistic aims, which both encompassed and transcended the desires of his audience, provided the final molding of the poems, the novels, and the more than seventy short stories comprising the Dunbar canon.

His statement reveals a great deal. The young high school graduate clearly hoped to be an artist and a worthy one. Like the Black writers who preceded him, he saw his role not only as a belletrist, however, but as an educator, an interpreter of Black people. His comment indicates that his proper audience was white, and it was to them that he apparently hoped to prove his people's humanity through his characterizations and, even more significantly, through his own example.

Ironically, despite Howells's conclusion after reading Dunbar's *Oak and Ivy*—"a race which has reached this effect in any of its members can no longer be held wholly uncivilized; and Dunbar makes a stronger claim for the Negro than any Negro has yet done."[6] Others, like Dr. W. C. Chapman, with whom Dunbar shared the speaker's platform at the Toledo West End Club, singled him out as the exception that proved the rule of Black inferiority.

Moreover, the contrast that Dunbar himself saw between the "human" and the "African" explains why he could never fulfill his "absorbing desire." Did Dunbar actually accept, to some degree at least, the racist preconceptions of that white audience? Or was he willing to forego his characters' humanity, to paint them as traditional stereotypes, in order to plead his own case as a "worthy singer" in the accepted mold? The answer, of course, is yes to both ironic possibilities.

It is now well known that Dunbar considered his dialect verse, the poetry that made him famous, to be secondary to his serious poems in literary English. The traditional verse is the "Oak" of *Oak and Ivy,* the "Majors" of *Majors and Minors,* making up almost two-thirds of his poetic output. William Dean Howells and the public preferred the dialect and the image of Black people that the dialect poems convey. By his own statement, Dunbar wished to write honestly, yet his stories and novels, more than those of any of his predecessors, are haunted by discredited spectres from plantation fiction. It is essential to realize, however, that his picture is not totally false. His books include some stories that completely contradict the magnolias and moonlight of his most popular treatments of the antebellum South. Moreover, within what appear to be conventional tales of the plantation type appear incidents and characters, Black and white, that give the lie to nineteenth-century America's comfortable view of itself.

Yet, these radical images seem to exist independently of their author. Unlike Griggs, Dunbar seldom examines the complexities of Black/white relationships with the intent of satirically showing the contradictions present in the democratic system and pointing toward political possibilities for change. On the contrary, he is almost completely apolitical, even antipolitical. Whatever the truths that he really understood about his people, he accepted literary stereotypes for literary purposes. It is as though he finally divorced his artistic aims from both the dialect poems and most of his fiction, producing those for the public and the critics, writing his serious poetry and a few serious stories for himself. Stubbornly, however, the artist within the popular writer, the slave's son inside the celebrated citizen, would not be entirely stilled and, consciously or not, finds a voice in a few stories, in a particularly telling monologue, in a few compelling characters, or in a complex relationship between some slave and his master. These lapses from the conventional occur seldom, and even when they do, they are often not the focus of concern in the story. But their very surfacing in a sea of conventional images, their very incongruity, indicates that the same contradictions troubled Dunbar's writing as disturbed his life. His books were meant to entertain; more than he realized, they instruct.

When Dunbar deviates from the well-trod path of Black stereotype, his prints are as clear as any other runaway's. It is true, as Saunders Redding remarks, that "nearly all the folk stories are limited to burlesque";[7] but not every one of them can be dismissed so easily, and in even the most apparently conventional often overlooked ironies of antebellum life appear. Appropriately for a Black artist with the paradoxical intent of popularity and honesty, Dunbar's artistic guns are double-barreled. While one side fires blanks that snap, crackle, and pop "in the good old way that always charmed and always will charm, Heaven bless it,"[8] the other sprays a scatter-shot of truthful observations that pierce the soft-scented veils of plantation life and provide the reader with quick glimpses of the bones beneath. This duality can be found in his treatment of all four of his major fictional topics: antebellum days, Black religion, migration to the North, and the Black middle class.

Although only about one-third of his poems are in dialect, by far the largest number of his stories deal with the situation in the old South before the war. Born in Dayton, Ohio, in 1872, the writer, obviously, had no firsthand knowledge of the antebellum South. Moreover, he never gained much firsthand knowledge of post-Reconstruction conditions below the Mason-Dixon line. But the contradictory picture of plantation life that emerges from his poems and stories cannot be attributed simply to ignorance. His parents related tales of the old days to him, and when he moved to Washington, he developed the habit of inviting into his home old-timers who lived in the "Camp," a Black settlement close to Howard University, and listening to their stories of the South before the war.[9] Moreover, since he had a high school education, he could not have escaped the popular literary version of slavery times. Therefore, the pictures that Dunbar offers in his plantation tales appear to be deliberately constructed and demonstrate choices that he made both because he desired commercial success and because he was himself unsure of the "truth" about the masses of his people. A close examination of the stories is essential to determine accurately the quality of these choices; and since, as Dunbar himself realized, they do not reveal a progression of understanding, they will be treated thematically rather than chronologically.

While Dunbar's picture of antebellum Blacks and of racial relationships is of primary interest, as in the books of his predecessors, his concept of whites is also revealing. In keeping with the plantation tradition, there are no "poor white trash" in his works. He treats the cream of the southern aristocracy, plantation owners noteworthy not only for their wealth and culture but also for the kindly interest that they take in their slaves. They are amused and entertained by them, allow themselves to be bullied by them, and have their best interests foremost in mind, particularly when affairs of the heart are concerned. Often, because of lovers' quarrels and family feuds of their own, these white masters and mistresses find themselves helpless and dependent on the special assistance of their trusted servants. Perhaps because of the unconscious awareness of this dependence, although Dunbar never probes this interesting area, the master of a plantation will insist upon a special relationship between his cherished heir and a bright,

loyal servant and is always willing himself to rely on the services of an established old mammy or cook. These special slaves invariably evoke the most
sentimental responses from the whites, and the masters inevitably attempt to
mask their soft hearts with authoritative demeanors. Few of Dunbar's whites are
cruel or unscrupulous to their slaves; those who are most often are overseers, not
members of the master class. Significantly, only one of his white characters
recognizes the complex evils of the slavery system.

Aunt Fanny's and Martha's mistresses are typical of Dunbar's white
females.[10] They conscientiously visit the old women when they are sick: Aunt
Fanny's lady brings her special treats from the kitchen and flannels to help ease
her rheumatism, and Martha's mistress assigns another servant to sit with the old
woman during the day and to get her husband's meals. Like *Clotelle*'s Gertrude,
Margaret Fairfax pleads with her determined father for kindness to his slaves and
wins the undying love and loyalty of Aunt Fanny and her son when she succeeds
in keeping Dick from being sold (*IOPD*, ''Dizzy-Headed Dick,'' pp. 120–29).

Moreover, Dunbar's white males are usually as tender-hearted as their women.
The master in ''The Brief Cure of Aunt Fanny'' announces plans to retire most of
the old servants and, in Mam Henry's words, ''let 'em res' fur' de balance o' dy
days, case dey been faifful, an' he think dey 'serve it'' (*IOPD*, p. 212). Another
plantation owner frees all his slaves in the middle of the Civil War and sends
medicine and the family doctor to his coachman, who has fallen ill; his wife
offers the former slave three months of back wages when he recovers (*IOPD*,
''The Stanton Coachman,'' pp. 217–25). Fairfax joyously gives all his field
hands the day off to celebrate the birth of his son,[11] and Stuart Morduant and
Master Fullerton show an even warmer regard for their servants. Morduant
refuses to sell a troublesome slave to his overseer—''I'm no nigger-trader''—but
agrees to give the man to him if he will promise to keep him on the plantation so
that Morduant can ''look after him if he got into trouble'' (*IOPD*, ''Mr. Gorby's
Slippery Gift,'' pp. 95–107). When the slave runs off and his brother, Jim, steals
food, stays out all night, and stubbornly refuses to explain his actions, Morduant
sadly orders Jim whipped. The runaway, however, returns just as Jim is about to
be lashed, confesses that his brother had been stealing for him, and offers to take
his beating. Human sympathy wins out over Morduant's fear of runaways and
thievery; the soft-hearted master emotionally forgives Jim with a cry of ''Oh, you
fool nigger—God bless you'' and takes Joe back onto his own plantation. In a
similar overflow of feeling for the happiness of his slaves, Fullerton in
''Ash-Cake Hannah and her Ben'' chooses to overlook the fact that Hannah's
husband has run off from a distant plantation to be with her at Christmas (*IOPD*,
pp. 108–19).

If one is to believe Dunbar, the antebellum whites found their slaves a continual source of delight and entertainment, when not coping with their mischief,
and gleefully allowed themselves to be bullied by them. Black children and
musicians seem to captivate them. The ''little black rascal'' after whom the tale
''Cahoots'' is entitled is given that nickname by his master and proudly carries it

with him to his grave; Lucius of "A Blessed Deceit" "first came to the notice of Mr. Daniels when as a two-year-old pickaninny he was rolling and tumbling in the sand about the quarters. Even then, he could sing so well, and was such a cheerful and good-natured, bright little scamp that his master stood and watched him in delight" (*IOPD*, pp. 190–202). Occasionally, the whites are coy about their interest in the lives of their servants. The "mirth-loving master, Stuart Morduant," for instance, gossips with his wife about the romantic entanglements of her maid and hides, with his entire family, behind the smokehouse to watch when Sophiny's two suitors battle for the honor of taking her to a dance (*IOPD*, "The Trouble About Sophiny," pp. 83–94).

The love affairs of the slaves, as a matter of fact, seem to exert an inescapable fascination over Dunbar's aristocrats. They will go to great lengths to find out about them and to aid in their satisfactory resolution. When Aunt Tempe begs Morduant, who is filled with "mischievous joy" at the tales of romantic goings-on in the slave quarters, to buy Tom from the distant Norton plantation so that he and Morduant's Laramie Belle can marry, the white man checks his romantic tendencies in favor of a comfortable self-image: "I'm not a nigger trader, and I won't have anyone making me one. You let me alone, Tempe, and don't concern yourself in this business" (*IOPD*, "Aunt Tempe's Revenge," pp. 12–26).

Concern herself she does, of course; and after three days of fretting about the situation, Morduant sheepishly goes to Tempe's cabin and thrusts a roll of bills into her hands, assuring her that since she had served him long and faithfully, he had been intending to make her a present for quite a while. As he expects, she uses the money to buy Tom for Laramie Belle. Dudley Stone, another plantation owner, takes such an interest in the matings on his property (and of his property) that in fatherly fashion he can assure the newly affianced Gideon, "You couldn't have done better if the match had been made for you." Stone is so fond of his slaves that he is willing to elaborate drastically on the typical slave "wedding": "Marry her, yes, and with a preacher."[12] The mistress of "The Easter Wedding" assumes a major role when she learns that Lize plans to marry Ben. She personally purchases her maid's wedding gown, and her young widowed daughter "brought out a once used orange wreath and a veil as filmy as a fairy spider's web, and both the white mother and daughter took as deep an interest in the affair as did the two black women" (*IOPD*, pp. 226–35).

One of the whites' favorite entertainments is observing the slaves' dances, and one of their most frequent acts of benevolence is lavishing attention upon a particularly talented Black musician, like Old Ben in "The Memory of Martha," who sits in the evenings "before his cabin door, picking out tune after tune, hymn, ballad or breakdown . . . always sure of an audience." The most extreme instance of white fascination with Black doings occurs in "A Supper by Proxy," in which Stuart Morduant, disguised as a tramp, returns early from a family holiday for the express purpose of spying upon his servants' antics. He is not concerned about attempts to escape, rebellion against the overseer, or danger of looting or arson; incredibly, he is merely curious about what his servants will do to amuse themselves while he is away. When Morduant discovers that the house servants have appropriated his parlor for a grand party, he pretends to be outraged, but is actually hard pressed to contain his amusement at this attempt to imitate white manners and social customs. The only punishment that he delivers is to the ringleader, Anderson the butler—one day's missed meals (*IOPD*, pp. 71–82).[13]

Aunt Tempe, the mammy, pushes her influence to the breaking point when she insists upon giving away Miss Eliza her "Lammy," at her wedding. Morduant is allowed to bluster and refuse for a few pages, but every Dunbar reader knows that Tempe will indeed triumph. True to form, when she pops up at the crucial moment at the ceremony to reply, "I does! Dat's who," to the minister's question "Who giveth this woman?" she is not punished. "When it was all over," Dunbar insists, "neither the father, the mother, the proud groom, nor the blushing bride had one word of reproach for mammy, for no one doubted that her giving away and her blessing were as effectual and fervent as those of the nearest relative could have been" (*IOPD*, "Aunt Tempe's Triumph," pp. 1–11).

Clearly, it is Dunbar, at least in this instance, who does not doubt the sincerity and humanity of Aunt Tempe and who transfers his feelings to the Morduants and their guests. He fails to convince the reader, however, that antebellum whites would have sanctioned the interruption of an only daughter's wedding by her Black mammy as "effectual and fervent" when Blacks themselves were considered such a low form of life that their own marriages were effected by "jumping over the broom" and could be dissolved at a master's whim when he needed the male to sell or the female to breed. Dunbar does not bother to try to resolve such contradictions because he knows that he does not need to. His audience was of a mind with the critic who praised the sketches in *Folks From Dixie:* "they touched us so deeply because they gave us what we asked for—the flow of a warm heart thrown on a little and hitherto almost unknown corner of our country's many-sided life."[14] The darkest corners of that life could very well go unlighted.

His white characters' benevolence is proof of Dunbar's "warm heart" presumably, and the Morduants' sympathy with Aunt Tempe is simply one instance of the general concern for their slaves that his aristocrats repeatedly demonstrate. One of his most unintentionally ironic expressions of this interest is his picture of a master gifting a slave with a fat shoat on the occasion of his family's earning enough money working overtime to buy his wife's freedom. When it appears that the newly freed wife intends to take all their money and head north, his sympathetic master offers Ben his free papers on the spot: "You can go North with her and you can pay me back when you find work" (*SOG*, "Viney's Free Papers," pp. 53–71).

This benevolence works both ways, for the Blacks in Dunbar's books play special roles in the lives of their masters and mistresses, often coming to their aid when the whites get into trouble. Their help can be as inconsequential as retrieving a love token from an improper suitor, a service that Dely renders Miss Emily in "A Lady Slipper" (*IOPD*, pp. 175–89), or as serious as Lucius's saving his young master from death in a fire in "A Blessed Deceit." Jube Benson nurses the town's white doctor through a serious bout with typhoid: he "nursed me as if I were a sick kitten and he my mother" (*HHH:* "The Lynching of Jube Benson," pp. 221–40). "The Colonel's Awakening," a tale of gothic sentiment, presents Colonel Robert Esteridge, who lost his mind when two sons died in the Civil War. He and his run-down plantation are cared for by the two remaining old servants, Ike and Lize. The old white man is unaware of the passage of time, and the servants help maintain his fantasy world by knitting him Christmas gloves, just as a long-dead acquaintance formerly did every year, and pretending that his sons are alive and will return for the holidays.[15]

Colonel Esteridge's case, however, is an unusual one, since most of the white dependence upon Blacks in Dunbar's stories is due to the problems that they bring upon themselves due to overweening family pride. The foolish young girl in "A Lady Slipper" cannot resist teasing a rejected suitor because his adulation flatters her. When she catches him glancing with admiration at her expensively shod foot, she is thrilled, for "she was rather proud of that pretty, aristocratic foot of hers, not so much because it was pretty and aristocratic as because it was hereditary in the family and belonged by right of birth to all the Stuarts" (*IOPD*, p. 175). Her birthright also includes, of course, a Black servant who will extricate her from the predicaments in which her Stuart vanity places her. Other young girls in Dunbar's tales pledge themselves to men of whom their fathers violently disapprove, and, invariably, the intervention of a kindly mammy is necessary to reconcile the outraged father and the disinherited couple. As in "Dizzy-Headed Dick" and "A Family Feud" (*FFD*, pp. 137–56), there are happy reunions in the end. In "The Intervention of Peter" (*FFD*, pp. 171–81) a servant prevents a duel between his young master and a former friend by popping out of the bushes with an ancient fowling piece and threatening to shoot his master's opponent in the back of the leg. The ridiculousness of the situation distracts the young foes, and common sense is restored. Significantly, although Dunbar makes only comic use of the fact, common sense is the slave's contribution: " 'Pete,' said his master, 'don't you know that it is dishonest to shoot a man from behind? You see you haven't in you the making of a gentleman.' 'I do' know nuffin' 'bout mekin' a gent'man, but I does know how to save one dat's already made.' " (*FFD*, pp. 180–81).

The whites frequently insist upon a special relationship with a particular slave. One would like to attribute this linking of characters to the author's desire to indicate the unconscious white dependence on Blacks during slavery days, but it is more likely that he is simply following plantation fiction's dictum of love and loyalty between slave and master. Two-year-old Lucius, who later saves his young master's life, begins their relationship by being appointed his "companion in chief, and amuser in general" (*IOPD*, "A Blessed Deceit," p. 192); He is taken up to the big house to live. "I want you to help your young Mas' Dud look after his mother and Miss Ellen," Gideon is charged by his aging owner. "Now that's the one promise I ask of you—come what may, look after the women folks" (*SOG,* "The Strength of Gideon," pp. 15–16). What comes is the Civil War, and Gideon's pledge is reinforced as young Dudley rides away to his death in battle: " 'You remember father's charge to you, take care of the women folks.' He took the servant's hand, and, black man and white, they looked into each other's eyes, and the compact was made" (*SOG,* p. 19).

Cahoots and his young master are introduced to each other shortly after their births in a similarly dramatic ritual solemnly initiated by old Fairfax himself: "the master took the black child's hand and put it in that of the white's . . . . 'they have made a silent compact of eternal friendship, and I propose to ratify it right here.' . . . he knelt and offered a prayer, and asked a blessing upon the two children just come into the world" (*HHH,* pp. 151–52). The Black boy becomes the white's childhood companion, and their relationship provides another example of the contradictions in Dunbar's treatment of Blacks. Commenting upon the vast amount of mischief that the two boys get into, he explains, "As was natural, the white boy planned the deeds, and the black one was his willing coadjutor in carrying them out" (*HHH,* p. 151). Yet, when Cahoots and Master Dudley get into trouble for a misadventure in one of the key scenes in the first part of the tale, it is the Black boy who rescues them with a clever turn of phrase, which earns him the nickname that he carries from then on. His response is treated comically, however, not seriously—as proof of his intelligence—because Dunbar is interested not in what is "natural" in the real world, but only in the world of plantation fiction.

In that rarefied atmosphere, when a master must reprimand his slaves, especially the bossy house servants, he is usually unsuccessful (Stuart Morduant is a fine example). The white man manages to maintain his composure for as long as it takes to deliver a halfhearted tongue-lashing to them and then dissolves in a "peal of laughter" (*IOPD,* "The Trouble About Sophiny," p. 93) as soon as the blacks are out of earshot—which is almost never. Aunt Doshy reports on Master Thornton's "furious" upbraiding of a fellow servant for interference in family affairs: "He was tryin' to talk an' look pow'ful stern, but I seed a twinkle in his eye" (*FFD,* "A Family Feud," pp. 137–56).

Dunbar paints almost no white owners who are brutal to their slaves. Lectures are given with suppressed smiles and twinkles; rare beatings for disobedience are mild and half-hearted. The few whites who are actually cruel to their servants are treated comically, as is Mr. Leckler, "a man of high principles," in "The Ingrate" (*SOG,* pp. 89–103) or Tyler, the stupid master of Ben who is so easily decoyed by Mr. Fullerton's wine cellar that he allows his runaway slave to spend the entire Christmas week with Ash-Cake Hannah and promises not to beat him when he returns. (*IOPD,* "Ash-Cake Hannah and Her Ben," pp. 108–19). Or they are of the lower class, like Groby, the overseer held in contempt by Stuart Morduant.

Life on Dunbar's plantations seems an unconscious reverse image of the "real" world—the bosses are bossed; the slaves master the masters; the Blacks show "white" common sense; and the whites are unconsciously vain, stupid, childish, and dependent. Thus, it is no surprise that only one of his white characters expresses any genuine awareness of the evils of the slavery system. In "The Lynching of Jube Benson," when Dr. Melville attempts to explain to a group of friends, and to himself, why he participated in the murder of a Black man who had befriended him, he comes closer than any other of Dunbar's characters to revealing the writer's own awareness of conditions in the antebellum South. His unraveling of the diverse cultural and psychological strands of racism that led him to tighten the rope around Jube's neck provides the only piece of writing in the Dunbar canon that approaches the vision of Sutton Griggs:

> "Why did I do it? I don't know. A false education, I reckon, one false from the beginning. I saw this black face glooming there in the half light, and I could only think of him as a monster. It's tradition. At first I was told that the black man would catch me, and when I got over that, they taught me that the devil was black, and when I had recovered from the sickness of that belief, here were Jube and his fellows with faces of menacing blackness. There was only one conclusion: The black man stood for all the powers of evil, the result of whose machinations had been gathering in my mind from childhood up" (*HHH*, p. 236).

Dr. Melville stands alone as a white man who recognizes not his own guilt alone, but the complex evils of the system that psychologically enslaved Blacks and whites alike. [16]

As would be hoped, Dunbar's portrait of the slaves is more complex and realistic than that of their masters. The possibilities for stereotyping were greater here, of course, and his tales contain their share of familiar nods and grimaces. The Stanhope coachman, for one, is the traditionally loyal, old retainer, as is Cahoots and as Jube Benson showed every promise of becoming if he hadn't been lynched first. The ironies of the coachman's choosing to live out his freedom in poverty, Cahoots' remaining "as great a [rebel] . . . to the day of his death as his master," and Jube's being lynched by the man to whom he was devoted seem not wholly, but largely, to have escaped Dunbar. Dr. Melville's announcement of white society's guilt is shocking precisely because it is unexpected in a volume of plantation tales pleasantly entitled *The Heart of Happy Hollow*.

"A Family Feud," "Mammy Peggy's Pride" (*SOG*, pp. 27–49), and "Aunt Tempe's Triumph" all depend on the machinations of a conventional mammy, outspoken in the defense of her charges and humoured by her white owner. If Dunbar's comic darkies are not buffoons of the most degraded type, they are, nevertheless, absurd enough to amuse Stuart Morduant and the turn-of-the-century reading public. Some, like Peter in "The Intervention of Peter" are drawn as buffoons even while they are performing acts as significant as saving human lives. "The Memory of Martha" concentrates upon the old, Black banjo picker lodged as a permanent fixture in cabin doors throughout fictional plantations, and "Ash-Cake Hannah and Her Ben" offers the obligatory image of carefree slaves at holiday time, "stamping or tripping along through the damp snow like so many happy children."

Christmas, in particular, spurs Dunbar and other writers of the plantation tradition to an indulgence in image upon image of mindless festivity. A southern Christmas of *In Old Plantation Days* wraps the big house and cabin alike in warm blankets of light and good fellowship:

Negro Tom was tuning up his fiddle in the barn, and Blophus, with his banjo, was getting the chords from him, while Alec was away out in the woods with his face turned up to the gray sky, letting the kinks out of his tenor voice. All this because the night was coming on. Christmas Eve night was the beginning of a week of joy. The wind freshened and the snow fell faster. The walks were covered. Old gnarled logs that had lain about, black and forbidding, became things of beauty. The world was a white glory. Slowly, so slowly for a winter's night, the lights faded out and the lamps and candles and torches like lowly stars laughed from the windows of big house and cabin. In fireplaces great and small the hickory crackled, and the savory smell of cooking arose, tempting, persistent. The lights at the big house winked at the cabin, and the cabin windows winked back again. Laughter trickled down the night and good cheer was everywhere (*IOPD,* "Ash-Cake Hannah and Her Ben," p. 109).

Although this decription appears in a potentially moving story about the separation of a slave and his wife, Dunbar spends so much time portraying the joyous mood of both the whites and the servants that when Ben must run away to spend the holiday with Hannah, the reader is neither saddened nor alarmed by their plight. Later, when it is clear that, because of the stupidity of his master, Ben has not really put himself in danger, the reader feels neither surprise nor relief. All of the usual responses on which Dunbar should have been able to count to maintain interest in his tale are eliminated by his muting of the actual drama of the situation that he is describing. Hannah's and Ben's troubles are of so little concern even to the other slaves that after serenading the master and his guests, they joyfully "filed through the hall, one by one each with a 'Me'y Chris'mus' and each receiving some token from the master and mistress. Laughing, joking, bantering, they went out to their holidays, some to their cabins to dance or eat, others to the woods with the dogs and the newly sharpened axes to look for game." It is not until one reads Dunbar's stories set in the North after the Civil War that the reader is given any perspective on his fond image of slavery life.

If one of the gentle failings of Dunbar's aristocrats is their inordinate pride of family, it is a failing shared by their slaves. Many of the Blacks are as proud of their white folks as the whites are of themselves. Aunt Tempe, Aunt Doshy, Old

Ike, and Lize all would have shared Mammy Peggy's disgust at hearing her young charge, the last member of an impoverished postwar family, observe realistically, "Oh what a pity one cannot sell one's quality for daily bread or trade off one's blue blood for black coffee." Indignantly asking, "Whaih's yo' Ha'ison pride?" the old woman almost ruins the girl's chances for a successful marriage and an escape from poverty. Dunbar's concern here, however, is not with the irony of the Black woman's clinging to the pretensions of a family that, through the maintenance of its proud traditions by the slavery system, has stripped her of her own African heritage. Instead, he focuses on the thwarted lovers and ends his sentimental tale with a conventional reconciliation scene, quenching the glimmer of enlightenment that Mammy Peggy achieves. Retreating again into the dark tradition, she is not accorded the dignity of recognizing the self-deception of her imitative pretensions; she is merely Miss Mima's "bad, stupid, dear old goose."

None of the faithful old retainers in the tales of the southern apologists are any more loyal to their white aristocrats before or after the war than Dunbar's Dizzy-Headed Dick, who "would have died for" his mistress, or the Stanton coachman, whose attitude is explained by another old Black man: "W'y dat man seemed lak he got proudah dan evah, 'case hit wuzn' de money he wuz lookin' aftah, hit wuz de fambly. Anybody kin git money, but Gawd got to gin yo' quality." When the house servants of "A Supper by Proxy" decide to celebrate, it is in imitation of the mode of entertainment that their master and mistress would have chosen. They give a dinner and invite house servants from the neighboring plantations, but no field hands.[17] "It was a well-dressed assembly, too," Dunbar observes. "Plump brown arms lay against the dainty folds of gleaming muslin, and white-stocked, brass-buttoned black counterparts of their masters strode up the walks."

Despite the abundance of such examples, these tales are peppered with realistic elements that the slave narratives insist made up the antebellum experience. Black independence, for example, historically a threat to the slavery system and a quality that led to discontented runaways like Frederick Douglass and violent rebels like Nat Turner, is shrunken in Dunbar's stories to the comic proportions of incurable meddling in their masters' affairs, but the picture of slaves with secret knowledge and the cunning to use it is a persistent and true image. Dick's, Doshy's, and Aunt Emmerline's spying is intended to amuse because such action and the knowledge that it brings are incongruous with their servile positions. But to one familiar with the slave narratives, the only incongruous aspect to their keeping an alert eye and ear on what is going on around them is their inordinate interest in reconciling feuding whites and their lack of interest in anything concerning themselves. "I knows I ain't got no bus'ness meddlin' in you 'fairs," pleads Aunt Emmerline, climbing in the window outside which she has been listening, "but I cain't see you all qua'l dis way." While the comic purposes to which it is put is a distortion, the spying itself is realistic.

Moreover, Black awareness of white affairs is not limited to the knowledge that Aunt Tempe demonstrates, a general acquaintance with "all the traditions of the section, and the histories of all the families thereabouts." Also present is Dinah's more useful ability to see beneath the surface of white action, to discard appearance for the real intentions concealed in her master's heart. When his daughter runs off to marry against his wishes, Master Bradley whips Dick for failing to stop them. Dinah knows, however, that the whipping is only an empty demonstration of authority: "an' Mas' Bradley he gwine fu'give de young folks anyhow. Ef he ain't, huccome he didn't taih Dick all to pieces?" Of course, no slave on Dunbar's plantations is ever torn "all to pieces" or even greatly discomfited, but real slaves sometimes were, and their ability to read sensitively their masters' moods and predict their actions frequently saved their skins, as Frederick Douglass's narrative demonstrates.

In addition to understanding the whites better than the whites understand themselves, several of the Black characters display other traits that make them more believable than mere stereotype would permit.[18] While in most ways Aunt Fanny is conventional, her brief introduction suggests that Dunbar may have had a more realistic portrayal in mind when he first conceived of her:

> Some people grow old gracefully, charmingly. Others, with a bitter reluctance so evident that it detracts from whatever dignity might attach to their advanced period of life. Of this latter class was Aunt Fanny. . . . She had been good-looking in her younger days, sprightly, and a wonderful worker, and she held to the belief in her capabilities long after the powers of her youth and middle-age were gone. . . . She had danced beyond the time when all her comrades had grown to the state of settled and unfrivolous Christianity. Indeed, she had kept up her gayety until she could find no men old enough to be her partners, and the young men began to ignore her; then she went into the Church (*IOPD*, "The Brief Cure of Aunt Fanny," pp. 203–16).

Clearly, such a character could have been used for the basis of a story about the problem of aging, a universal theme, or, more particularly, about the attitudes of other Blacks to the antics of such an individualist in their midst. Instead, she is put to the services of a traditional, humorous tale of the difficulties that the white aristocrats faced with their kitchen help. After her introduction, none of Aunt Fanny's qualities that make her unique, rather than being just one of a score of cantankerous, old servants who plague their tender-hearted masters, is developed. Nevertheless, a note of pathos is inadvertently struck, which leaves the reader regretting that Dunbar did not choose to follow its tone.

Somewhat better realized is Joe of "Mr. Groby's Slippery Gift." While both he and his brother are field hands, "Jim went his way and did his work rejoicing," while "Joe was the bane of the overseer's life." Giving the lie to the image of field hands being equally docile, Joe and his brother "could hardly have been more unlike." Dunbar, however, obviously shares Groby's disapproval of Joe, for "a lazier, more unreliable scamp . . . could not have been found within a radius of fifty miles. . . . He would seize every possible chance of shirking, and it was his standing boast that he worked less and ate more than any other man on the place.''

Dunbar also sympathizes with Stuart Morduant's fear that Joe ''will corrupt the whole plantation'' if strong measures are not taken: ''Joe literally carries out the idea that he doesn't have to work, and is there a servant on the place who will work if he thinks he doesn't have to?'' When Morduant raises this question, overseer Groby replies, ''Yes, one—Joe's brother Jim. . . . He's what a nigger ought to be—as steady and tireless as an ox.'' Dunbar disapproves of the vulgar Mr. Groby and permits Morduant to remark that the reason that Joe has not corrupted his brother is because Jim is too loyal and sensible to allow it to happen, not because he ''ain't got sense enough to be corrupted as long as he gets his feed,'' as Groby maintains. Nonetheless, Dunbar, too, favors the docile, cooperative Jim over his rebellious brother. Despite Dunbar's ambivalence, Joe is a significant portrayal because he is one of the few discontented slaves in the poet's antebellum world.

An even more interesting, although fragmented and undeveloped, portrait is that of Lucy, the mother of the ill-named Laramie Belle in ''Aunt Tempe's Revenge.'' Lucy, who ''closed her ears to all advice, remonstrances, and prophecy when warned as to the naming of her baby,'' is a law unto herself:

No one argues with Lucy, whatever they might say to her daughter. About the older woman there was a spirit fierce and free that would not be gainsaid. There was something of the wild nerve of African forests about her that had not yet been driven out by the hard hand of slavery, nor yet smoothed down by the velvet glove of irresponsibility.

When the other slaves are cruel to Laramie Belle, ''Lucy's eyes grew fierce. Something strange, foreign, even wild within her seemed to rear itself and call for release. But she held herself as if saying, 'A little while yet.' ''

Obviously, this story should be Lucy's rather than Aunt Tempe's or Laramie Belle's. Dunbar could have developed a fascinating character portrayal if he had examined how Lucy kept her wildness and freedom in the face of the deadening influence of slavery, especially when so few of the other slaves in his stories seem to maintain any trace of their African heritage. Or, he might have concerned himself with the callous responses of the other Blacks to Lucy and her lovelorn daughter. Thinking her to be traitorous for loving a slave from a rival plantation, the Morduant servants have very little sympathy for the girl's plight: ''When they saw that she would not yield, they cast her off. They would not associate with her, nor speak to her. She was none of theirs. Let her find her friends over at Norton's, they said. They laughed at her and tossed their heads in her face, and she went her way silent but weeping.''

Such cruelty links these slaves with all men and their frailties, and Dunbar could have examined their hatreds and jealousies and enriched the reader's experience of them as realistic human beings, as William Wells Brown's portrayal of Dinah, the cook who hates Clotelle, succeeds in doing. Or he could have delved deeper into the rivalries that apparently developed between slaves on neighboring plantations. Instead, he concentrates upon Aunt Tempe and her ability to manipulate soft-hearted and soft-headed Master Morduant into buying Tom. The focus in the story, then, is on the stereotypes rather than the humans, on conventional action rather than on either individualistic or universal responses that ring true.

However, the very fact that the central problem in "Aunt Tempe's Revenge" is the separation of the lovers caused by the conditions of slavery indicates that Dunbar does not totally ignore the realistic sufferings of antebellum Blacks; they are simply not his primary, or even secondary, concern and are usually glossed over. In contrast, his entire interest in "The Easter Wedding" is the breaking up of slave families on the auction block. Their bankrupt master "had fostered fidelity among them and he knew that now it would fall back upon them, bringing only suffering and pain, for wives and husbands who had been together for years must be separated and whole families broken up." Dunbar clearly realizes the ironic and cruel dilemma facing antebellum Blacks in their personal relationships. If they followed the teachings of their masters' Christianity and married with a lifetime's commitment in mind, they faced the chance of losing their life's partner in a few minute's bidding at the auction block. If they followed the tradition of casual alliances fostered on many plantations, they were in danger of being deprived of family stability and, ironically, condemned by whites for alleged inconstancy, immorality, and lack of feeling.[19] Despite the deep awareness that Dunbar shows in "The Easter Wedding," it is the only one of his stories to concentrate on this poignant aspect of slave life.

Another tragic feature of the slavery system that is seldom discussed in literature in anything other than a comic vein is the relationship between the Black mammy and her white charges. Dunbar's own focus on this theme is a humorous one, yet, despite himself, he conveys some of the complexities of the relationship for the Black woman. The paradox of being a mother and not a mother, charged with the responsibilities of motherhood, but blessed with few of its rights and rewards, is at issue here. Aunt Tempe poignantly voices an awareness of her dilemma when she confronts Stuart Morduant with the question,

> "Who raise up dat chile? Who nuss huh to'll de colic w'en she cried all
> night, an' she was so peakid you didn't know w'en you gwine lay huh
> erway? Huh? Who do dat? Who raise you up, an' tek keer o' you, w'en
> you' ol' mammy die, an' you wa'n't able even to keep erway f'om de
> bee-trees? Huh? Who do dat? You gin huh erway? You gin huh erway!
> Da's my child, Mas Stua't Mo'de'nt, an' ef anybody gin huh erway at de
> weddin', d'ain't nobody gwine do it but ol' Tempe huhself. You hyeah
> Me?"[20]

Such dissatisfaction and self-concern are rare in the Dunbar canon.[21]

As these passages dealing with the problems of the mammy, the slave couple, rebellion, individuality, and dissatisfaction prove, Dunbar was neither ignorant nor completely insensitive to the complexities of life for antebellum Blacks. He could include realistic elements in his stories when he chose. That he so seldom chose to do so attests to his sophisticated awareness of audience expectations. Yet, Dunbar's eye to the popular market is only a partial explanation. The high-school-educated, Ohio poet appears not entirely certain that the popular literary and social conventions about the masses of Blacks were completely false. In addition to being shaped by publishers' expectations, Dunbar's stories seem further limited by their author's own uncertainties about his people.

His ambivalence is best demonstrated in the four stories that are better written and contain fuller characterizations than the others dealing with antebellum life: "The Strength of Gideon," "Viney's Free Papers," "The Ingrate," and "The Wisdom of Silence" (*HHH*, pp. 191–204). Each of their main characters is independent and possesses a strong personal sense of identity. The Black family in each is depicted as suffering from the historically documented trials brought on by the slavery situation. In each of these tales exists a complex, rather than stereotypic, relationship between the bondsmen and the masters who control their destinies. In addition, elements of folk speech and incidents validated by the slave narratives ground these accounts in the verities of slave life.

While Dunbar apparently intends "The Strength of Gideon" to glorify the loyal slave celebrated in his minor tales, the effect of the story is just the opposite. Gideon, named after the Hebrew warrior of the Old Testament, is a young man who was made intensely conscious from the time of his childhood of his own identity and potential. His naming indicates his special role: "All the plantation knew the spiritual significance of the name, and from the day of his birth the child was as one set apart to a holy mission on earth." A politically aware reader of Dunbar's tale would naturally expect this "holy mission" to have something to do with fighting for the liberation of his people, just as Gideon of old led his troops to victory against the Midianites. That this expectation is to be dashed is clear when one realizes how conventional and timid the present-day Gideon is. As a child, he is the parent surrogate, the censor, the voice of law and order. He never went

> into the direction of the stables, where the other pickaninnies worried the horses, or into the region of the hen-coops, where egg-sucking was a common crime. . . . At a very early age his shrill voice could be heard calling in admonitory tones, caught from his mother's very lips, "You 'Nelius, don' you let me ketch you th'owin' at ol' mis' guinea-hens no mo'; you hyeah me?" or "Hi'am, yo come offen de top er dat shed 'fo' you fall an' brek yo naik all to pieces."

Gideon is clearly one of Thomas Bailey Aldrich's little good boys, the pusillanimous sort who drove Mark Twain into sputtering rages. Despite his precocious concern with acceptable behavior and caution, however, Dunbar insists he was "early destined to sacrifice and self-effacement."

Since these are the qualities of the leader, the prophet who isolates himself in the desert for purification before speaking the Word or leading the righteous army, the reader's trust in Gideon's future role is rekindled. As he grows, the other slaves recognize his difference from themselves. "The appointed man is always marked, and so Gideon was by always receiving his full name," Dunbar says. "No one ever shortened his scriptural appellation into Gid. He was always Gideon from the time he bore the name out of the heat of camp-meeting fervor until his master discovered his worthiness and filled Cassie's breast with pride by taking him into the house to learn 'mannahs and 'po'tment.' "

This move from the quarters into the big house subtly indicates the actual nature of Gideon's future leadership. There is ample evidence in the story that the plight of his people is something almost completely absent from his awareness: "As a house servant he was beyond reproach, and next to his religion his Mas' Dudley and Miss Ellen claimed his devotion and fidelity." Cassie, his mother, is not mentioned again. Like several of Dunbar's slaves, Gideon is further singled out by being given the special charge to "look after the women folks" if anything should happen to the white men. Thus, even though Gideon, and apparently Dunbar, is oblivious to any such interpretation, his responsibilities are aligned with the master class.

When the Civil War erupts, and with it an awareness among the slaves of its implications for freedom, Gideon alone fails to rejoice. By his pact with the whites, the favored house servant has abrogated any position of leadership with the Blacks. Instead of being guided openly out of bondage, they are forced to slip away in darkness; instead of magnificently leading his people as did his namesake of old, Gideon keeps silent and tries to ignore what is taking place all around him. Rather than being in the forefront of those claiming their manhood, Gideon refuses even to follow and, ironically, perpetuates the slavery-born sundering of Black families, for his wife Martha will not stay behind. As she leaves with the others, Dunbar paints a pathetic scene for Gideon, who "drew out a pace after the troops, and then, turning, looked back at the house. He went a step further, and then a woman's gentle voice called him, 'Gideon!' He stopped. He crushed his cap in his hand, and then the tears came into his eyes. Then he answered, 'Yes, Mis' Ellen, I's a-comin'.' "

The sad irony of the "warrior" deserting even the tail end of the troops is clear to the reader, but is obviously not the response that Dunbar intends. Not only does the writer seem to sympathize with Gideon's misguided self-sacrifice, he seems oblivious to the sexual implications of the Black man's separation from his wife to obey the requests of his white mistress. The emphasis at the end of the story is on the pathos of his hero's situation as he slowly loses sight and sound of the army, the liberated slaves, and Martha. Dunbar's last comment, "Gideon had triumphed mightily," cannot, as much as one might wish, be taken as sardonic. Given the characterization and tone of the rest of the story, this observation seems intended, instead, to reinforce the image of the generous servant caught in the conflict between self-interest and responsibility. To the modern reader, the warrior who ignorantly and unnecessarily surrenders to his foe is a figure of scorn rather than admiration. Of course, the Stones are never depicted as "foes," for they are never physically cruel to their slaves. But, clearly, they are selfish, blind to the destruction that they are inflicting on those over whose lives they hold sway, incapable of caring for themselves, and content to play upon Gideon's misplaced sense of loyalty to maintain his servitude. The other slaves realize this well enough to leave as soon as they can, but none of these qualities is apparent to Gideon, or, it appears in this instance, to Dunbar.

Like "The Strength of Gideon," "Viney's Free Papers" presents a major character with an intense sense of her own identity. Viney's self-awareness, however, does not stem from an unusual name or from being chosen for special service to her owners. Rather, her identity manifests itself from within once she becomes a free woman.

After three years of working overtime to buy her freedom, her husband Ben at last hands Viney the piece of paper certifying that she is no longer a slave. At first, she is overwhelmed at the meaning of the thing and cannot even bring herself to take the piece of paper into her hands. Ben, however, persists, recognizing that the paper is an important symbol of her new status and that her accepting it and holding it in her own hands will be the first act in her new life of self-determination: "Dat's de way to git used to bein' free. Wenevah you looks at yo'se'f an' feels lak you ain' no diff'ent f'om whut you been you tek dat papah out an' look at hit, an' say to yo'se'f, 'Dat means freedom.'"

Logically enough, Viney moves from one symbol of her status to another and decides that the name she was given by her master is no longer appropriate. Oddly, however, Dunbar at this point turns her into a pompous harridan who is so vain about her new importance that she alienates all her former friends. "Oomph!" an acquaintance exclaims, "You done gone now! Yo' naik so stiff you can't ha'dly ben' it. I don' see how dat papah mek sich a change in anybody's actions. Yo' face ain' got no whitah." Claiming "I's free, an' I kin do as I please," Viney even begins to alienate Ben. He agrees that she should discard their slavery name, but asks her to wait until he is free and can change his, too. "Viney tossed her head," however, "and that night she took out her free papers and studied them long and carefully."

At her suggestion that they move north when Ben is freed, her husband reacts as though she has spoken a blasphemy: "No, I won't go Nawth! I was bo'n an' raised in de Souf, an' in de Souf I stay ontwell I die. Ef I have to go Nawth to injoy my freedom I won't have it. I'll quit wo'kin fu' it." Dunbar clearly sides with Ben in this dispute and places himself in the awkward position of asserting the value of the South over the importance of being free.

He stacks the deck against Viney. He depicts her as selling her laying hens, which she had been tending to help Ben buy himself, and using these funds to increase her savings for a trip north by herself. Moreover, when Ben accuses her of really wishing to go north because Si Johnson, a free Black acquaintance, is going, her weak denial is meant to be unconvincing.

The reader can't help but be confused about the author's intentions in this story, until it becomes clear that although ''Viney's Free Papers'' appears to tell the story of bondage and freedom from the slave's point of view, it is just another plantation fiction done up in Black face. The conventional point of the story becomes abundantly clear as selfish, fickle Viney, whom freedom has ruined, plots and schemes, and true-blue Ben seeks advice from his master, Mr. Raymond.

The story ends, however, with Viney's last-minute change of heart, which is as unexplained as the rest of her arbitrary characterization. Significantly, she blames her previous attitude upon ''dese pleggoned free papahs'' and burns them in the fireplace: '''Thaih,' she said, 'thaih, now, Viney Raymond!''' Since the deed of sale was established at the beginning of the story as a symbol not only of her emergence from slavery, but also of her concomitant self-awareness and sense of identity, the burning of the papers and resumption of her slave name strikes the reader as either an extremely careless artistic choice or a deliberate ritualistic action rejecting freedom. But then, Dunbar is obviously not taking his own symbols or characters seriously. Significantly, after Viney destroys the symbols of her freedom, she and Ben are completely reconciled, and ''that night singing was heard from Ben's cabin and the sound of the banjo.''

The resolution of ''The Wisdom of Silence'' is even more disturbing. When Jeremiah Anderson, after Emancipation, decides he has ''been fattenin'' frogs fu' othah people's snakes too long now'' and takes out a mortgage on his own farm, instead of staying on the plantation to work, his former master warns him that he might have to come crawling back. Sure enough: a combination of bad weather and his own wastefulness and laziness lead inevitably to failure. But, Jerry ''was proud with an obstinate pride and he shut his lips together so that he might not groan. He would not go to his master. Anything rather than that.''

Dunbar overlooks the fact that Samuel Brabant is no longer master. Moreover, as in Viney's tale, he damns the Black man's desire for self-sufficiency as obstinate pride rather than seeing it as a sign of ambition and self-confidence. Only whites in Dunbar's South are permitted the luxury of pride, apparently. When Jerry borrows enough from moneylenders to recover during his second year on the farm, Brabant's resentment of his success is neatly excused. He does not bear any malice toward Jerry, Dunbar explains, but is displeased ''for the reason that any man with the natural amount of human vanity must feel himself aggrieved just as his cherished prophecy is about to come true. . . . He had been ready to help Jerry after giving him admonitions, but here it was not needed. An unused 'I told you so,' however kindly, is an acid that turns the milk of human kindness sour.'' ''Kindly'' Samuel Brabant, then, is excused for demonstrating a ''natural amount of human vanity'' while he waits for Jerry to come begging at his door, but the former slave reveals only ''obstinate pride'' for refusing to do so.

When Jerry alienates the town's whites and his fellow Blacks by carelessly bragging about his success, leading some local vigilantes to burn his house, crops, and barn, his desperate wife urges him to appeal to their old master: "Jerry rose up, his eyes flashing fire. 'Cindy Ann,' he said, 'you a fool, you ain't got no mo' pride den a guinea hen, an' you got a heap less sense. W'y, befor' I go to ol' Mas' Sam Barbant fu' a cent, I'd sta've out in de road.' 'Huh!' said Cindy Ann, shutting her mouth on her impatience."

Thus, in "The Wisdom of Silence," Dunbar reverses the actors in the conflict that he treated in "Viney's Free Papers"—marital discord in a Black family occasioned by overweening pride that surfaces after freedom. Significantly, in both stories, the virtuous Black is the one who maintains a state of psychological slavery. Cindy Ann goes to Brabant behind Jerry's back, and the white man offers his former slave the money that he needs to rebuild. When Jerry refuses his aid, Brabant threatens to give it to Cindy Ann in her own name. At this, Jerry relents and accepts the loan. Once again, Dunbar seems insensitive to the historical sexual overtones of the Black man/Black woman/white master triangle. Moreover, he asserts a postwar need for the slave's trick of hiding his true feelings when he allows the repentant Jerry to assert, "An' nex' time ef I evah gets a sta't again, I'll keep my mouf shet. Fac' is, I'll come to you, Mas' Sam, an' borry fu' de sake o' hidin'.' " In this perverted, but prophetic, version of Black cunning, the former slave works in cahoots with the master to hide his self-sufficiency.

That such pretense was essential for survival during slavery times is a fact to which the slave narratives amply testify, and Reconstruction, it is true, hardly provided a healthier climate than antebellum days. But Dunbar never probes the horror of this situation. He does not portray Jerry as a flawed human being wrestling with the problem of trying to succeed from scratch in the white man's South. Nor does he examine in any depth the emotional and historical conflicts in the sexual triangle that provides the resolution for his tale. Instead, he presents a foolish Black buffoon who is saved through the sagacity of his wife and the benevolence of his white master and who, despite the "sobs someplace back in his throat," doesn't recognize the degradation of his final decision to live by the slavery-time role of self-abasement and appeasement. Jerry does not recognize the significance of his actions because Dunbar does not. Or if he does, it is not his real concern.

Nevertheless, Dunbar wrote one story set in Civil War times that presents the Black man as something other than a child or a fool. As a matter of fact, "The Ingrate" shows a slave successfully tricking his owners in much the same manner that Frederick Douglass used to effect his escape. This tale is actually modeled on the experiences of Dunbar's father, Joshua, when he ran away to Canada from Kentucky before the Civil War, and such grounding in reality, rather than popular fiction, must explain its unique portraiture and theme.

Like Douglass, Dunbar's Josh uses every opportunity to learn to read and learns very quickly when his owner, Leckler, instructs him in order to keep Josh from being cheated when he hires him out. Leckler's interest becomes clear when it is revealed that he keeps nine tenths of Josh's wages.

Once the slave discovers books, there opens up to him a world that makes his condition intolerable. Braving the wrath of whites and the scorn and misunderstanding of his fellow slaves, he smuggles books into his cabin and spends his few hours of leisure rapt in their pages. Like Douglass, the more he reads, the more he yearns to be free. The aspirations motivating him are presented with a power found in none of Dunbar's other characterizations: "He was being swayed by ambitions other than the mere fathering of slaves for his master. To him his slavery was deep night. . . . To own himself, to be master of his hands, feet, of his whole body—something would clutch at his heart as he thought of it; and the breath would come hard between his lips." Like the successful slaves of the narratives, he bides his time, meeting his master "with an impassive face, always silent, always docile."

On Joshua's trek north with his forged pass in his pocket, Dunbar utilizes several motifs from the slave narratives. The hounds put on his trail "came yelping back, pawing their noses and rubbing their heads against the ground. They had found the trail but Josh had played the old slave trick of filling his tracks with cayenne pepper." Like William Wells Brown, he is befriended by Quakers, agents on the Underground Railway. And, like Jerome, Brown's protagonist in *Clotelle*, he is saved from capture when the Quakers trick the local slave catchers.

Once free, "it was a new thing for [Josh] to feel himself a man and to have his manhood recognized by the whites with whom he came into free contact," Dunbar remarks. "It was new, too, this receiving the full measure of his worth in work. He went to his labor with a zest that he had never known before, and he took a pleasure in the weariness it brought him." Clearly, in this almost isolated story, Dunbar appreciated the psychological and emotional differences between slavery and freedom.

Mr. Leckler's curse, "oh, that ingrate, that ingrate," is offered ironically at the end of Josh's tale, but it should be remembered that Jerry in "The Wisdom of Silence" was judged by Dunbar, as well as by his other characters, as just such a proud, stubborn, reprobate as Leckler considers Josh. Since Jerry's tale was published later than "The Ingrate," a development in Dunbar's understanding of the antebellum South cannot account for the difference. Rather, Dunbar's treatment of Jerry depends on the same reason that Brown imagined a burlesque fox-hunting scene for Jerome: both writers were following a sterile literary tradition. In "The Ingrate," on the other hand, Dunbar based his description upon real escapes and the universal longings of human beings rather than upon the wish fulfillment of pro-slavery apologists.

The aspect of plantation life that interests Dunbar more than any other is that traditional subject of the southern humorists, Black religion. The uses to which the whites put their Christianity merited sarcastic comment from many escaped slaves, Henry Bibb and Solomon Northup, for example; Frederick Douglass, too, was outraged by "how pious priests whip Jack and Nell."[22] The nineteenth-century humorists, who helped mold the popular imagination, however, concentrated upon the vagaries of Black religious practices, not white, and it is important to note that Dunbar's tales diverge from their pattern of burlesque only when he shifts his scene from the plantation to the town. His biographers agree that he once contemplated going into the ministry, and his empathy with characters like the protagonists of "Old Abe's Conversion" (*HHH*, pp. 105–21) and "The Ordeal at Mt. Hope" (*FFD*, pp. 29–65) is obvious, as is his distance from the plantation exhorters and old-fashioned "desk-thumpers" who populate most of his tales on this theme.

Four of his antebellum tales, in particular—"The Walls of Jericho" (*IOPD*, pp. 27–38), "How Brother Parker Fell from Grace" (*IOPD*, pp. 39–49), "Jim's Probation" (*SOG*, pp. 165–75), and "The Trousers" (*IOPD*, pp. 50–59)—reveal the same uncritical picture of paternalism and humorous condescension between Blacks and whites in the religious area as imagined in economic and social matters.[23]

In at least two stories centered in Black congregations in the North, however, Dunbar seriously utilizes the motif of separation and reunion that Frances Harper employed to good effect in *Iola Leroy* and that figures so prominently in the slave narratives. Admittedly, both "The Finding of Martha" (*IOPD*, pp. 236–58) and "One Christmas at Shiloh" (*HHH*, pp. 35–52) are sentimental renderings of this theme, since they are grounded in the coincidences, chance meetings, and improbable happy endings common to popular fiction. Nevertheless, these stories demand attention, for both involve characters from earlier tales, and the topic of slave partings and reunions links them to one of the consistent themes of the Black literary tradition.

"The Finding of Martha" reintroduces the disturbingly loyal Gideon. Like Josh, Gideon "learns to read by hook and by crook," attends one of the freedman's schools, the chief business of which was "the turning out of teachers and preachers," completes his ministerial training, and sojourns to Washington, D.C., where he believes Martha, whom he has not seen for over five years, is living. No details of his life on the deserted Stone plantation after the war are given.

It is clear from the beginning that this time Dunbar intends a happy ending for his self-sacrificial protagonist; and, as the reader expects, after a long period of Gideon's disappointed and faithful searching, Martha suddenly appears. Improbably, she simply walks through the door of Shiloh Church one evening as he is starting services.

The most interesting note to this tale is the congregation's response to the reunion. Dunbar's explanation of its sympathy indicates his seldom expressed sensitivity to the facts of bondage: "So many of them were just out of slavery. So many of them knew what separation and fruitless hope of remeeting were, that it was an event to strike home to their hearts. Some wept, some rejoiced, and all gathered around the pastor and his wife to grasp their hands." The ending of this tale, then, is one of believable celebration, of jubilee for families united and hardships overcome. Yet, Dunbar cannot refrain from dulling its point by depicting the parting church members as looking back fondly, "seeing the yellow fields, the white cabins, the great house, in the light of other days."

This conventional note of nostalgia for the prewar South is a persistent one in Dunbar's stories set in the North, although occasionally he undercuts it by painting a rare picture of desolation. The study in color contrasts that appears in "Anner' Lizer's Stumblin' Block" (*FFD*, pp. 3–26), symbolizing conflicting lifestyles in the big house and the quarters, is an example of his more sensitive treatment of this subject. His almost naturalistic rendering of the big house with its promise of comfort and the slave shacks with their assurance of squalor differs sharply from his conventional paeans to "yellow fields" and "white cabins" among Shiloh's congregation. An almost identical tale is "One Christmas at Shiloh."

If social satire can be found anywhere in Dunbar's fiction, it occurs in the scenes in which he pokes fun at the hypocrisy and jealousy rampant in church-goers. In "The Defection of Maria Ann Gibbs" (*IOPD*, pp. 259–72), Maria and her "bosom friend," Lucindy, "come to'oo" [come through] on the same night because they are rivals for the attention of the Reverend Eleazer Jackson: "Thus were the Rev. Eleazer Jackson's meetings a great success, and his name became great in the land." At least half of Dunbar's congregations are rife with such hypocrisy, but it is essential to note that the focus of his satire is on materialistic, northern ministers and gullible, self-deceptive congregations, not on the religion itself.[24]

As a matter of fact, Dunbar obviously appreciated the power and spiritual nourishment of certain manifestations of the Black church. Some of his most effective writing appears in scenes of sincere mourners being prayed into church fellowship. The rhythmic dialogue between the minister and the church members in "Anner' Lizer's Stumblin' Block," for instance, successfully conveys the excitement and emotional release that Griggs's Aunt Molly missed when her insecure, middle-class congregation decided to bleach the fervor out of its religion.

Dunbar's ministers can stand their people's hair on end with fire-and-brimstone sermons or set them quietly weeping with promises of a heavenly city to replace their squalid huts. Anner' Lizer's preacher's voice is so enticing that he soon has the entire church on its feet:

Leaning over the pulpit and stretching out his arms before him, [he coaxes] in his softest tone, "Now come, won't you, sinnahs? De Lawd is jes' on de othah side; jes' one step away, waitin' to receibe you. Won't you come to him? Won't you tek de chance o' becomin' j'int 'ars o' dat beautiful city whar de streets is gol' an de gates is pearl? Won't you come to him, sinnah? Don't you see de pityin' look he's a-givin' you, a-saying' Come, come?"

His effective pleas soon inspire a stalwart young man to begin to writhe and twist into every possible contortion, crying,

"O Lawd, de devil's a ridin' me'; tek him off—tek him off!"

"Tek him off, Lawd!" shouted the congregation.

Then suddenly, without warnings, the mourner rose straight up into the air, shouting, "Hallelujah, hallelujah, hallelujah!"

"He's got it—he's got it!" cried a dozen eager worshippers, leaping to their feet and crowding around the happy convert: "bless de Lawd, he's got it." A voice was raised, and soon the church was ringing with "Loose him and let him go, Let him shout to glory." On went the man shouting "Hallelujah," shaking hands, and bounding over seats in the ecstasy of his bliss.

This scene abounds in comic possibilities, but Dunbar does not exploit them as he does in "The Defection of Maria Ann Gibbs." Instead, he seems sensitive in this instance to the powerful role of the Black church in offering hope and emotional and psychological release to African-Americans both before and after the Civil War. Furthermore, despite Brother Parker's comic treatment and the satire leveled at northerners like the Reverend Eleazer Jackson, Dunbar draws several preachers with great sympathy. Gideon and the Reverend Silas Todbury of "One Christmas at Shiloh" are good examples, but "Old Abe's Conversion" and "The Ordeal at Mt. Hope" indicate the writer's appreciation of the Black minister's role better than any of his other stories on this topic.

Despite his skepticism about the preacher whose talents are limited to "thumping the desk" and raising funds, he feels nothing but respect for ministers with a social and humanitarian concern. "Old Abe's Conversion" introduces examples of both types.

A year after his rejection as a preacher by his father's smug, old-fashioned congregation, the seminary-trained Robert Dixon shows the old man around his city pastorate. This odyssey introduces Old Abe to a way of life of which he has been completely ignorant. Engaging in his favorite, almost naturalistic, description of city scenes, Dunbar conjures up an atmosphere so unlike rural Danvers that the father must turn to the son for guidance.

This is a story of contrasts, of rural and urban life, old and new preaching styles and training, and, most importantly, traditional notions of the minister's elitist role and modern concepts of his social duty. After following his dedicated, hard-working son around the slums of his city mission, Old Abe is compelled to admit "his own conceit and vainglory, the pride of his age and experience," and he confesses, "Why, people, . . . I feels like a new convert!"

The need for a church that involves itself meaningfully in people's everyday lives and of ministers concerned with social and economic problems is the entire focus of "The Ordeal at Mt. Hope." It is significant that at the optimistic end of this tale, Mt. Hope's young men are working at trades rather than attending Sunday morning services or shouting at revival meetings. The ministers whom Dunbar respects are those who are more interested in inspiring self-confidence and industry in their people than in bringing them quaking to the mourner's bench. The antebellum Parker promised heavenly cities; Dixon and Dokesbury cope with the squalor of southern small towns and northern slums.

These young ministers, who could represent an image that Dunbar had of himself if he had chosen a religious vocation, do benefit from their move to urban areas, but his stories abound with discontented nonreligious Blacks who are destroyed by the false glitter of the city. The dangerous lure of the metropolis is as consistent a theme in his work as in the domestic romances and temperance tracts of the first part of the century.

Self-liberated slaves fleeing north were the forerunners of the thousands migrating to the cities at the time of Dunbar's writing. Thus, the image of the hopeful Black headed away from his roots was one of the firmest in the African-American imagination. In Dunbar's stories, as in the slave narratives, the physical change of locales is accompanied by a psychological shift that prohibits migrating Blacks from ever returning comfortably to their former homes. But true to the literary image of a benevolent Southland and to his agrarian sentiments, Dunbar almost invariably paints such moves to the urban North as destructive of some natural goodness.[25]

One realistic note is his emphasis on the isolated quality of rural Black life that limits experience and makes a journey to the city or off to college seem such a momentous occasion that the traveler is transformed into another kind of being in his peers' eyes. All levels of Black society in Little Africa, the locale of "The Home-Coming of 'Rastus Smith'" (*HHH*, pp. 277–92), "from Douglass Street to Cat Alley," were "prepared to be dazzled" when he comes back on a visit. Explains Dunbar, "So few of those who had been born within the mile radius which was 'Little Africa' went out into the great world and came into contact with the larger humanity that when one did he became a man set apart." Erastus, moreover, proves that a move to the city is a change for the worse.

But he is no exception. Life in New York either victimizes children, as it does thirteen-year-old Jimmy in "An Old-Time Christmas" (*SOG*, pp. 231–39), who is arrested on Christmas Eve for gambling for pennies, or encourages the vices of weak men like Sam, the numbers player in "The Trustfulness of Polly" (*SOG*, pp. 257–68), who steals the few dollars that his wife has saved to buy a second-hand silk dress and loses it gambling. Silas Jackson, in the story named after him (*SOG*, pp. 341–62), is changed for the worse before he ever sets foot off the farm by the suggestion of a wealthy white acquaintance that he go to the Springs and wait tables at one of the resort hotels. As soon as this move becomes a possibility,

> The farm looked narrower to him, the cabin meaner, and the clods were harder to his feet. He learned to hate the plough that he had followed before in dumb content, and there was no longer joy in the woods he knew and loved. . . . He began to see that the cabin was not over clean, and for the first time recognized that his brothers and sisters were positively dirty. He had always looked on it with unconscious eyes before, but now he suddenly developed the capacity for disgust.

Ironically, but with a predictable appropriateness, Dunbar uses the white man,

Murston, to voice his own reservations about Silas's change after a few seasons at the Springs. Silas's patron longs for the good, old Uncle Remus image and regrets the increasing sophistication of a "simple" people. His assessment, "You've grown too fast. You've gained a certain poise and ease at the expense—of—I don't know what, but something that I liked better," seems Dunbar's own admonition.

And if the Springs are not ruinous enough, Broadway beckons. While developing his singing talent, Silas quickly appropriates all the vices that Dunbar assumes to be rampant in the theatrical world. Proving his complete decadence, Silas eventually even forgets "the people down in a little old Virginia cabin." "The pity of it was," the author laments, "he was proud of himself, and utterly unconscious of his own degradation. He looked upon himself as a man of the world, a fine product of the large opportunities of a great city."

Such blissful villainy cannot last for long, and Silas falls heir to a catalogue of disasters: as rehearsals for the opera in which he is to star are beginning, he takes sick and is replaced; his money runs out; his false friends desert him; the chorus girl whom he was dating marries someone else; and, finally, he is completely dropped from the company when the opera is abandoned. "Then spent, broken, hopeless, all contentment and simplicity gone," Dunbar's prodigal returns to the shabby farm and the knowing eye of Mr. Marston. Although the tone of the ending of this story is somber rather than humorous, it reminds the reader of that of "The Wisdom of Silence," with its defeated protagonist, and is equally disturbing.

The ending of "Jimsella" (*FFD*, pp. 113–121) is far less deterministic and gloomy. As a matter of fact, its unreality is of a completely other sort, providing a sentimental tidying up of an apparently hopeless situation. Nevertheless, the tale is unusual for its relentlessly grim portrayal of northern Blacks. The marital conflict between Mandy and Jim, the result of their coping with "one room in a crowded tenement house, and the necessity of grinding day after day to keep the wolf—a very terrible and ravenous wolf—from the door" are the subject of the story. In the city there are no concerned white masters and mistresses, no conjure doctors with potions and spells, not even any charitable friends to help a man and wife settle their differences. Mandy's tenement neighbors dislike her because "she was only a simple, honest, country-woman, who did not go out with them to walk the avenue."

After a violent argument over money, Jim deserts her and establishes what is to be the pattern of their relationship. He will return in a month or two, stay a while, then drift away again. Such a distressing situation demands more realistic dialogue than Dunbar is prone to write; nevertheless, he succeeds in making the grievances of the trapped couple believable.

Their shrill and bitter dialogues are Dunbar's farthest remove from pleasant plantation banter: "'Oh, cry!' he exclaimed. 'Cry all you want to. I reckon you'll cry yo' fill befo' you gits me back. What do I keer about de baby! Dat's jes de trouble. It wa'n't enough fu' me to have to feed and clothe you a-layin' 'roun' doin' nothin', a baby had to go an' come too.'"

Mandy's threat to destroy herself and their child is another radical departure from the traditional sunny pictures of Black life that one expects from Dunbar. "It's yo'n," the distraught woman cried, "an' you got to tek keer of it, dat's what you have. I ain't a-gwine to waih my soul-case out a tryin' to pinch along and sta've to def at las'. I'll kill myse'f an' de chile, too, fus.'' Jim's bitter retort is: "Kill yo'se'f. . . . Who evah yeahed tell of a niggah killin' hisse'f?'' Despite the incongruity of the tale's happy ending, such dialogue and the desperation of the southern couple unable to cope with an indifferent environment make "Jimsella" a significant forerunner of Dunbar's naturalistic novel, *The Sport of the Gods*.

While Mandy and Jim are unfortunate because their rural ignorance did not prepare them for the callous demands of New York, educated members of the Black middle class fare almost as badly in Dunbar's cities. He divides his attention between bitter tales of racism that thwart the aspirations of young African-Americans and cynical exposés of political life, in which the unscrupulous of the race are rewarded. Although he never approaches Sutton Griggs's absorption in satirizing imitative Blacks, a sizable portion of his work centers on this segment of the citizenry. These stories range from his comic look at trivial feuds in "The Triumph of Ol Mis' Pease" (*HHH*, pp. 207–20) and "Johnsonham, Junior" (*SOG*, pp. 297–306) to the satiric study of racism, "One Man's Fortunes" (*SOG*, pp. 131–164).

In the latter, Bertram Halliday, protagonist of this tale of the loss of innocence, is first seen as a hopeful, midwestern college graduate who rejects the cynical view of his roommate that Blacks are given no opportunity. He returns to his southern hometown expecting to begin a law career. Interestingly, his foes turn out to be not only the powerful whites of Broughton, who thwart his career, but also his Black peers, who resent his ambition.

As in Griggs's books, other middle-class Blacks offer no help, only criticism. Pressure is put on the disappointed young man to go south to teach—the traditional, if overcrowded, outlet for Black talents at the turn of the century. He resists until his neighbors begin to claim that he does not genuinely wish to work and is using his job hunting only as an excuse for laziness. Stung by this criticism, he finally takes a position as a janitor in a factory where he had unsuccessfully applied for the position of clerk. Paradoxically, "The people who had accused him of laziness now made a martyr of him, and said what a pity it was for a man with such an education and with so much talent to be employed so menially." Eventually, because of white duplicity and Black passivity, he is forced to go south, after all, to search for a teaching position.

The only thing that Halliday achieves from his hopeful homecoming is an initiation into the bitter truths of race relations and a new sympathy for other educated members of his race. "One thing, my eyes have been opened anyway," he realizes, "and I no longer judge so harshly the shiftless and unambitious among my people. I hardly see how a people, who have so much to contend with and so little to hope for, can go on striving and aspiring. But the very fact that they do, breeds in me a respect for them.''

The last image in this uniquely bitter tale is of his former college roommate, to whom he writes of his ordeal. A cynical, worldly-wise self-promoter, he is a type to which Dunbar will often return. Unlike Halliday, he has found a way to succeed in the racist system by cunningly supporting the whites in their notions of racial superiority. Despite his college training, Davis is a hustler who "had worked in a hotel, saved money enough to start a barbershop and was prospering. His white customers joked with him and patted him on the back, and he was already known to have political influence. Yes, he sympathized with Bert, but he laughed over the letter and jingled the coins in his pockets."

The hustler figure fascinated Dunbar, and it is not improbable that much of his interest may have derived from the connection that the acclaimed poet saw between himself and other Blacks who survived by their wits. The faith-cure man, in the story of that name (*SOG*, pp. 307–14) sells the ignorant, trusting Martha a bottle of "liquified prayer and faith" that cannot save the life of her daughter; the unscrupulous protagonist of "The Promoter" (*HHH*, pp. 163–90) preys upon the pitiful aspirations of Blacks newly released from the South; and the charming con man of "The Mission of Mr. Scatters" (*HHH*, pp. 53–86) is acquitted of fraud against the Blacks of Miltonville when he cleverly appeals to the family pride of the whites in power.

Politics, Dunbar knew, was the arena in which urban Blacks felt that they could even out America's lopsided distribution of its riches. The midwestern writer is nowhere more cynical than in his examination of the effect on individuals and on the African-American community of attempts to play the political power game. The protagonist of "Mr. Cornelius Johnson, Office-Seeker" (*SOG*, pp. 209–27) is broken spiritually, physically, and financially when he places his faith in white politicians. Young Tom Swift in "A Mess of Pottage" (*SOG*, pp. 240–68) sells his vote to the Democrats for five dollars, signaling the end of the shrewdness and perception of the slave generation and heralding the greed and vanity of the new middle class.[26]

There are only two successful African-Americans involved in politics in Dunbar's tales, the wily Mr. Asbury of "The Scapegoat" (*HHH*, pp. 3–34) and the conniving Miss Kirkman of "A Council of State" (*SOG*, pp. 317–40). The first sells his soul just as surely as the naive Tom Swift of "A Mess of Pottage," and the second sells not only her own integrity, but the fortunes of her people as well.

Like the cynical college graduate of "One Man's Fortunes," Mr. Asbury opens a barbershop in the Black section of town and wins the allegiance of his customers by hanging up the sign "Equal Rights Barber-Shop," although there are no whites in the area. "But it was a delicate sop to the people's vanity," Dunbar explains, "and it served its purpose." Its purpose, the motive behind everything Mr. Asbury does, from running the numbers racket to opening a law office, is to gain influence in the African-American community and, thereby, power with the white politicians. Asbury is a hustler, Dunbar implies, because he has to be if he wishes to succeed in his white-dominated society. A political crony, Judge Davis, remarks admiringly, "Asbury . . . you are——well, you ought to be white, that's all. When we find a black man like you we send him to

State's prison. If you were white, you'd go to the Senate.'' By the end of his tale, Asbury has manipulated both his Black and his white political enemies to his own advantage and wins the grudging admiration of Dunbar, because the barber-turned-lawyer has simply analyzed the rules of the game and used them to his own advantage without victimizing his people.

Miss Kirkman of ''A Council of State,'' however, is shown to be a traitor to Black aspirations, fattening on the blood of her kinsmen, whom she callously sacrifices to the political bosses. Like Carrie Wynn of W. E. B. DuBois's *Quest of the Silver Fleece,* she aligns herself with those in power and helps them to manipulate Black voters. Miss Kirkman, who does not look Black, is ''in reality . . . colored 'for revenue only.' '' While she could pass for white, she realizes that as a white woman she could never have assumed her powerful position as troubleshooter for Congressman Hamilton: ''So she was colored, and without having any sympathy with the people whom she represented, spoke for them and uttered what was supposed by the powers to be the thoughts that were in their breasts.''

Besides reporting to Hamilton on Black hopes and grievances, she also spies on leading African-American spokesmen and rewards proadministration speakers with money that he provides. Ironically, despite her services, Hamilton subtly makes sure that she remembers her racial and social inferiority. Her reactions to his racism are also ironic. After instructing her to spy on the Afro-American Convention, where it is rumored that a denunciation of the government will occur, Hamilton then asks her, in a completely casual way, to drop off his wife's jewels at the bank:

> This was one of the ways in which Miss Kirkman was made to remember her race. And the relation to that race, which nothing in her face showed, came out strongly in her willingness thus to serve. The confidence itself flattered her, and she was never tired of telling her acquaintances how she had put such and such a senator's wife's jewels away, or got a servant for a cabinet minister.

This assessment echoes Griggs's white labor leader's complaint about the complacency of Blacks in *Overshadowed*. Dunbar will bitterly return to the theme of Black vanity in his last novel.

Miss Kirkman's own willingness to be a messenger, however, stems from her vanity and ambition and certainly does not reflect the attitudes of the political leaders who organize the rebellious convention. Pragmatism is her moral standard. Writing a deceptively antiadministration speech for her fiancé, she snorts, ''Look here, don't talk to me about convictions. The colored man is the under dog, and the under dog has no right to have convictions.'' Due to her efforts, the convention is a miserable failure, the antiadministration spokesmen are fired from their jobs, and her fiancé is rewarded with a patronage position.

The response of the Black leaders to her deception is difficult to interpret, however. One of her victims, an organizer of the meeting, recognizes her role in sabotaging it and asks another member of the group, "But why do you allow this base deception to go?" His friend calmly replies,

> "Because these sagacious whites among whom we live are really a very credulous people; and the first one who goes to them with a good front and says 'Look here, I am the leader of the colored people; I am their oracle and prophet,' they immediately exalt and say 'That's so.' Now do you see why Miss Kirkman has a pull?"

This dialogue is extremely confusing. The first speaker appears to be asking not why Miss Kirkman "has a pull," but why knowledgeable Blacks allow her to attend their meetings to spy upon them. The second speaker, however, suggests that such a tool of the whites can actually be manipulated by the Blacks whom credulous white politicians believe she represents. If this is his point—and it is not entirely clear that it is—the events of the story do not bear him out. Miss Kirkman and her white patron are completely successful in undermining the convention and, by extension, any Black attempts for power. The only failures at the tale's end are the Black leaders who speak truthfully and wish to organize an effective opposition. Not only do they lose political power; they also lose their jobs.

If these political stories accurately reflect Dunbar's assessment of turn-of-the-century possibilities for northern Blacks, his is a much bleaker picture than Sutton Griggs's southern view. In Dunbar's works there are no enlightened white liberals willing to risk their careers for social justice. Not only must African-Americans overcome the traditional opposition of white politicians, but they must ferret out and eliminate the traitorous Miss Kirkmans in their midst.

The idea of a Black aiding whites against his own people is a particularly striking one. There are numerous accounts in the slave narratives, as well as in the early African-American novels, of drivers in the fields who were more vicious toward their fellow slaves than the white overseers because they had been relieved from field work and placed in a tenuous position of relative comfort and authority. There are also many accounts of Blacks who were paid by whites to pretend to befriend runaways, then turn them over to kidnappers to be taken back to the South. Thus, the portrait of Miss Kirkman is given additional depth by its grounding in the realities of the Black experience and her interaction between the powerful and the powerless made more depressing because they demonstrate, as Griggs's novels do in a more general way, a continuation of the effect of antebellum Black insecurity. Despite apparent changes in Black/white relations, Dunbar implies that, in reality, late nineteenth-century conditions in the North were basically the same as they had been in the antebellum South. One cannot help wonder if Dunbar caught a grim glimpse of his own popular success in the astute Mr. Asbury and even the fawning Miss Kirkman.

When Dunbar turned from the limitations of the short story to try his hand at novels, two departures resulted: he began to experiment widely with narrative forms, and he abandoned Black characters for white. While, with only a few exceptions, his shorter works fall into the general category of popular romance, each of his novels is of a different type, which indicates his interest in artistic experimentation, even if it is within accepted limits. His last novel reveals, furthermore, a sensitivity to late nineteenth-century literary developments quite beyond the scope of popular demands.

Dunbar produced four novels. *The Uncalled* (1898) is both a semiautobiographical tale of maturation and an exposition of small-town mores of the type later made famous by Sherwood Anderson and Sinclair Lewis. Moving from the Midwest to Colorado, Dunbar offers a conventional romance and adventure story in *The Love of Landry* (1900). *The Fanatics* (1901), on the other hand, is a historical novel, an ambitious attempt to capture the spirit of the Civil War period as it developed in the closed environment of small-town Ohio.[27] Most significant is *The Sport of the Gods* (1901), which returns to Black characters and traces the effect of fate and environment upon one fragmented southern family. Dunbar's experimentation in these novels ranges, then, from romance and adventure to naturalistic gloom.

His choice of characters presents a much thornier problem than his style. Except for a handful, his short stories concern themselves with African-Americans, believable or otherwise, but only one of his novels contains significant Black characters. Oddly, the novel that comes closest to revealing Dunbar's assessment of his own development, *The Uncalled,* presents as its protagonist Freddie Brent, a young white boy. Since the decision to employ Blacks at the center of their books is one of the revolutionary hallmarks of the early Black novelists, linking them in important ways to the slave narrators, Dunbar's failure to follow their lead is significant in the development of African-American fiction and offers an opportunity for critical speculation.

Victor Lawson very generously accounts for Dunbar's use of white characters by judging it "a reflection of the optimism of *some* in that day, who thought the Negro author should feel himself simply an American citizen, with all marks of race a thing of the past." Lawson urges the reader to view Dunbar's decision on this score as "The sweeping embrace of an unreal freedom, the reaction from bonds apparently destroyed, which led a good part of a generation of Negroes to write 'Just like white men.' "[28]

One wonders who the "some" are, who, according to Lawson, were so eager at the turn of the century to forget race. They could not have been the popular writers of the breed of Thomas Dixon, Jr., who made a career out of inflaming race hatred, or the general reading public, who devoured his fiery books as well as gentler works depicting an illusory antebellum world. They could not have been the northern landlords and politicians who exploited newly urbanized Black citizens in the first years of the new century. Nor could they have been Charles Chesnutt's editors and publishers, who counseled him to keep his racial identity a secret, nor even William Dean Howells, who appreciated Dunbar's verse precisely because it revealed qualities that set Blacks apart from whites. No, race was hardly a dead issue by 1900. Perhaps Lawson is referring to the optimism engendered in the African-American population by Theodore Roosevelt's invitation to Booker T. Washington to dine at the White House and his appointment, despite southern protest, of William D. Crum to the collectorship of the Port of Charleston, South Carolina. Since Roosevelt's friendship greatly inspired Dunbar, Lawson's feeling about the writer's trust in the nonracial essence of art might be accurate; as Addison Gayle, Jr., points out, "He did not want to be known as a Negro poet, but simply as a poet."[29]

Gayle's own interpretation of Dunbar's reliance on white characters in *The Uncalled* is that it was a master stroke of irony: "Why not make his characters white, creating a situation in which a black man pleads for a white man's freedom."[30] This view is appealing, but grants the young writer more insight and independence than the bulk of his work will support. It would be heartening to believe that Dunbar is being bitterly sardonic when he refers to Aunt Tempe as "chief authority and owner-in-general" of the Morduant plantation. But this interpretation would be a gross misreading of his characterizations, tone, and general intent. He is writing sentimental fiction, and the comment about Aunt Tempe is meant only to evoke knowing smiles from his readers for an old Black woman who good-naturedly bosses her good-natured boss. It would also be satisfying to examine his plots and conclude that he consciously took the realities of slavery and twisted them around for ironic effect, so that reunions in the North are condemnations of partings in the South, and servants' saving the love affairs, family relationships, and even lives of their masters are bitter commentaries on the destruction of their own loves, relations, and lives that slavery assured. The tales involving incidents of this sort, however, are riddled with Black stereotypes and always end on a comic note. Therefore, although there are exceptions to the rule, Dunbar's works point to an acceptance and use of the fictional traditions of his time, rather than an ironic manipulation of them for racial statement. As he asks in "A Family Feud" about Aunt Doshy, who delights in telling stories about her white folks, of whom she is "inordinately proud," "What if some of the harshness of reality was softened by the distance through which she looked back upon them; what if the glamor of memory did put a halo round the heads of some people who were never meant to be canonized?" He, too, is willing to sentimentalize. Hagiography at the turn of the century proved much more popular than muckraking.

Saunders Redding's explanation of Dunbar's use of whites in *The Uncalled* seems more probable than Lawson's or Gayle's. He points out the obvious: "Dunbar, writing his autobiography, had to portray himself as a white youth because what happened to him could not, in the limits of the pattern and the view of the general public—what happened to him could not have happened to a Negro."[31] Moreover, that reading public, as publishers intuited, would not pay to read accounts of Black lives written by Blacks; Dunbar's first two books were printed at his own expense and sold by him on his elevator.

The Uncalled is both a psychological study of the maturation of a young midwestern boy and a sociological exposé of small-town rigidity. After the death of his mother, Freddie is "adopted" by Miss Prime, a puritanical old maid whose name suggests her character and whose motto is "Everything in order."[32] Even the flowers in her garden are planted with such exactness that they look cramped and artificial. Freddie's natural impulses are similarly suppressed. He is forbidden to fish, play marbles, swim, or fly kites with the other children; "the word 'duty' burned like a fiery cross upon his heart and brain" (p. 75). Miss Prime's fond ambition is for her ward to testify to her proper rearing by becoming a minister in Dexter.

The most compelling passages in the work are those exposing small-town religious hypocrisy and cruelty. As in his short stories, the strict Christians in *The Uncalled* are generally not the sort to inspire the trust of an honest, young boy. At Freddie's mother's funeral, the Rev. Mr. Simpson delivers a bombastic sermon accompanied by "much slapping of his hands and pounding of the table." Toward the end of the services

> he lowered his voice and began to play upon the feelings of his willing hearers, and when he had his meed of sobs and tears, when he had sufficiently probed old wounds and made them bleed afresh, when he had conjured up dead sorrows from the grave, when he had obscured the sun of heavenly hope with the vapors of earthy grief, he sat down, satisfied (pp. 17–18).

Later, when the boy forgets himself in church and laughs aloud at a ridiculous remark made by an irascible old man, he is treated to threats of being devoured by she-bears, confined to prison in later life, or thrown eventually into the yawning pit of hell, and he is ignominiously marched out of church by Miss Prime. "He felt revolted," Dunbar says, "child as he was, at the religion that made so much of his fault. Inwardly, he vowed that he would never 'get religion' or go into a church when he was big enough to have his own way" (pp. 60–61).

Miss Prime's training, however, is too strong for him, and when revival time comes around again, "as, sure as death it must come," Freddie "worked himself into the proper state, and then, somewhat too coldly, it is true, for his anxious guardian, 'got religion' " (p. 76). Yet, he resists mightily when Miss Prime begins to pressure him to enter the ministry, surprising himself by bitterly releasing emotions that he had been taught to repress since childhood: "I'm tired of doing right. I'm tired of being good. I'm tired of obeying God. . . . I hate duty. I hate obedience. I hate everything, and I won't obey—" (p. 117). Obey he does, of course; Dunbar is already toying with the notion of determinism. And to his surprise he enjoys his training, the companionship of the other students, and even preaching after his ordination, until he realizes that the congregation is watching him in much the same way that Robert Dixon was scrutinized in "Old Abe's Conversion" and is anticipating some fatal flaw in the orphaned son of the town's drunk. When he refuses to censure crudely an acquaintance who does not abide by the town's moral code, the Dexterites have what they want. Rumors spread that he is the girl's partner "in sin."

After exposing the hypocrisy and ignorance of his neighbors, Brent moves along the same well-worn path to maturation that fictional heroes from Hawthorne's Robin to Ellison's Invisible Man have trod: he goes to the city. However, in this instance, Dunbar prefers the anonymity and possibility of Cincinnati to the imprisoning public atmosphere of small-town life. He notes unselfconsciously,

> It is one of the defects of the provincial mind that it can never see any good in a great city. It concludes that, as many people are wicked, where large numbers of human beings are gathered together there must be a much greater amount of evil than in a smaller place. It overlooks the obvious reasoning that, as some people are good, in the large mass there must be also a larger amount of goodness (p. 196).

Of course, Cincinnati is not New York—even today—and Dunbar's growing sense of determinism steers Brent to reject even this smaller city's mildly attractive dangers. Brent does not fall into urban pitfalls because he cannot break away from the rigid morality with which Miss Prime imbued him. Just as he could not fail his final examination at ordination, no matter how desperately he wished to give the wrong answers, in Cincinnati "when the hour to assert his freedom had come, he found that the long years of rigid training had bound his volition with iron bands." Instead of reveling in once forbidden pleasures, he finds "his sensibilities revolting from everything that did not accord with the old Puritan code by which they had been trained" (p. 209). Dunbar, then, even in this first novel is intrigued by the concept of environmental determinism that he is to explore more fully in *The Sport of the Gods*. Like Huck Finn's conscience, Miss Prime's admonitions provide an "internal monitor," which the young man is to carry with him all his life.

His next novel offers an abrupt shift of scene and style. *The Love of Landry* is Dunbar's obeisance to the sentimental adventure story full of daring escapades among the romanticized mountains of the far West. Written while the author was in Denver seeking in the clear, mountain air a cure for the tuberculosis that finally killed him, the story centers on Mildred Osborn, an effete easterner, who has also moved to Colorado for health reasons. In the tradition of such popular tales, Mildred is easily swept off her feet by Landry, the dashing, guitar-playing cowboy with a mysterious past, who saves her life in a stampede. Despite its conventionality the book offers two points of interest: a quick return to Dunbar's mistrust of urban "civilization" and his condescending portrait of the only Black who appears in the story, a porter on the train that the Osborns take west.

The novel is primarily concerned with painting vivid genre pictures of western scenery and ranch life and with uniting the lovers despite a stampede, the displeasure of a stuffy aunt in the East, the sudden appearance of a former suitor, several lovers' quarrels, and the mysterious cowpuncher's secret past. Landry, it turns out, has abandoned the East because of its general corruption, which manifested itself melodramatically by his being cheated of his inheritance by an adventuress and by his brother's ruin and suicide.

The wisdom gained from these experiences is summed up by his Thoreauvian claim to Mildred:

> "Nothing is quite so conceited as what we call civilization; and what does it mean after all, except to lie gracefully, to cheat legally, and to live as far away from God and Nature as the world limit will let. If it must mean that out here, pray God that it may never come to this part of the country. If it does, then some of us will have no refuge."[33]

Dunbar takes a less melodramatic swipe at eastern values in his comic characterization of Mildred's Aunt Anna, who begs her niece not to disgrace the family by becoming involved with a common cowboy or, worse, by no longer riding sidesaddle in the approved eastern style. "It has been brought to my ears," she confides in dismay,

> "that the women of Colorado are advocating riding their horses astride. Horrors! And have made an appeal to the country on the score of humanity. Oh, Mildred, I cannot even contemplate the spectacle of a niece of mine *astride* a horse. . . . Don't do it, my dear. Propriety in a girl of your station is very much more necessary than humanity. The poor can afford to be humane. The rich cannot afford to be less than proper" (pp. 102–3).

To Dunbar, then, the East and the large cities associated with it are centers not only of vice and corruption but also of foolishness, snobbery, and self-deception.

When asked at one point if he doesn't consider ranch work a waste of his talents and if he wouldn't rather do something important, like becoming a soldier in the Philippines, Dunbar's hero drawls, "every man to his liking. But I do say that a good many of those boys who are out there wasting their lives under suns that weren't made to shine on anybody but niggers, might be better employed out here in God's country" (pp. 78–79). The book's only other mention of Blacks is the stereotypic portrait of the porter on the train that Mildred and her father take west.

This porter is suddenly summoned by the frail young girl to fetch her father and, after being assured that there is nothing he can do to help, dashes off to find Mr. Osborn. "If that porter had been a blackbird instead of a black man," Dunbar observes, "he would have flown, so great was his excitement. As it was, he came as near accomplishing that impossible feat as Nature, a narrow aisle, and a rolling car would allow him" (p. 44). It turns out that the excitable Mildred has been captivated by the appearance of prairie dogs along the railroad tracks and wanted only to share the unusual sight with her father. "Why, you nearly startled that porter out of his wits," Mr. Osborn scolds. "He didn't say it, but he looked as though you might be in a fit":

> And, indeed, the colored man was still staring at them with wide, white eyes, and when he saw them burst anew into laughter, he left the door and went back to his place, in disgust no doubt with the thought in his mind that here was aother instance of white people tramping on, and making a fool of, the black man.
> "I didn't mean to frighten him," said Mildred. "But it was such a new sight to me! I'll give him an extra tip before we leave."
> "You should make him pay you for turning him so near white, even for such a short space of time" (pp. 46–47).

The intention of this scene is to characterize Mildred as charmingly impetuous and to provide comic relief with a humorous portrayal of the porter. It is a dismaying portrayal straight out of southern humor, however, despite Dunbar's attempts to second-guess the aggrieved reactions of the Black man.

A similar character is dealt with at greater length in *The Fanatics*. One of Dunbar's major concerns in this novel is the psychological and social effects of the violent attitudes aroused by the Civil War in Dorbury, a small Ohio town. "Nigger Ed," the town's most conspicuous Black resident, its bell ringer, becomes an ironic symbol of the change in Dorbury itself.

The reader's first view of Ed is through the reflections of Mary Waters, one of the white girls parted from their lovers by the outbreak of conflict. Her view of Ed and the war echoes the feelings of many of her fellow citizens. "What had she to do with all those black men down there in the South," she wonders resentfully:

> it was none of her business. For her part, she only knew one black man and he was bad enough. Of course, Nigger Ed was funny. They all liked him and laughed at him, but he was not exemplary. He filled, with equal adaptability, the position of town crier and town drunkard. Really, if all his brethren were like him, they would be none the worse for having masters.[34]

When the war intensifies, Ed goes to battle as a camp aide and returns to Dorbury on leave with the white troops. The experience in battle changes Ed, as it changes the feelings of the town itself. Dorbury becomes intensely respectful of anyone associated with the Union Army. Ed, too, undergoes a metamorphosis and returns quieter and more reflective. "The sight of camps, the hurry of men and the press of a real responsibility had evoked a subtle change in the negro," Dunbar explains, and he answered with humor the sallies made at him, he capered no more in the public square for the delectation of the crowd that despised him. He walked with a more stately step and the people greeted him in more serious tones, as if his association with their soldiers, light though it had been, had brought him nearer to the manhood which they still refused to recognize in him (p. 122).

As the battle drags on, however, and the South appears to be winning, a hatred for all Blacks, judged to be the cause of the conflict, grows in Dorbury. One night back home on leave again, Ed innocently drifts into the midst of an antiwar mob and is manhandled and threatened. Dunbar's assessment of Ed's reaction to this treatment is as ambiguous as some of the portraits of Blacks in his short stories. It is as though he, too, is not quite sure what kind of creature Ed, as a representative Black man, is. "What he felt is hardly worth recording," he remarks, but then goes on to record it:

He was so near the animal in the estimation of his fellows (perhaps in reality) that he could be presumed to have really few mental impressions. He was frightened, yes. He was hurt, too. But no one would have given him credit for that much of human feeling. They had kicked a dog and the dog had gone away. That was all. Yet Ed was not all the dog. His feeling was that of a child who has tried to be good and been misunderstood. He should not have felt so, though, for he knew Dorbury and the times by an instinct that was truer than conscious analysis, and he should have known, if he did not, that the people who mistreated him were not sane and accountable. But the underdog does not stop to philosophize about his position. So Ed went his way in anger and in sorrow (pp. 182–83).

Anger and sorrow are precisely the same emotions that the town is experiencing about the war. And once again, as in "The Walls of Jericho," and "The Wisdom of Silence," whites are easily excused for their mistreatment of Blacks. Nigger Ed, Dunbar appears to argue, is not driven mad by anger and sorrow—as Dorbury is—but is to blame for his pain because he does not use his childlike, animal instinct to interpret white attitudes properly.

The third scene involving Ed and his relationship to Dorbury occurs after the war, when the violent emotions of battle have given way to sentiment. A former resident of the town sends for Ed to come down to Virginia, suggesting that work on a plantation might suit him better than bell ringing. Ed politely refuses, commenting that the pay for his job is better than it had been. "And it was true," Dunbar says.

There were men who had seen that black man on bloody fields, which were thick with the wounded and dying, and these could not speak of him without tears in their eyes. There were women who begged him to come in and talk to them about their sons who had been left on some Southern field, wives who wanted to hear over again the last words of their loved ones. And so they gave him a place for life and everything he wanted, and from being despised he was much petted and spoiled, for they were all fanatics (pp. 311–12).

The parallel in these three scenes between Ed's development and that of the town seems intentional. He moves through successive stages, beginning with unreflective stupor, then pride of battle, anger and frustration, and finally melancholy reminiscence. Dorbury's development is identical. Ironically, the residents never recognize this relationship, but change from despising Nigger Ed to petting him, without ever accepting him as a citizen like themselves. The injustice of Dorbury's reactions would have been sharper, however, if Dunbar's own attitude toward the bell ringer were clearer. He vacillates between condemning the blindness of the townspeople and wondering if Ed isn't really part-animal/part-child after all.[35]

Dunbar's attitude toward the Blacks who appear in minor roles in this novel is consistently ambiguous. He does show understanding of the forces driving one of the few other African-Americans to whom he gives individual attention. But his description of him as a "primitive" with the "glare of an animal brought to bay in his eyes," who stabs a man and runs "into the night to be lost forever," seems unnecessary, a focusing on a sensational type from the Dixon school of race baiting. Although he also characterizes him as "stalwart" and "strong-limbed" and spurred to action by his mother's tears, the boy is ultimately not heroic because of Dunbar's ambiguous attitude (p. 176). Obviously, this is not to say that the episode is totally unrealistic, that no Black man ever knifed a racist white. Nor is it to demand, along with the early Black reading public, that the violent aspects of the race's life be deliberately ignored or glossed over. However, since Dunbar chose to portray so few Blacks, if he were concerned with accurately representing his race, he could have chosen some other examples than his "wild-eyed boy" or Nigger Ed, who fit so easily into the southern apologists' stereotype of "black beast" or "black buffoon." In a novel containing many Black characters, one violent boy would not have commanded the reader's attention. *The Fanatics,* however, contains only Nigger Ed as a counterbalance.

His last novel, *The Sport of the Gods,* is Dunbar's most intriguing. All of its themes and much of its treatment had been tested in the short stories, but he pulls them together in this last, long work to make an ironic and timely statement about the types of degradation and the helplessness of all individuals in the face of fate. The book shifts psychological terrain from the complacency of the Oakleys, a well-to-do white family, to the desperation of their servants and cycles the reader from the South to the North and back again in Berry and Fannie Hamilton's fruitless attempt to escape their destiny.

At the beginning of his novel, Dunbar promises that his book will be different from other novels set in the South because it will tell the truth. "Fiction," he observes, "has said so much in regret of the old days when there were plantations and overseers and masters and slaves, that it was good to come upon such a household as Berry Hamilton's if for no other reason than it afforded a relief from the monotony of tiresome iteration."[36] His statement cannot be considered a repudiation of the plantation tradition (*In Old Plantation Days* and *The Heart of Happy Hollow* were yet to be published). Nevertheless, the picture of southern life that Dunbar paints in this book is certainly not a William Gilmore Simms tribute to chivalry and old lace nor a celebration of benevolent masters like Stuart Morduant or happy buffoons like Brother Parker. Berry and Fannie Hamilton are no shuffling darky and broad-beamed mammy. They are industrious, proud people who have managed through hard work and thrift to attain a middle-class status for their family. Their downfall exposes a civilization (as in "The Lynching of Jube Benson" and "The Mission of Mr. Scatters") in which family pride and traditional stereotypes of Blacks as thieves and liars blind whites to the existence of individual human beings behind individual dark skins. As represented by Mrs. Oakley, white women in this culture are, indeed, powerless, timid, unthinking creatures; the darker side of their portrayal in southern romance as languid, lovely drawing-room decorations becomes clear. The fact that Berry Hamilton has for many years held a place of trust in both the aristocratic Oakley home and the Black community does not save him from imprisonment when Maurice Oakley's pride of family and his racism are aroused. The fact that Fannie Hamilton has held a similar position does not keep her and her children from being evicted from their cottage behind the main house after Berry is gone. Even years later, after a repentant Francis writes to his brother confessing that he had fabricated the theft for which Berry was imprisoned, Maurice refuses to sully his brother's name by revealing the truth. It is only when Scaggs, a white newspaper reporter from New York, confronts him with bits and pieces of the story, obtained from Berry's son, that Maurice is forced to admit the family's guilt.

For revealing the Oakleys's family secret, Scaggs, the outsider, suffers a verbal attack by an old member of the town's aristocracy, which suggests Dunbar's understanding of the self-deceptive mentality of the slave master. This enraged southerner declares,

"The trouble is that the average Northerner has no sense of honor, suh, no sense of honor. If this particular man had, he would have kept still, and everything would have gone on smooth and quiet. Instead of that, a distinguished family is brought to shame and for what? To give a nigger a few more years of freedom when, likely as not, he don't want it; and Berry Hamilton's life in prison has proved nearer the ideal reached by slavery than anything he has found since emancipation. Why, suh, I fancy I see him leaving his prison with tears of regret in his eyes" (p. 240).

Dunbar's argument is not solely with such self-serving southern conclusions, however. He also condemns the motive behind the New York *Universe*'s exposé of Berry's story as far less than altruistic. Scaggs is hardly a humanitarian, rather just a curious reporter on the trail of a human interest story. When Berry is released and brought by the *Universe* to New York, he is treated with as little compassion as he might have expected in the South:

> Now that the *Universe* had done its work, it demanded the right to crow to its heart's satisfaction. . . . He had to be photographed—before he could seek those whom he longed to see. They printed his picture as he was before he went to prison and as he was now . . . and in the morning that it all appeared, when the *Universe* spread itself to tell the public what it had done and how it had done it, they gave him his wife's address (pp. 244–45).

Moreover, callous white attitudes alone are not the source of evil in this novel. The Hamiltons have always belonged to the Black middle class and have prided themselves upon their home, their solvency, and their well-dressed children. For this reason, other Blacks in the town have long resented them and crow when their downfall comes. "Tell me, tell me," said one, "you needn't tell me dat a bird kin fly so high dat he don' have to come down some time. An' w'en he do light, honey, my land, how he flop!" (pp. 50–51).

Nor is Dunbar content to leave the Hamiltons entirely blameless. Because of their comfortable position, both Fannie and Berry have spoiled their children and allowed Joe to develop into a snob and a dandy. After his father's imprisonment, the jibes of his fellow employees at the barbershop force him to quit. Realizing that he must now assume the role of family breadwinner, Joe decides to try to find another job and tells his sister, "I'll go an' see what I kin do anyway, Kit. 'Tain't much use, I reckon, trying to get into a bahbah shop where they shave white folks, because all the white folks are down on us. I'll try one of the coloured shops" (p. 66). "This was something of a condescension for Berry Hamilton's son," Dunbar remarks. "He had never yet shaved a black chin or put shears to what he termed 'Naps' and he was proud of it" (p. 66). His prejudice is well known, however, and he is unable to find a position in even a Black barbershop. Joe then "remembered with a pang the words of an old Negro to whom he had once been impudent, "Nevah min', boy, nevah min', you's bo'n, but you ain't daid!' " (p. 69).

Unable to survive in the South, the Hamiltons move to New York. Once again, Dunbar's city is evil and enticing, an environment in which all the weaknesses in one's character are discovered and exploited. And, Joe, weak and impressionable, vain and selfish, is immediately intoxicated by the fast pace and the worldly crowd of the drinking clubs.

Kitty holds out a little longer, for "there was a sound quality in the girl's make-up that helped her to see through the glamour of mere place and recognize worth for itself. . . . She had a certain self-respect which made her value herself and her own traditions higher than her brother did his'' (p. 89). Joe's downfall is hurried by his introduction to the Banner, a drinking club that figured in "The Finding of Zach" (*SOG,* pp. 287–96) and that caters to the lonely city dweller's need for society: "Of course the place is a social cesspool, generating a poisonous miasma and reeking with the stench of decayed and rotten moralities" (p. 118).

Kitty's ultimate betrayer is not the saloon, but that other age-old entrancer of youth, the theater. After witnessing her first glittering performance,

> Kitty was enchanted. The airily dressed women seemed to her like creatures from fairyland. It is strange how the glare of the footlights succeeds in deceiving so many people who are able to see through other delusions. The cheap dresses on the street had not fooled Kitty for an instant, but take the same cheesecloth, put a little water starch into it, and put it on the stage, and she could see only chiffon (p. 102).

For Dunbar, the theater is the logical extension of unreality in a city made up of artificial people expressing false emotions. Through Joe, Kitty becomes acquainted with actors and actresses, and her doom is sealed.

Even Fannie is influenced by big-city ways. Crushed by Berry's imprisonment and the uprooting of her family, she nevertheless attempts at first to continue to protect Joe and Kitty. First, Joe goes to live with Hattie, an actress; then Kitty goes on the stage; and Fanny is finally persuaded to remarry. Her new friends convince her that her southern marriage was not legal, anyway, so she enters into an unhappy alliance with Mr. Gibson, a bookie, and ceases to write to Berry.

However, Dunbar is on the trail of darker forces than the Oakleys' and Hamiltons' cruelty and weakness. "Whom the Gods wish to destroy they first make mad" (p. 88), he agrees, and that list includes just about everyone in *The Sport of the Gods.* In this last novel, the young Black writer turns aside, as he promised, from the sunny artificialities of plantation fiction to the grim, bitter ironies of contemporaries like Stephen Crane and Frank Norris.

As with all naturalistic plots, when it seems that nothing worse can happen, it inexorably does. Joe kills Hattie in a drunken stupor, is convicted, and is sent to prison for life; Kitty spins on a downward spiral that can result only in a fate similar to Hattie's; and, as a last joke on the disintegrating family, Berry is abruptly released from prison and, knowing nothing of what has happened to his kin, comes searching for them.

When he discovers from Fannie all that has happened, his animallike, anguished response further establishes him as a protagonist in a bleak study of man's struggle against overwhelming forces beyond his control:

> He rushed forward and seized her by the arm. "Dey sha'n't do no mo', by God! Dey sha'n't, I say!" His voice had risen to a fierce roar, like that of a hurt beast, and he shook her arm as he spoke. . . .

He turned to the door, murmuring, ''My wife gone, Kit a nobody, an'
Joe, little Joe, a murderer, an' then I—I ust to pray to Gawd an' call him
'Ouah Fathah.' '' He laughed hoarsely. It sounded like nothing Fannie had
ever heard before.

''Don't, By'y, don't say dat. Maybe we don't un'erstan'.''

Her faith still hung by a slender thread, but his had given way in that
moment.

''No, we don't un'erstan','' he laughed as he went out of the door. ''We
don't un'erstan' '' (pp. 248–51).

This naturalistic depiction of Berry's anguished cry as a ''fierce roar, like that of
a hurt beast,'' suggests Norris's portrayal of the hulking, dim-witted McTeague.
Berry's ironic laughter as he echoes Fannie's plea, ''We don't un'erstan','' is a
clear indication of Dunbar's apparent conclusion toward the end of his short life
that man is unable to make sense of his situation or to alleviate its pain. When
Berry finally can realize what has happened, he tries to strike out in the only way
that seems open to him, by killing the man whom Fannie married while he was in
prison. But the same capricious fate that punished him despite his innocence
seems now to save him from himself: Gibson is stabbed to death at the racetrack
by another gambler before Berry can make his attempt.

The gods, however, have not spared the aristocrats, either. After the disclosure
of his brother's guilt and his own culpable silence, Maurice Oakley goes mad.
His wife, repentant for the wrongs done the Hamiltons, fixes up their former
cottage behind the main house, and Berry and his wife move back to the South.
Although the geographical movement of Dunbar's characters has come full circle
by the end of the novel, there is no return for them to the seemingly secure, joyful
life that they lived before Francis Oakley's fateful visit. Of their last days,
Dunbar concludes, ''It was not a happy life, but it was all that was left to them,
and they took it up without complaint, for they knew they were powerless against
some will infinitely stronger than their own'' (p. 255).

Both fate and environment seem equally strong in uprooting and destroying the
Hamiltons. The force of environment is at work in Maurice Oakley's defensive
and unexamined charge against his Black butler. His instinctive assumption of
Berry's guilt is a result of the same kind of training that freed Mr. Scatters and
drove Dr. Melville to lynch Jube Benson. The environmental influence is also
present in their Black neighbors' lack of charity toward the helpless family and
reaches its most destructive impact in the manifold pitfalls of New York City.
Fate brings Francis on his rare visit home and places Scaggs at Joe's table just
when the boy, inspired by drink, is in a mood to reveal details about his past. It
is also fate, rather than the usual, omnipresent coincidence of popular fiction,
that eliminates Gibson on the very day that Berry decides to murder him.

Kitty's decline into the underworld of New York theatrical life can be attributed to the powerful influence of society to change moral values. Even Fannie
does not escape. With Joe, however, Dunbar's formula of determinism breaks

down. After the boy begins to succumb to the fast pace of the city, Dunbar remarks,

> One might find it in him to feel sorry for this small-souled, warped being, for he was so evidently the jest of Fate, if it were not that he was so blissfully, so conceitedly, unconscious of his own nastiness . . . he had started out with false ideals as to what was fine and manly. He was afflicted by a sort of moral and mental astigmatism that made him see everything wrong (p. 100).

This observation suggests that had Joe's ideals been truer, he would have been able to resist the temptation represented by Hattie and the Banner. Kitty, however, is shown to have higher ideals than Joe, and she, too, is unable to resist temptation for long. Dunbar's ambivalence toward Joe is further demonstrated by his remark that "what Joe Hamilton lacked more than anything else in the world was someone to kick him. Many a man who might have lived decently and become a fairly respectable citizen has gone to the dogs for the want of someone to administer a good resounding kick at the right time. It is corrective and clarifying" (p. 142). No kick, lecture, or example, however, will correct the behavior or clarify the standards of the protagonist in a naturalistic novel. However correct and clear his ideas, he will still be the pawn of fate, as Berry Hamilton's life demonstrates. Despite Dunbar's moralistic tendency, which leads him to try to judge Joe responsible for his actions when everyone else around him is determined, the novel is clearly in the naturalistic mold and links Dunbar at this stage in his career with the experiments of serious fiction writers both in America and in Europe at the end of the nineteenth century.

In any attempt to assess the value of Dunbar's fiction, it is helpful to remember that a story teasingly entitled "The Race Question" (*HHH*, pp. 125–30) is a humorous monologue by a self-deceptive old Baptist at the racetrack. Except in a handful of stories and one novel, his work does not present a serious look at the lives of Black people, not nearly as serious a look as that in the frequently flawed books of his predecessors. He is more interested in following a successful tradition of Black portrayal than in subverting that tradition with satire or, even, counterstereotype. He wished to be an artist; America turned him into a hustler. At the time, such a stereotype was an unfamiliar one to whites, so it is no wonder that even Howells—generally so sensitive to nuances of character—would not recognize the role that Dunbar was playing. But Dunbar knew. He recognized in his catering to popular tastes the slavery-born need for trickery that led to code languages and forged passes. He did not want to be a slave, one generation after Emancipation; he wished to speak the common language, but to speak it so eloquently that not only his worth, but that of all Blacks, would be obvious. Instead, he found his freedom to write dependent upon his ability to forge a pass in a broken tongue. His fiction is contradictory, fragmented, and more poignantly representative of thwarted ambitions than that of his contemporary Charles Waddell Chesnutt.

5

Charles Waddell Chesnutt: Art or Assimilation?

> ... if Judge Tourgée with his necessarily limited inter-
> course with colored people, and with his limited stay in the
> South, can write such interesting descriptions, such vivid
> pictures of southern life and character to make himself rich
> and famous, why could not a colored man, who has lived
> among colored people all his life, who is familiar with their
> habits, their ruling passions, their prejudices, their whole
> moral and social condition, their public and private ambi-
> tions, their religious tendencies and habits, ... and who
> besides, had possessed such opportunities for observation
> and conversation with the better class of white men in the
> South, as to understand their modes of thinking; who was
> familiar with the political history of the country, and espe-
> cially with all the phases of the slavery question—why
> could not such a man, if he possessed the same ability,
> write as good a book about the South as Judge Tourgée has
> written? But the man is yet to make his appearance; and if I
> can't be the man, I shall be the first to rejoice at his debut,
> and God speed to his work.
>
> Charles Chesnutt, journal entry, March 16, 1880

Charles Waddell Chesnutt could have been created by Sutton Griggs. A transitional figure, Chesnutt defines through his long career the limits of African-
American artistic and social acceptance in the United States at the turn of the
century. With Griggs's politically oriented professionals, he represents the small
African-American middle class of the 1880s and 1890s; like Belton Belmont and
Ensal Ellwood, Charles Chesnutt was dedicated throughout his long artistic and
public career to gathering the fruits of American civilization for a people whose
parents had nurtured the country's roots during slavery.

Born in Cleveland in 1858 of free mulatto parents, Chesnutt was reared in
North Carolina, but, following the footsteps of Blacks before him, returned to the
North early in his life and established himself in the city of his birth. Because of
his talent, ambition, and fair skin and because of the opportunities that these

assets provided for him in New York and Cleveland, Chesnutt—even more than Griggs's educated southern Blacks—secured a foothold on America's political and economic ladder.

Although he lived until 1932, he appears strangely distant from the Harlem Renaissance, the most important African-American cultural movement of his lifetime. Critic Sylvia Render finds it to his credit "that he did not seek to express his art as distinctly Negro and therefore different, as was often the case during the so-called Negro Renaissance of the Twenties, but rather through his writings to make himself and his people an integral part of American life."[1] Other critics, however, are disturbed by his concentration on the middle class, specifically on the mulattoes, who represent only a fraction of the Black experience in this country.[2]

Despite Chesnutt's acclaim as the country's first well-known African-American novelist and his important contribution to the postwar realistic movement in American fiction,[3] it is precisely this concentration that makes his accomplishment paradoxical and provides yet another disturbing picture of what happened to the Black artist who wished to tell the truth about American society and, at the same time, to succeed in that society. Chesnutt's progress toward assimilation and away from the common Black experience can be traced easily in his business and social careers; its development is stunning in his art. By comparing Uncle Julius, the narrator of *The Conjure Woman* (1899), Chesnutt's first book, with Colonel French, the protagonist of his last published work, *The Colonel's Dream* (1905), the reader with an eye for paradox is struck by Chesnutt's gradual identification with the liberal, white middle-class and his simultaneously deepening pessimism about his country's racism.

At the age of eight, Chesnutt moved with his parents from Cleveland to their former home, Fayetteville, North Carolina. The eldest of thirteen children, he was formally educated at one of the schools established in North Carolina by the Freedman's Bureau.[4] His most important learning, however, was achieved on his own. He read voraciously in the classics, in English, French, and German literature, and in world history. The solitary nature of this pursuit was not lost on him. "I would above all things like to enjoy the advantages of a good school, but must wait for a future opportunity," he confided to his journal on October 16, 1878. "In some things I seem to be working in the dark . . . . As I have been thrown constantly on my own resources in my solitary studies, I have acquired some degree of self-reliance."[5] When only fourteen, Chesnutt became an assistant teacher at the Howard School, where he was still a student, and the next year, after teaching at a number of other rural schools, he was appointed a full-fledged instructor at the State Normal School in Charlotte, North Carolina, where he became principal in 1880.

Clearly, there was an ambitious side to Chesnutt that had little to do with financial and social aspirations and that must have served as one source of his artistry. No one who reads Helen Chesnutt's account of her father's life can fail to recognize in both the boy and the man an incredible intellectual vitality that led him into areas of study unrelated to public and monetary success. After his marriage in 1878, out of interest rather than need, he gave music and Latin classes at his home in his spare time. His journal entries during this period reflect the dual path of artist and public figure that he was to follow throughout his career. On May 29, 1880, he announced to himself, "I think I must write a book . . . . I feel an influence that I cannot resist calling me to the task" (*CWC*, p. 21). A month later, reflecting on both the lowly position of his people and his own role as teacher, he wrote,

I wish to inspire the young men with ambition—honorable ambition, and earnest desire for usefulness and I would point them to the heights of knowledge, and tell them how to attain them; to the temple of fame and how to reach it. It is true they cannot all be lawyers, doctors, and divines, but they will all be better men, if they cherish high aspiration (*CWC*, p. 23).

When Chesnutt decided to leave the South, he did not originally think of the move as ensuring a development of his talent. Rather, in union with his idol, Frederick Douglass, for whom he later expressed "a profound and in some degree a personal sympathy with every step of Douglass's upward career," he envisioned his escape from the narrow road of southern life as guaranteeing financial success, an achievement that he deemed essential for both personal and racial progress.[6] "I will go North," he promised himself self-confidently on October 16, 1878,

where although the prejudice sticks, like a foul blot on the fair scutcheon of American liberty, yet a man may enjoy these privileges if he has the money to pay for them. I will live down the prejudice, I will crush it out. If I can exalt my race, if I can gain the applause of the good, and approbation of God, the thoughts of the ignorant and prejudiced will not concern me" (*CWC*, p. 17).

Thus, it was with both personal and racial success in mind that Chesnutt made the break to the North in 1883. He found immediate employment in New York as a reporter for Dow-Jones and Company, while contributing a daily column of Wall Street gossip to the *New York Mail and Express*. After six months, he returned to his birthplace in Ohio and took a job in the accounting department of Cleveland's Nickel Plate Railroad Company; after a year and a half, he was transferred to the legal department and began reading law in the office of Judge Samuel R. Williamson, where he remained for two years. At the end of this period he was admitted to the Ohio bar, but gave up this profession for the more lucrative job of court stenographer. All this while, he was developing his art.

As many critics have noted, when the *Atlantic* accepted Chesnutt's "Goophered Grapevine" in 1887, it was the first time that a major literary journal in this country had published fiction by an African-American. It was not, however, the first time that Chesnutt had been published. The Fisk University

Archives contains a bit of doggerel, "A Perplexed Nigger," that he humorously penned in January 1882, predicting that since the ambitious young Chesnutt had "no great predilection, / For living on bacon and greens, / [he would] adopt a respectable calling, / And write for the magazines."

His first story had been published in a southern Black weekly when he was only fourteen.[7] But it was during this mature period of professional growth in Cleveland that Chesnutt began turning more and more often to something longer lasting than court stenography and business ledgers; "he would write down all the interesting incidents of the day, storing up material for his stories" (*CWC*, p. 35). He launched his professional writing career more surely a second time, with an entry in the story contest run by the S. S. McClure syndicate in 1885. Writing in the evenings with that tremendous reserve of energy that never failed him, Chesnutt began placing stories regularly in such popular journals and newspapers as *Family Fiction,* the *Youth's Companion,* the *Chicago Ledger,* and the *Cleveland News and Herald.*[8]

In 1889 he took the bold step of sending to George Washington Cable, the noted regionalist and a fellow North Carolinian, an essay entitled "An Inside View of the Negro Question" for his comments and criticism. Chesnutt also shyly asked the well-known writer to advise him about adopting literature as a career. Cable was sufficiently impressed to invite him to take the position of his private secretary, and until Chesnutt was certain that his $2,000 yearly income as court stenographer was secure, he seriously considered accepting. Instead, he remained at his comfortable post in the business world of Cleveland, considering literature essentially an avocation, despite his dedication to it. Chesnutt's commitment during this period was to security, a comfort that literature provides for neither Blacks nor whites. Even as late as November 18, 1891, he was complaining to the editors at Houghton Mifflin that "the money returns from literature are so small and so uncertain that I have not had the time to spare from an absorbing and profitable business to devote to it, and therefore my stories are so far between that the reading public has forgotten my name before they see it again."[9]

Like Cable's, Chesnutt's roots remained in the South, even after he had established himself and his family as a thriving part of the Black middle-class community in Cleveland; he "kept on his mind both sweet and bitter memories of his childhood, adolescence, and early majority in North Carolina."[10] Chesnutt himself attests to this close tie in an article, "Superstitions and Folk-Lore of the South," in which he tries to account for his use of conjuration, with which he feels he "took . . . considerable liberty" in his folk stories, and to explain some of his examples of folk magic. He realizes "that the brilliant touches, due, I had thought, to my own imagination, were after all but dormant ideas, lodged in my childish mind by old Aunt This and old Uncle That, and awaiting only the spur of imagination to bring them again to the surface."[11]

Despite his success in the Cleveland business world, he kept his thumb to the pulse of movements in Black political life at the end of the century. In addition to several visits back to North Carolina over the years, one of which led to his questioning of old Aunt Harriet, "a dreamer of dreams and a seer of visions,"[12] Chesnutt visited Tuskeegee Institute, thereafter corresponding frequently with Booker T. Washington. He joined the Open Letter Club, "a product of a number of Southerners to help the race situation by making more readily available various clarifying 'information of every sort, and from every direction, valuable to the moral, intellectual, and material interests of the South,' " and exchanged literary and political ideas with southern authors like Cable and Walter Hines Page.[13] In a letter of November 11, 1905, he admitted honestly, "I could never be so placed that I should not have an abiding interest in the welfare of our people in the South."[14] This regional and racial interest remained the impetus behind his writing.

Like the slave narrators before him, Chesnutt wished to educate whites, thereby freeing Blacks from the "subtle almost indefinable feeling of repulsion toward the Negro, which is common to most Americans" (*CWC,* p. 21). His work, he concluded in a journal entry of May 29, 1880, would be aimed primarily at the white audience, and its goal would be "not so much the elevation of the colored people as the elevation of the whites." In 1880 this educative intent was foremost in his mind. He recognized that the public had been glutted with Black stereotypes that increased its unwillingness to grant the African-American full citizenship. Like the cunning slaves before him and unlike his contemporary, Paul Dunbar, Chesnutt sought to transform popular attitudes. The "organized crusade" that he would lead would not be "a fierce indiscriminate onset, not an appeal to force, for this is something that force can but slightly affect, but a moral revolution. . . . " His artistry would "lead people out, imperceptibly, unconsciously, step by step, to the desired state of feeling" (*CWC,* p. 21).

Although later he is to praise the mulattoes' white ancestry for "an intellectual and physical heritage of which social prejudice could not entirely rob them, and which helped them to prosperity in certain walks of life," when he set to writing his first book, *The Conjure Woman,* he chose the mode of his Black forebears.[15] Unlike the Uncle Remus tales of Joel Chandler Harris, Chesnutt's stories in this collection were essentially the fruit of his own imagination and bear the same relationship to folk tales as the art ballad does to the ballad composed by successive anonymous contributors. Nevertheless, because of his rearing in the South and his youthful acquaintance with some of its old tale tellers, his stories ring true as representations of slavery times. Furthermore, his clever use of the frame story and of old Uncle Julius as narrator reinforces with subtle power the meanings of the enclosed tales.

After reading a story, "Reminiscences," by Harriet Beecher Stowe in the *Atlantic* of March 22, 1899, Chesnutt commented in a letter to Walter Page that "the dialect story is one of the sort of Southern stories that make me feel it my duty to write a different sort, and yet I did not lay it down without a tear of genuine emotion" (*CWC,* p. 106). It is in keeping with his conflicting attitudes toward things southern, then, that Chesnutt began the major phase of his writing career with a book of plantation tales. In one very real sense he was sliding along the accepted track of popular fiction with *The Conjure Woman;* in another, more vital, way he clearly recognized the liberating force of the Black tradition and identified with his narrator, old Uncle Julius, who through his wisdom and artistry manipulates his white listeners to do his bidding.[16]

Walter Page had replied on March 30, 1898, to Chesnutt's submission of a manuscript of short stories to Houghton Mifflin Company, encouraging him to resubmit five or six of the "conjure" stories. Once the stories were accepted, the eager new author advised his publishers against revealing his racial identity.

I should not want this fact to be stated in the book, nor advertised, unless the publisher advised it, first because I do not know whether it would affect its reception favorably or unfavorably, or at all; second, because I would not have the book judged by any standard lower than that set for other writers. If some of these stories have stood the test of admission in the *Atlantic* and other publications where they have appeared, I am willing to submit them all to the public on their merits (Fisk University, September 8, 1891).

It is clear from this comment that Chesnutt's desire for personal success had taken precedence over his earlier hopes for public recognition of Black talent. Yet, even in this self-serving gesture, he was reflecting the Black wisdom of his forebears. One of the first lessons learned by the slaves was the necessity of disguise.

Although, as shown in this study, elements of Black folklore appeared briefly in the works of his predecessors, Chesnutt was the first Black fiction writer to recognize the psychological thrust of this element of African-American culture and to reproduce it in the same vein as it originated. As Sterling Stuckey insists, if the slaves "did not regard themselves as the equals of whites in many ways, [their] folklore indicated that the generality of slaves must have at least felt superior to whites morally. And that, in the context of oppression, could make the difference between a viable human spirit and one crippled by the belief that the interests of the master are those of the slaves."[17] Stuckey's description of Old John, the folk hero, could easily be applied to Chesnutt's Uncle Julius:

John, characterized by a spiritual resilience born of an ironic sense of life, was a secular high priest of mischief and guile who delighted in matching wits with Old Marster, the "patter-rollers," Old Missy, and the devil himself. He was clever enough to sense the absurdity of his predicament and that of white people, smart enough to know the limits of his powers and the boundaries of those of the master class. While not always victorious, even on the spacious plane of the imagination, he could hardly be described as a slave with an inferiority complex. And in this regard it is important to note that his varieties of triumphs, though they sometimes included winning freedom, often realistically cluster about ways of coping with everyday negatives of the system.[18]

When the reader applies these criteria to Chesnutt's conjure tales, he has to agree with Jules Chametzky that they constitute "the first conscious, fictional form given to the black ethos in America."[19]

Unfortunately, *The Conjure Woman* is a goopher that wears off. Its magic resides in Chesnutt's identification with the trickster hero who imaginatively transforms the world for his physical and emotional survival. Like Dunbar, Chesnutt was intensely aware of the demands of the white book-buying public; unlike the younger author, however, he "puts on ole massa" by appearing to offer plantation tales in the accepted mode, while he is actually luring his audience into confronting slavery as it really was, thereby suggesting a role for the Black artist far different from the one expected by readers reared on Uncle Remus.

The conjuring power of the artist is at the root of this collection of antebellum stories. Uncle Julius, Chesnutt's alter ego, spins his southern web with the apparent intent of catching his employer's approval in the same genial way that Remus delighted his white folks. Julius's stories do not merely entertain, however; they charm. Julius's two secret goals are to obtain some immediate material good from John, his white employer and the narrator of the frame in which Julius's tales are contained, but also to ensure an important long-range benefit, the development of an enlightened consciousness about racial and social conditions in Annie, John's wife. Significantly, the young white couple has moved to the South for Annie's health. It is with her spiritual well-being, representative of that of whites in general, that Chesnutt is concerned.

Conjure depends upon supernatural powers and trickery to alter human events. In the American experience, it is Black power irresistibly reshaping a world molded by whites. In *The Conjure Woman,* the conflict between white and Black forces is fierce, despite a deceptive overlay of southern romance. The most obvious force is that of the slaveholders and of John: a power composed of money, autonomy, and ownership. Undermining this class, however, is the subterfuge of the devious slaves, the magic of the conjurers, and the artistry of Uncle Julius. Theirs are the power of language, a loving relationship with nature, and an easy acquaintance with supernatural forces. And behind it all stands Chesnutt, the master magician, creating a new world of awareness with a potion that he hopes is strong enough to transform the old. As observed earlier, Black writing has always been a weapon. *The Conjure Woman* is not the bludgeon of propaganda, however; it is the much more potent elixir of folklore, which works miracles from within.

Chesnutt's dual narrators serve to clarify the important difference between white and Black power. With his telling of "The Goophered Grapevine," the story of a conjured slave whose fate is magically and materially linked with the success or failure of his master's vineyard, Uncle Julius's role becomes apparent. Like the author, Julius is of mixed blood: 'He was not entirely black, and this fact, together with the quality of his hair, which was about six inches long and very bushy, except on the top of his head, where he was quite bald, suggested a slight strain of other than negro blood."[20] In an ingratiating way intended to assure his acceptance by the whites, he humbly refers to himself as just "a ole nigger" (p. 12) and distracts John's and Annie's attention from the seriousness of his tales by acknowledging that some whites do not believe in goopher. He ensures his audience's sense of racial security by deliberately reinforcing their stereotypic view of Blacks: "Now, ef dey's an'thing a nigger lub, nex' ter 'possum, en chick'n, en watermillyums, it's scuppernon's. Dey ain' nuffin dat kin stan' up side'n de scuppernon' fer sweetness; sugar ain't a suckumstance ter scuppernon' " (p. 13). He so successfully works this ploy that John contentedly accepts him as nothing more than a nostalgic old darky reliving his happier, youthful days: "As he became more and more absorbed in the narrative, his eyes assumed a dreamy expression, and he seemed to lose sight of his auditors, and to be living over again in monologue his life on the old plantation" (pp. 12–13).

Unlike Julius, John tries—but is incapable of—deception. He attempts a conventional literary deceit at the opening of the book as he explains where in the South he and Annie intend to settle. He calls their destination "Patesville, because, for one reason, that is not its name" (p. 3). Immediately, however, he describes the village square in great detail and reveals that Patesville "was one of the principal towns in North Carolina, and had a considerable trade in cotton and naval stores" (p. 3). John is simply no good at subterfuge, although he would like to be, and in this is similar to Mars Dugal of the book's first tale.

When the slave, Henry, is goophered by eating conjured grapes from Dugal's plantation and, consequently, withers with the vines in the winter and flourishes with them in the summer, his crafty white master recognizes in this peculiar circumstance, as in all others, a chance to make money. He sells Henry to neighboring plantation owners without telling them that, come fall, he will begin to stiffen up, lose his hair and energy, and finally have to take to his bed. When they complain that Dugal made a bad bargain with them, he "generously" agrees to buy Henry back for a small sum, intending all the while to sell him to some other unsuspecting white acquaintance the following spring—and the following, and the following. "He tuk good keer uv 'im dyoin' er de winter," Julius remarks, "give 'em w'iskey ter rub his rheumatiz, en terbacker ter smoke, en all he want ter eat,—'caze a nigger w'at he could make a thousan' dollars a year off'n din n' grown on eve'y huckleberry bush" (p. 27).

But Mars Dugal is not the only white in the tale who is willing to trick other whites, nor is he the sharpest. He meets his match in the Yankee who convinces him to apply "modern" farming methods to his grape culture. "En ole Mars Dugal des drunk it all in, des 'peared ter be bewitch' wid dat Yankee. W'en de darkies see dat Yankee runnin' 'roun' de vimya'd en diggin' under de grapevimes, dey shuk dere heads, en 'lowed dat dey feared Mars Dugal' losin' his min' " (pp. 28–29). What he loses is his grape crop. "Dyoin' all er dis time, mind yer, dis yer Yankee wuz libbin' off'n de fat er de lan', at de big house, en playin' kya'ds wid Mars Dugal' eve'ry night; en dey say Mars Dugal' los' mo'n a thousan' dollars dyoin' er de week dat Yankee wuz a'ruinin' de grapevimes" (p. 28).

Dugal is also tricked by Aunt Peggy, the conjure woman, to whom he turns for a method to keep the slaves from stealing his valuable scuppernongs. She agrees to put a goopher on the vineyard, but, showing where her true loyalties lie, also agrees to fix it so that Henry can eat all the grapes that he wants in exchange for a ham from the plantation smokehouse. Significantly, Aunt Peggy lives among the "free niggers on de Wim'l'ton Road" (p. 15), not among the slaves. Her conjuring powers make her an awful force to Blacks and whites alike.

The next tale in the collection, "Po' Sandy," a disturbing account of a slave whose wife is forced to turn him into a tree to keep him from being sent to another plantation, offers the following poignant dialogue, imaginatively illuminating the dehumanizing quality of slavery life and the desperation of escape attempts:

> "Den Tenie ax 'im ef he doan wanter be turnt inter a rabbit.
> Sandy say, 'No, de dogs mought git atter me.'
> 'Shill I turn you ter a wolf?' sez she.
> 'No, eve'ybody's skeered er a wolf, en I doan want nobody ter be skeered er me.'
> 'Shill I turn you ter a mawkin' bird?'
> 'No, a hawk mought ketch me. I wanter be turnt inter sump'n w'at'll stay in one place.'
> 'I kin turn you ter a tree,' sez Tenie. 'You won't hab no mouf ner years, but I kin turn you back oncet in a w'ile, so you kin git sump'n ter eat, en hear w'at's gwine on.'
> Well Sandy say dat'll do. En so Tenie tuk 'im down by de aidge er de swamp, not fur fum de quarters, en turnt 'im inter a big pine-tree, en sot'im out 'mongs' some yuther trees" (pp. 46–47).

When Sandy is cut down along with a lot of other trees and sent to the sawmill, the scene is one of the grisliest in all of Chesnutt's works and a wrenching metaphor for the powerlessness and grotesque suffering inherent in slavery. Tenie rushes to the mill and starts to turn Sandy back into a man, but

> de mill-hands kotch holt er her en tied her arms wid a rope, en fasten' her to one er de posts in de sawmill; en den dey started de saw up ag'in, en cut de log up into bo'ds en scantlin's right befo' her eyes. But it wuz mighty hard wuk; fer of all de sweekin', en moanin' en groanin', dat log don w'iles de saw wuz a-cuttin' thoo it. De saw wuz one er dese yer ole-timey, up-en-down saws, en hit tuk longer dem days ter saw a log 'en it do now. Dey greased de saw, but dat did n' stop de fuss'; hit kep' right on, tel fin'ly dey got de log all sawed up (p. 55).

In death as in life, the dehumanized Sandy is only a merchandisable piece of property.

By the end of this second story, Uncle Julius' intentions and artistic role become clear. When he finishes "The Goophered Grapevine," Annie "doubtfully, but seriously" asks, "Is that story true?" John scoffs at the old man's affirmative reply and buys the supposedly conjured vineyard anyway. Julius's immediate object, a mercenary one—to keep the grapes for himself—is not entirely thwarted, however, for John hires him as coachman. "Po' Sandy" was occasioned by Annie's desire to have a kitchen built behind the main house, southern fashion, and by John's plan to tear down an old schoolhouse and use that lumber to build it. According to Julius, Sandy's body had gone into the building of the schoolhouse, and his spirit continues to haunt it:

> Annie had listened to this gruesome narrative with strained attention.
> "What a system it was," she exclaimed, when Julius had finished, "under which such things were possible!"
> "What things?" I asked, in amazement. "Are you seriously considering the possibility of a man's being turned into a tree?"
> "Oh, no," she replied quickly, "not that;" and then she murmured absently, and with a dim look in her fine eyes, "Poor Tenie!" (pp. 60–61).

Significantly, she refuses, over John's protests, to allow the kitchen to be built from the schoolhouse lumber and even persuades her husband to allow Uncle Julius to use the old building for his church meetings:

> "And I'll venture to say,"I continued, "that you subscribed something toward the support of the new church?"
> She did not attempt to deny it (p. 63).

Annie's response is in direct contrast to her husband's. As a northerner, he is not callous to the hardships of slavery; but as a businessman, his outlook is much more akin to Mars Dugal's and Mars Maraboo's than to Julius's or Tenie's. He easily dismisses his wife, "who takes a deep interest in the stories of plantation life which she hears from the lips of the older colored people," as being "of a very sympathetic turn of mind" (p. 41). As for himself, he comfortably categorizes "some of these stories" as "quaintly humorous; others wildly extravagant, revealing the Oriental cast of the negro's imagination; while others, poured freely into the sympathetic ear of a Northern-bred woman, disclose many a tragic incident of the darker side of slavery" (pp. 40–41).

This contrast between Annie and John is sharpened in the next, and most strangely compelling, story in the collection, "Mars Jeems's Nightmare." At its beginning John betrays an interest in old Julius, an appreciation of his familiarity with all the hunting and fishing spots of the area, his knowledge of soil quality, and his ease in handling horses and dogs. However, despite his grudging recognition of Julius's cunning, John indulges himself in the belief that his abilities were doubtless due to the simplicity of a life that had kept him close to nature. Toward my tract of land and the things that were on it—the creeks, the swamps, the hills, the meadows, the stones, the trees—he maintained a peculiar personal attitude, that might be called predial rather than proprietary. He had been accustomed until long after middle life, to look upon himself as the property of another. When this relation was no longer possible, owing to the war, and to his master's death and the dispersion of the family, he had been unable to break off entirely the mental habits of a lifetime, but had attached himself to the old plantation of which he seemed to consider himself an appurtenance'' (pp. 64–65).

But, Julius is no Gideon or Stanton Coachman, and while his relationship with nature is integral, it is not simple. Nor are his dealings with the whites subservient. The frame surrounding the nightmare of Mars Jeems involves Julius's efforts to secure a job for his nephew, whom John has determined to fire:

> "Yas, suh," replied Julius with a deep sigh and a long shake of the head, "I knows he ain' much account, en dey ain' much 'pen'ence ter be put on 'im. But I wuz hopin' dat you mought make some 'lowance fuh a 'ign'ant young nigger, suh, en gib 'im one mo' chance."
>
> But I had hardened my heart. I had always been too easily imposed upon, and had suffered too much from this weakness. I determined to be firm as a rock in this instance (p. 67).

In the story within the story, a rigid and inflexible master is turned into a slave himself and must discover to his horror what it is like to be at the mercy of others. Before the transformation, "Mars Jeems didn' make no 'lowance fer nachul bawn laz'ness, ner sickness, ner trouble in de min', ner nuffin; he wuz des gwine ter git so much wuk outer eve'y han', er know de reason w'y'' (p. 72). Afterwards, in a complete reversal, he fires Old Nick, the overseer who had given him a taste of his own whip, and "tol' de han's dey neenter wuk on'y fum sun ter sun, en he cut dey tasks down so dey din n' nobody hab ter stan' ober 'em wid a rawhide er a hick'ry'' (p. 98). As Julius observes, "Aun' Peggy's goopher had made a noo man un 'em enti'ely'' (p. 98).

Mars Jeems's transformation must represent the dream of every slave: to plunge the cruel master into the nightmarish depths of his own system. It was a revenge that, most often, could be satisfied only in the imaginary world of magical Black power.

In order to reinforce his point about the benefits to kind masters, Uncle Julius asserts that Jeems's sweetheart, Miss Libbie, who had earlier refused his offer of marriage because she was afraid of anyone who would treat his slaves as cruelly as he did, agrees after his remarkable change of heart to marry him. Also, ironically, because of his new liberality with his workers, "eve'ybody 'mence' ter say Mars Jeems McLean got a finer plantation, en slicker-lookin' niggers, en

dat he 'uz makin' mo' cotton en co'n, dan any yuther gent'eman in de county''
(p. 99). Kindness can be good business, too, the old man implies. And, in order
to make the immediate application of his point crystal clear to a boss whom he
must suspect of obstinate obtuseness, he pointedly remarks, ''Dis yer tale goes
ter show . . . dat w'ite folks w'at is so ha'd en stric', en doan make no 'lowance
fer po' ign'ant niggers w'at ain' had no chanst ter l'arn, is li'ble ter hab bad
dreams, ter say de leas', en dat dem w'at is kin' en good ter po' people is sho' ter
prosper en git 'long in de worl''' (p. 100).

With Annie, at least, Julius's goopher succeeds. Although John discharges
Tom, Annie gives the lazy hand another chance. John is ''seriously enough
annoyed'' by this benevolence ''to let [his] cigar go out.'' Yet, while he does not
share Annie's hopes for Tom, he admits, ''as I did not wish the servants to think
there was any conflict of authority in the household, I let the boy stay'' (p. 102).

Thus far in the book, Uncle Julius's artistry both reveals old truths about the
master/slave relationship and modifies present-day white behavior. However,
Chesnutt blunts the force of his magic by following the effective ''Mars Jeems's
Nightmare'' with ''The Conjurer's Revenge,'' an amusing, but inconsequential,
tale about the stubborn slave Primus, who, appropriately enough, is turned into a
mule for stealing the conjure man's shoat.

Like Aunt Peggy, the conjure man is a free Black,

> a Guinea nigger . . . his daddy wuz a king, er a guv'ner, er some sorter
> w'at-you-may-call-'em, 'way ober yander in Affiky whar de niggers come
> fum, befo' he was stoled erway en sol' ter de spekilaters. De conjuh man
> had he'ped his marster out'n some trouble ernudder wid his goopher, en his
> marster had sot him free, en bought him a trac' er land down on de
> Wim'l'ton Road. He pur ten' ter be a cow-doctor, but ev'ybody knows
> w'at he r'al'y wuz (pp. 121–22).

The most cogent feature of this slight tale is the implied understanding that
animals were better off during slavery times than men. Once he realizes what has
happened to him, Primus, now a mule, is free to indulge his enormous appetites
in a way that he never could when he was a human being. Primus devours two
whole rows of tobacco plants, then nudges the lid off the wine barrel and drinks
two or three gallons before he is stopped. ''Co'se de niggers tol' dey marster
'bout de mule's gwines-on. Fust he did n' pay no 'tention ter it, but atter a w'ile
he tol' 'em ef dey did n' stop dey foolis'ness, he gwine tie some un 'em up. So
atter dat dey did n' say nuffin mo' ter dey marster, but dey kep' on noticin' de
mule's quare ways des de same'' (p. 120). This refusal to accept the reality of
powers beyond their own is a frequent response of Chesnutt's whites.

Nevertheless, although this story, like the others, is about a magical transformation, Annie listens to it with only mild interest and, at its end, remarks, ''That
story does not appeal to me, Uncle Julius, and is not up to your usual mark. It
isn't pathetic, it has no moral that I can discover, and I can't see why you should

tell it. In fact, it seems to me like nonsense'' (p. 127). At this rebuke, ''the old man looked puzzled as well as pained. He had not pleased the lady, and he did not seem to understand why'' (p. 127).

He assumes that she dislikes the tale because she thinks it is too farfetched and so begins to vouch for its veracity. He compares its believability to that of a statement that an educated, young Black made to him, which he judges completely improbable:

> F' instance, dey's a young nigger gwine ter school in town, en he come out heah de yuther day en 'lowed dat de sun stood still en de yeath turnt roun' eve'y day on a kinder axletree. I tol' dat young nigger ef he did n' take hisse'f 'way wid dem lies, I'd take a buggy-trace ter 'im fer I sees de yeath stan'in' still all de time, en I sees de sun gwine roun' it, en ef a man can't b'lieve w'at 'e sees, I can't see no use in libbin'—mought 's well die en be whar we can't see nuffin (p. 128).

But Julius has just told a tale of a man who looks like a mule and of slaves who could ''see'' deeper into reality than their master. With the old man's skeptical attitude toward the young, educated Black, Chesnutt skirts dangerously close to William Wells Brown's undercutting of Jerome by involving him in buffoonery and even closer to Dunbar's ''old darky preacher'' in ''Silas Jackson.''

This depiction seems a sad diminishing of Julius, the cunning artist, but might be seen as thematically linked to the crassly material motive behind his telling the tale, for he successfully convinces John to buy a horse in which the coachman has an interest, rather than the mule that he was contemplating. This trickery to accomplish a totally material gain, rather than to preserve his contact with nature or to ensure a meeting place for his church or a job for his nephew—combined with the fact that the horse that he urges John to buy is blind, spavined, and will die after three months—links the old trickster in his greed to the whites in his tales. Primus was transformed for stealing from another Black; Julius momentarily loses his identity for cheapening his art. Annie's early judgment of the tale, ''what ridiculous nonsense!'' (p. 107), might constitute a conscious comment by Chesnutt about the sort of material common to the weakest of the Uncle Remus tales—exotic tales of slavery superstitions and misadventures, like Primus's, published most often because they were lucrative.

But having inserted ''The Conjurer's Revenge'' in the middle of his book, Chesnutt uses his next story, ''Sis' Becky's Pickaninny,'' to redeem Uncle Julius both in Annie's eyes and in the reader's. Chesnutt's ordering appears deliberate, for at the beginning of this tale John reveals that Annie's health has deteriorated. Although she improved a great deal the first year that they were in the South, as if in reaction to the weakening of Julius's truth potion, ''toward the end of [the] second year . . . her ailment took an unexpected turn for the worse. She became the victim of a settled melancholy, attended with vague forebodings of impending misfortune'' (p. 132). Appropriately, the tale that Uncle Julius concocts to improve her spiritual and emotional health, the account of the slave mother sold away from her little son, is one of his most poignant depictions of slavery life. It also contains one of his most evocative renderings of man's imaginative longings in the scene in which Aunt Peggy works her roots and turns the child into a hummingbird so that he can fly to the distant plantation where Becky is working:

> "So little Mose flewed, en flewed, en flewed away, 'tel bimeby he got ter de place whar Sis' Becky b'longed. He seed his mammy wukkin' roun' de ya'd, en he could tell fum lookin' at her dat she wuz trouble' in her min' 'bout sump'n, en feelin' kin er po'ly. Sis' Becky heared sump'n hummin' roun' en roun' her, sweet en low. Fus' she 'lowed it wuz a hummin'-bird; den she thought it sounded lack her little Mose croonin' on her breas' way back yander on de ole plantation. En she des 'magine' it wuz her little Mose, en it made her feel bettah, en she went on 'bout her wuk peartner'n she'd done sence she'd be'n down dere'' (p.147).

Eventually, through her conjure and magical knowledge of the ways of white folks, Aunt Peggy restores Sis' Becky to her son.

In sharp contrast to his motive for telling about Primus, with this story Uncle Julius is interested only in demonstrating another sad facet of slavery life and in revealing the power of the Black imagination. Before he begins the story, he shows his young employers a talisman, a rabbit foot, that he always carries with him. This display occasions a mocking reproof from John:

> "Julius," I observed, half to him and half to my wife, "your people will never rise in the world until they throw off these childish superstitions and learn to live by the light of reason and common sense. How absurd to imagine that the forefoot of a poor dead rabbit, with which he timorously felt his way along through a life surrounded by snares and pitfalls, beset by enemies on every hand, can promote happiness or success, or ward off failure or misfortunes!"
>
> "It is ridiculous," assented my wife with faint interest (pp. 132–35).

Annie's interest is subsequently piqued, however, by the story of Sis' Becky. While Julius is narrating, "her countenance . . . had expressed in turn sympathy, indignation, pity, and at the end lively satisfaction" (p. 158). When Julius finishes the tale, John responds to it in the same way that he had responded to the rabbit's foot. Annie's reaction, on the other hand, not only differs from his but also indicates that she has regained her former interest in life and some of her lost vitality:

> "That is a very ingenious fairy tale, Julius," I said, "and we are much obliged to you."

"Why, John!," said my wife severely, "the story bears the stamp of truth, if ever a story did."

"Yes," I replied, "especially the humming-bird episode, and the mocking-bird digression, to say nothing of the doings of the hornet and the sparrow."

"Oh, well, I don't care," she rejoined, with delightful animation; "those are mere ornamental details and not at all essential. The story is true to nature, and might have happened half-a-hundred times, and no doubt did happen, in those horrid days before the war" (p. 159).

John retreats on that point, but cannot help kidding the old man about the rabbit's foot. When he professes to be puzzled because the tale didn't have anything to do with rabbit's feet, Uncle Julius remarks, "Hit's plain 'nuff ter me, suh, . . . I bet young missis dere kin 'splain it herse'f" (p. 159). And, sure enough, Annie guesses that Sis' Becky had not been carrying a rabbit's foot and that that mistake was the cause of all her trouble. Moreover, Annie starts carrying a rabbit's foot herself. She has moved a significant distance: from wishing to imitate the southern white custom of building a kitchen behind the main house to adopting an element of Black superstition. "My wife's condition took a turn for the better from this very day," John remarks in surprise, "and she was soon on the way to ultimate recovery" (p. 160).

If Chesnutt had ended his collection with this story, it would have been a coherent and powerful work. Unfortunately, he includes two more tales that dilute the potency of Uncle Julius's role. "The Gray Wolf's Ha'nt," it is true, is a sad, harrowing, and haunting tale of love, hate, death, and revenge. Centered on relationships of Black to Black, it has little directly to do with the slavery situation. Possibly, Chesnutt hoped by this point that Uncle Julius's listeners and his own readers would be well enough aware of white and Black power struggles that he could concentrate on some of the tensions within Black antebellum society. If this were his intent, he apparently realized that a grasp of the complexities of Black life was extremely difficult even for well-meaning whites, like John and Annie.

"The Gray Wolf's Ha'nt" tells of the thwarted love of Dan and Mahaly after Dan accidentally kills another of her suitors, the conjure man's son. Moreover, it offers one of the book's few instances of "black magic"—that is, supernatural forces used to harm rather than to help—when the conjure man, rabid for revenge, turns the lovers into animals and tricks Dan into killing Mahaly.

The stunning effect of this story is due in part to the frightening images of the wolf and the black cat. Even more compelling than these nightmarish transformations, however, is the unwarranted misfortune dealt the lovers. They were guilty of nothing; their unhappiness and death were due to the conjure man's hatred and desire for vengeance. His magical oppression of Dan and Mahaly can be construed as an extension of the unwarranted economic destruction of all Blacks by the slavery system, but Chesnutt does not encourage the reader to strain after a social interpretation. Instead, the story finally focuses on Uncle Julius's warning that Dan's ghost, in the form of the gray wolf, haunts a certain plot of land that John is thinking of clearing. Julius's purpose, similar to the motive behind "The Goophered Grapevine," is to keep secret and secure for himself "a bee-tree in the woods, with an ample cavity in its trunk, and an opening through which convenient access could be had to the stores of honey within" (p. 194). This tale of violent death and unmerited loss has no thematic connection with Julius's self-serving desire for a monopoly on the bee tree. And this disjunction in meaning is so complete that at the story's end Annie, always sensitive to the old man's double meanings, makes no comment whatsoever. It is possible, of course, that she could be speechless in the face of Dan and Mahaly's undeserved misery. She could also be stunned by the strangely compelling and horrible images of the wolf and the cat. Yet, since the story is one of Black vengeance and Black hatreds, it is more likely that Chesnutt recognizes the impossibility of any appropriate response from even this genuinely sympathetic, northern white lady. Annie has learned enough about the value of Black culture that she cannot easily dismiss such tales as "nonsense," as she does the abstruse philosophical extracts that John reads to her, yet her silence reveals an inability to respond to such an imaginative presentation of the unhappiness of the human condition when no social and historical connections are clearly established.

Chesnutt's book should have ended here, at least. Unfortunately, he concludes with "Hot-Foot Hannibal," the most stereotypic tale in the collection. Although this story once again demonstrates how slavery twisted the lives of its victims and tore lovers and families apart, although it reveals the rivalry between the house servants and the field hands, and although it points out the white man's skeptical, but insecure, attitude toward conjure, its interest is almost entirely with the comic sufferings inflicted on Hannibal by Aunt Peggy's conjuring. The most distressing aspect of this story, however, is Julius's motive for telling it.

The frame story begins with a lovers' quarrel between Annie's sister and Malcolm Murchison, the young southerner whom she had been expected to marry. Although the quarrel was the result of the clash of two proud, stubborn wills, John wishes them reconciled because "the match thus rudely broken off had promised to be another link binding me to the kindly Southern people among whom I hadn't long before taken up my residence" (p. 197). Mabel's and Malcom's love problems can in no way compare to those of Jeff and Chloe in the main tale, a couple whose relationship is destroyed not only because of their own human frailties but also because of slavery.

Nevertheless, Uncle Julius's main concern is reuniting the young white folks. While driving them home one pleasant afternoon, he tells his story, it appears at first, to explain why his mare will not continue on the road they have chosen. He explains that she is afraid of coming upon "Chloe's ha'nt," which comes "eve'y ebenin' en sets down unner dat willer-tree en waits fer Jeff, er e'se walks up en down de road yander, lookin' en lookin', en waitin' en waitin', fer her sweethea't w'at ain' neber, neber come back ter her no mo' " (p. 225). Since the mare will not go along the road, Uncle Julius takes another route home and, lo and behold, encounters Malcolm Murchison's servant, who informs them that the young man is leaving that very day for New York, never to return. As planned, Mabel is now given the opportunity to walk ahead and reconcile with Malcolm. The traditionally happy ending of the white lovers' problems is in stark contrast to the fate of Chloe and Jeff, but this irony is completely ignored. As a matter of fact, aside from its use to establish a sadly romantic atmosphere, their tale is forgotten.

John speculates that Uncle Julius and Murchison had prearranged the meeting with Mabel with the understanding that once the couple was married, the old man would enter their service. Such a materialistic motive, present in the other tales, is not the case in this one, however. Julius remains with Annie and John and seems to have agreed to arrange the meeting purely out of affection for his white folks. Like Dunbar's servants, he eagerly fills out the lineaments of one of the devoted "Black folks from Dixie." His revolutionary role as the trickster artist is reduced to the self-deception of Aunt Doshy retrieving lost love tokens. Significantly, although Annie responds sympathetically to the story of Jeff and Chloe, she indicates no development of understanding at the end of this tale as she has done at the end of most others. In a letter to Walter Page on September 18, 1898, just before the publication of *The Conjure Woman,* Chesnutt comments on the ordering of the tales and the revisions that he was making in them for their appearance in book form and observes that "Hot-Foot Hannibal" "winds them up well and leaves a good taste in the mouth" (*CWC,* p. 101). This taste is the evanescent sweetness of spun-sugar fantasy, not the pungent, bitter root of racial reality.

When *The Conjure Woman* was accepted for publication, Walter Page wrote to Chesnutt, congratulating him on the quality of the stories, but expressing doubt as to "whether the present interest in this side of the Negro character is sufficient to carry the book to the success we hope for" (*CWC,* p. 100). The citizens of Cleveland, nevertheless, were so interested in their local author that the book headed the best-seller list for the month of April, and the members of the Rowfant Club convinced Houghton Mifflin to issue a special, limited large-paper edition of the book at the same time as the trade edition appeared. One hundred fifty numbered copies of this edition were subscribed for. The large-paper edition was printed on handmade linen paper and bound in linen-colored buckram, while the trade edition was bound in brown cloth and carried a picture of Uncle Julius, looking very much like Uncle Remus, sitting between two white rabbits on a red background (*CWC,* p. 106).

Just as the decision was made to publish *The Conjure Woman,* Chesnutt's short story "The Wife of His Youth" appeared in the July 1898 volume of the *Atlantic* and aroused a great deal of favorable comment. Public interest in this tale, plus the response to *The Conjure Woman,* led Chesnutt boldly to suggest a second volume of stories to his publishers.

On December 8, 1900, he wrote to Houghton Mifflin to report that he was in the process of arranging the order of these new stories and remarked that Walter Page had suggested the name *The Wife of His Youth and Other Stories of the Color Line* for the forthcoming volume. ''I have not been able to think of any better title,'' Chesnutt admitted.

> I would like to hope that the stories, while written by depicting life as it is in certain aspects that no one has ever before attempted to adequately describe, throws a little light upon the great problem on which the stories are strung; for the backbone of this volume is not a character, like Uncle Julius in *The Conjure Woman,* but a subject as indicated in the title—the Color Line (Fisk University).

This subject was a pressing one for Chesnutt; he commented in 1901, ''My friend, Mr. Howells, who has said many nice things about my writings . . . has remarked several times that there is no color line in literature. On that point I take issue with him. I am pretty fairly convinced that the color line runs everywhere so far as the United States is concerned'' (*CWC*, p. 178).[21]

The Wife of His Youth pulls Chesnutt from the imaginative flights of folklore to a grounding in social realism. His concern, as he indicated to Page, is not with the Black artist/magician, but with the day-by-day social, economic, and political problems facing African-Americans, especially those like himself, fair enough to pass for white or to be ranked among the elite of Black society, where, ironically, personal worth was also judged by skin color. Propaganda is not his predominant voice in this volume, however; and while these stories are not folktales, Chesnutt is still attempting to fulfill the highest purpose of art, to convey meanings through an imaginative and truthful presentation of life. In this quest, he moves away from both the stereotypes of Dunbar and the southern apologists and the counterstereotypes of his Black predecessors.

Chesnutt's characters, like Griggs's, are primarily from the middle or upper levels of Black society. Sounding very much like Griggs, indeed, he satirizes the Blue Vein Society in the lead story, ''The Wife of His Youth,'' as an organization whose ''purpose was to establish and maintain correct social standards among a people whose social condition presented almost unlimited room for improvement.''[22] In some degree at least, this group might correspond to the Cleveland Social Circle, which the Chesnutts were asked to join after they had lived in that city for several years. Chesnutt's daughter reports that this ''little club had been organized in 1869 by a group of young colored people who wanted to promote social intercourse and cultural activities among the better educated people of color. This was a very exclusive organization—membership in it was the *sine qua non* of social standing'' (*CWC*, p. 61). In Chesnutt's tale, ''by accident, combined perhaps with some natural affinity, the society consisted of individuals who were, generally speaking, more white than black. Some envious outsider made the suggestion that no one was eligible for membership who was not white enough to show blue veins'' (p. 1). Like J. McHenry Jones's Black aristocrats in *Hearts of Gold*, ''the Blue Veins did not allow that any such requirement existed for admission to their circle, but, on the contrary, declared that character and culture were the only things considered; and that if most of their members were light-colored, it was because such persons, as a rule, had had better opportunities to qualify themselves for membership'' (p. 2).

The next story, ''Her Virginia Mammy,'' opens on a scene at a dancing class similar, no doubt, to the ones that the Chesnutts attended in Cleveland. Miss Hohlfelder's first ''colored class'' was made up of

> people whom she would have passed on the street without a second glance, and among them were several whom she had known by sight for years, but had never dreamed of as being colored people. Their manners were good, they dressed quietly and as a rule with good taste, avoiding rather than choosing bright colors and striking combinations. . . . Among them . . . there were lawyers and doctors, teachers, telegraph operators, clerks, milliners and dressmakers, students at the local college and scientific school, and even a member of the legislature (pp. 37–38).

One class member indicates that, unlike Griggs's southern Black leaders, those in the North wish to put as much distance as possible between themselves and the masses of their people. Mr. Solomon Sadler explains,

> ''The more advanced of us are not numerous enough to make the fine distinctions that are possible among white people; and of course as we rise in life we can't get entirely away from our brothers and our sisters and our cousins, who don't always keep abreast of us. We do, however, draw certain lines of character and manners and occupation. You see the sort of people we are. Of course we have no prejudice against color, and we regard all labor as honorable, provided a man does the best he can. But we must have standards that will give our people something to aspire to'' (p. 38).

Chesnutt presents this pompous speech satirically. Like Grigg's Black ''aristocrats'' in *Overshadowed*, Sadler and his friends are aping white standards of behavior, while congratulating themselves for providing role models for less fortunate Blacks. Chesnutt good-naturedly pokes fun at this self-deception; he shared very little of it himself.[23]

Chesnutt was clearly troubled by the ''talented tenth'' mentality by the time he undertook *The Wife of His Youth;* this theme provides the fabric of the title story and is woven throughout the book. His fourth story, ''A Matter of Principle,'' offers a particularly incisive, if broadly humorous, look at the snobbishness evident in the Black middle class. From Mr. Cicero Clayton's first speech at the monthly meeting of the Blue Vein Society, advocating ''a clearer conception of the brotherhood of man'' (p. 94), to his final comeuppance for his own prejudices, Chesnutt starkly outlines his personal absurdities in order to bring those of his class into sharp focus.

Mr. Clayton is a racist. He resents the fact that whites have classified him with all other African-Americans, regardless of his light skin and social position, and has developed his plan for fighting back. ''If we are not accepted as white,'' he announces, ''we can at any rate make it clear that we object to being called black. Our protest cannot fail in time to impress itself upon the better class of white people; for the Anglo-Saxon race loves justice, and will eventually do it, where it does not conflict with their own interests'' (p. 95). Chesnutt cannot allow this final bit of stupidity to pass unremarked and observes quitely to the reader, ''Whether or not the fact that Mr. Clayton meant no sarcasm, and was conscious of no inconsistency in this eulogy, tended to establish the racial identity that he claimed may safely be left to the discerning reader'' (pp. 95–96).

Clayton's actions are consistent with his prejudices; he refuses to associate with Blacks whose skin is notably darker than his own. Moreover, he goes out of his way to enhance his non-Negroid appearance by emphasizing its Latin American cast, growing a Vandyke beard and waxing the ends of his mustache.

One serious consequence of such prejudice is a severe limitation of social contacts for the younger members of his class. Mr. Clayton's interest in the tale is to acquire a proper husband for his daughter, whose choice of mates is severely restricted by the group's exaggerated evaluation of her white blood. Miss Clayton and her friends ''would not marry black men, and except in rare instances white men would not marry them. They were therefore restricted for a choice to the young men of their own complexion. But these, unfortunately for the girls, had a wider choice'' (pp. 98–99). Unlike the color-conscious Viola Martin, Mrs. Seabright, and Miss Letitia of Griggs's books, Chesnutt's discriminating middle class has no political strategy in mind. Purely and simply, it has accepted the white society's standards of beauty and worth.

Chesnutt's view of these people is clearly a comic one. When Clayton's own prejudice leads him into a complicated series of mistakes that prevents his daughter from meeting a congressman whom Clayton deemed worthy of her, Chesnutt laments, tongue in cheek, ''Such luck is enough to disgust a man with trying to do right and live up to his principles'' (p. 128). At the end of his tale, Clayton is still mouthing his meaningless cant; and while Chesnutt's treatment of him and his circle is humorous, the author's hopelessness about changing middle-class Black prejudices is evident in the cyclic structure of the story. Experience teaches nothing here.

Clearly, Chesnutt's stance in a number of tales in *The Wife of His Youth* is satiric rather than tragic. ''Uncle Wellington's Wives,'' for instance, tackles with humorous detachment the long-standing taboo against Black/white sexual relations. A more seriously developed undertone in the story, however, connects this theme of sexual liberation with the turn-of-the-century migration of Blacks to the North in hope of economic and political freedom.

With something akin to Dunbar's mistrust of urban ways, Chesnutt shifts from his light tone to one of dark foreboding once Wellington heads north. From the very beginning of his protagonist's movement away from the South, images of darkness, loneliness, and death predominate:

> He went around to the dark side of the train, and climbed into a second-class car, where he shrank into the darkest corner and turned his face away from the dim light of the single dirty lamp. There were no passengers in the car except one or two sleeping negroes, who had got on at some other station, and a white man who had gone into the car to smoke, accompanied by a gigantic bloodhound . . . as the train rattled through the outskirts of the town, he saw gleaming in the moonlight the white headstones of the colored cemetery where his only daughter had been buried several years before (p. 226).

The journey to the city is infused with malevolent images that transform the story's previously easy tone. Wellington's sexual transgression there makes him swallow the bitter fruit of northern racism and opens his eyes to the impotency of unskilled Blacks.[24]

Nevertheless, Wellington himself is essentially a figure of fun, as illustrated in the following account of his mental circumlocutions as he struggles to convince himself that he is justified in stealing his first wife's savings:

> The lawyer had told him that his wife's property was his own; in taking it he was therefore only exercising his lawful right. But at the point of breaking open the chest, it occurred to him that he was taking this money in order to get away from Aunt Milly, and that he justified his desertion of her by the lawyer's opinion that she was not his lawful wife. If she was not his wife, then he had no right to take the money; if she was his wife, he had no right to desert her, and would certainly have no right to marry another woman. His scheme was about to go to shipwreck on this rock, when another idea occurred to him.
>
> "De lawyer say dat in one sense er de word de ole 'oman is my wife, an' in anudder sense er de word she ain't my wife. Ef I goes ter de Norf an' marry a w'ite 'oman, I ain't commit no brigamy, 'caze in dat sense er de word she ain't my wife; but ef I takes dis money, I ain't stealin' it, 'caze in dat sense er de word she is my wife. Dat 'splains all de trouble away" (p. 224).

In addition, unlike the Hamiltons in *The Sport of the Gods,* the chastened Wellington is treated to a homecoming that reestablishes this atmosphere of traditional humor and dilutes Chesnutt's naturalistic social commentary. It is apparent that the writer simply did not know what kind of tale he wished to write here, and his inconsistencies are its most striking feature.

There is only one story in this collection that presents a cunning Black like Uncle Julius; appropriately, "The Passing of Grandison" is also the only story set during slavery times. Once again, Chesnutt scrutinizes social standards, this time white society's. The word *principle* takes on satiric significance because of its frequent and careless use. The story begins with reference to the trial of a white man accused and convicted of helping a slave escape to Canada. After the trial, Dick Owens, a white "youth of about twenty-two, intelligent, handsome, and amiable, but extremely indolent, in a graceful and gentlemanly way" (p. 169), confesses "that while my principles were against the prisoner, my sympathies were on his side. . . . But father and the rest of them stood on the principle of the thing, and told the judge so, and the fellow was sentenced to three years in the penitentiary" (pp. 170–71). The principle at issue here is, of course, the same as in Clayton's tale—the superiority of the white culture and the necessity of laws that ensure its survival. When the young woman whom Dick wishes to marry asserts that she considers the convicted man heroic and observes, pointedly, "I could love a man who would take such chances for the sake of others" (p. 171), he decides to aid in the escape of Grandison, one of his father's slaves. Romantic love, true to the popular tradition, is a fair substitute for principles.

Chesnutt engages in a number of ironic dialogues between this servant and the colonel, intended to reveal the master's complacent self-deception. Grandison is consistently cunning, perceptive, and, like the trickster heroes, successfully deceitful. The following amusing example is representative:

> "I should just like to know, Grandison," says the colonel, "whether you don't think yourself a great deal better off than those poor free negroes down by the plank road, with no kind master to look after them and no mistress to give them medicine when they're sick and—and—"
>
> "Well, I sh'd jes' reckon I is better off, suh, dan dem low-down free niggers, suh! Ef anybody ax 'em who dey b'long ter, dey has ter say nobody, er e'se lie erbout it. Anybody ax me who I b'longs ter, I ain't got no 'casion ter be shame' ter ter tell 'em, no, suh, 'deed I ain', suh!"
>
> The colonel was beaming. This was true gratitude, and his feudal heart thrilled at such appreciative homage. What cold-blooded, heartless monsters they were who would break up this blissful relationship of kindly protection on the one hand, of wise subordination and loyal dependence on the other! The colonel always became indignant at the mere thought of such wickedness (pp. 178–79).

Aware that the old man is afraid that he will run away when he accompanies Dick Owen on a trip to the North, Grandison assures him that he would risk striking a white man rather than allow himself to be stolen from slavery. The colonel is so pleased by such loyalty that he promises the servant,

". . . if you please your master Dick, he'll buy you a present, and a string of beads for Betty to wear when you and she get married in the fall."

"Thanky, marster, thanky, suh," replied Grandison, oozing gratitude at every pore; "you is a good marster, to be sho', suh; yas, 'deed you is. . . ."

"All right, Grandison, you may go now. You need n't work anymore today, and here's a piece of tobacco for you off my own plug."

"Thanky, marster, thanky, marster! You is de bes' marster any nigger ever had in dis worl'." And Grandison bowed and scraped and disappeared round the corner, his jaws closing around a large section of the colonel's best tobacco (pp. 181–82).

Dick's repeated attempts to lose Grandison in the North, stratagems that give the slave every opportunity to escape to Canada, all go for nought. As he promised, Grandison proves "loyal." The young southerner finally is placed in the ridiculous position of having to hire kidnappers to steal his servant from him. Within a short time after Owen's return home, however, Grandison shows up and gravely reports to the colonel about his ordeal. Outraged and astonished at "the depths of depravity the human heart is capable of" (p. 197), the colonel reports proudly that "Grandison escaped, and, keeping his back steadily to the North Star, made his way, after suffering incredible hardships, back to the old plantation, back to his master, his friends, and his home. Why it's as good as one of Scott's novels! Mr. Simms or some other one of our Southern authors ought to write it up" (p. 199).

Like Ellison's Trueblood in *Invisible Man,* Grandison is valued and rewarded because he reinforces white notions of superiority: "His fame spread throughout the county, and the colonel gave him a permanent place among the house servants, where he could always have him conveniently at hand to relate his adventures to admiring visitors" (p. 200). However, "one Monday morning Grandison was missing. And not only Grandison, but his wife, Betty the maid; his mother, Aunt Eunice; his father, Uncle Ike; his brothers, Tom and John, and his little sister Elsie, were likewise absent from the plantation" (p. 200).

Clearly, Grandison returned from the North temporarily, to rescue his family from slavery's "blessings." His "passing" is not only his movement from the South to the North, from slavery to freedom, but also his successful pretense. He "passes" as a loyal, humble slave to ensure his family's passage out of bondage, an action reflecting the psychological freedom of Blacks presented in the slave narratives. Although its humor is satiric, then, this story is closer in tone to those in *The Conjure Woman* than most others in this volume.

Another story that conjures up the atmosphere and spirit of the Uncle Julius tales is "Cicely's Dream," a piece about portents and dreams that go "by contraries" (p. 135). Unlike "The Bouquet," a sentimental and predictable companion piece that also examines the ironies of relationships between white schoolmarms and their adoring, imitative Black pupils, "Cicely's Dream" is richly compelling. Its opening scenes create a fertile, southern Eden, which has nourished the girl whose "bare feet seemed to spurn the earth as they struck it" and whose "eyes were dreamy with vague yearnings" (p. 133). This dreamlike, pastoral atmosphere is maintained throughout the story, despite the sudden intrusion of the mysterious young man, the healing of whose physical and psychic wounds becomes Cicely's vocation, until Chesnutt shatters the mood with an improbable recognition scene at the end. The story finally fails because of this intrusion of the sentimental formula. Nevertheless, it remains an evocative blending of the real and the imaginative, of dream states and levels of consciousness.

A very different sort of tale, "The Sheriff's Children" deserves attention because of its probing examination of the ironies of miscegenation and the light that it might throw upon Chesnutt's self-image. He sets this tragic tale in a spot very different from the lush natural environment in which Cicely had grown to womanhood. Troy is a semiurban settlement symbolic of the stagnant, impoverished lives of southern poor whites. "If a traveler, accustomed to the bustling life of cities, could have ridden through Troy on a summer day," he observes,

> he might easily have fancied himself in a deserted village. Around him he would have seen weather-beaten houses, innocent of paint, the shingled roofs in many instances covered with a rich growth of moss. Here and there he would have met a razor-backed hog lazily rooting his way along the principal thoroughfare; and more than once he would probably have had to disturb the slumbers of some yellow dog dozing away the hours in the ardent sunshine, and reluctantly yielding up his place in the middle of the dusty road (p. 62).

The farm folk who come to town on Saturday are Faulknerian: "bearded men in straw hats and blue homespun shirts, and butternut trousers of great amplitude of material and vagueness of outline; women in homespun frocks and slat-bonnets, with faces as expressionless as the dreary sandhills which gave them a meagre sustenance" (p. 64).

This story of a young mulatto accused of killing one of the town's leading white citizens foreshadows the concerns that Chesnutt will express at greater length in *The Marrow of Tradition*. Of the members of the lynch mob that immediately forms outside the jail, Chesnutt explains, "They had some vague notions of the majesty of the law and the rights of the citizen, but in the passion of the moment these sunk into oblivion; a white man had been killed by a negro" (p. 66). The writer's interest is equally divided between the dangerous and endangered young Black and the sheriff whose duty is to safeguard the prisoner. The latter is a man out of place in his community, "far above the average in wealth, education, and social position," who "had graduated at the State University at Chapel Hill, and had kept up some acquaintance with current literature and advanced thought.'' He "had traveled some in his youth, and was looked up to in the county as an authority on all subjects connected with the outer world'' (pp. 71–72).

After facing down and dispersing the mob, the sheriff is startled to find himself confronting a gun in the hands of the prisoner. Despite his superior intelligence and education, it is clear from his response to this situation that the sheriff, too, is limited by stereotypes: "The sheriff mentally cursed his own carelessness for allowing him to be caught in such a predicament. He had not expected anything of the kind. He had relied on the negro's cowardice and subordination in the presence of an armed white man as a matter of course'' (pp. 80–81). When he lamely tries to convince the young man to trust in the course of justice, the prisoner only laughs sarcastically at this empty phrase and assures the sheriff that he is well aware of the consequences of southern "justice" for Blacks.

The life-and-death relationship between the helpless lawman and his armed prisoner becomes doubly ironic when the young man reveals himself to be the sheriff's son. In the past, despite his relative enlightenment, the sheriff had behaved according to the accepted mores of his race and class. The prisoner's mother was a slave whom he had callously sold to a speculator: "He had been sorry for it many a time since. It had been the old story of debts, mortgages, and bad crops. He had quarreled with the mother. The price offered for her and her child had been unusually large, and he had yielded to the combination of anger and pecuniary stress'' (pp. 84–85).

Informed of their real relationship, the older man gasps, "Good God . . . you would not murder your own father?'' (p. 84). Chesnutt uses the son's response to what the sheriff, no doubt, considered a rhetorical question in order to vent some of the anger and ambivalence that he must have felt about his own heritage:

> "My father?'' replied the mulatto. "It were well enough for me to claim the relationship, but it comes with poor grace from you to ask anything by reason of it. What father's duty have you ever performed for me? Did you give me your name, or even your protection? Other white men gave their colored sons freedom and money, and sent them to the free States. *You* sold *me* to the rice swamps'' (p. 85).

Chesnutt explains, "The Sheriff was conscientious; his conscience had merely been warped by his environment'' (p. 88).

This melodramatic, but generally effective, revelation scene is violently and abruptly ended by a shot fired from the passage behind the prisoner, wounding him in the arm and causing him to drop his gun. Coincidentally, it was fired by Polly, the sheriff's daughter, who arrived at the very moment that her half-brother had decided that he would have to kill his father for his own safety. After this close escape, the sheriff begins to brood about the errors of his life and determines to make up for the years of neglect by doing everything in his power to discover the real criminal in the murder of which his son stands accused. This reversal, which is not completely believable, is followed by Chesnutt's melo-dramatically ending his tale by having the wounded mulatto commit suicide by tearing the bandage from his arm and bleeding to death.

While such an ending underscores the futility of the son's life and the self-deception of the father's tardy plans for postponed justice, it seems facile and ineffective. As a matter of fact, although "The Sheriff's Children" is an attempt at social realism, the story is most successful as allegory. It is significant that the white child, Polly, attempted to kill the Black in order to preserve the white father/sheriff, the symbol of society's traditions and codes, just as the white father had, in his own way, exploited and killed the Black slave mother. The sheriff's dream for his son, his plan to make up to him for the death of his mother and the son's degradation, is completely incongruous in this pattern of social and racial conflict; on the allegorical level, then, the only possible outcome would have been the death of the Black man.

Although "The Sheriff's Children" is a stark and harsh reminder of the tangled web of miscegenation, the most despairing story in this collection is "The Web of Circumstance," a tale that rivals Dunbar's *Sport of the Gods* for naturalistic gloom. It concerns the thwarted dream of Ben, a self-confident, talented, and ambitious blacksmith, to rise by his own hard work and frugality in southern society. He lectures other Blacks about saving their money rather than wasting it on entertainments that profit the whites and points out the foolishness of their building churches rather than building homes for themselves. The white men who hear Ben's remarks agree with him and even go so far as to echo Booker T. Washington's beliefs by asserting, "Yo'r people will never be re-spected till they've got property" (p. 293). Ben brags to his "good-looking yellow wife," "I paid Majah Ransom de intrus' on de mortgage dis mawnin' an' a hund'ed dollahs besides, an' I spec's ter hab de balance ready by de fust of nex' Jiniwary; an' den we won't owe nobody a cent. I tell yer dere ain' nothing' like propputy ter made a pusson feel like a man" (p. 294).

However, Chesnutt never fully accepted Washington's belief that acquiring property would solve most of the Blacks' problems in the South. The fragility of such a scheme is obvious when Ben is accused of the theft of a buggy whip, and his well-known philosophy of acquiring property is used to convict him. The prosecuting attorney ironically labels him

"a man of dangerous character, a surly impudent fellow; a man whose views on property are prejudicial to the welfare of society, and who has been heard to assert that half the property which is owned in this country has been stolen, and that, if justice were done, the white people ought to divide up the land with the negroes; in other words, a negro nihilist, a communist, a secret devotee of Tom Paine and Voltaire, a pupil of the anarchist propaganda, which, if not checked by the stern hand of the law, will fasten its insidious fangs on our social system, and drag it down to ruin" (p. 298).

The actual thief is another Black who covets Ben's possessions, especially his "good-looking yellow wife." In the same corrupt southern court in which Ben is tried, a white man convicted of manslaughter is given a brief admonition and sentenced to one year in the penitentiary; a well-connected, young clerk guilty of forgery is sentenced to six months in the county jail and fined one hundred dollars; and Ben, for supposedly stealing a buggy whip, is given "the light sentence of imprisonment for five years in the penitentiary at hard labor" (p. 312). Like his predecessors, Chesnutt feels the need to establish the veracity of such incongruities and explains in a footnote that "there are no degrees of larceny in North Carolina, and the penalty for any offense lies in the discretion of the judge, to the limit of twenty years" (p. 312).

As in all naturalistic fiction, the fortunes of the main character rapidly deteriorate after his first slip. The formerly hopeful, ambitious dreamer steels himself against emotion as he hears his sentence read: "There was one flash of despair, and then nothing but a stoney blank, behind which he masked his real feelings, whatever they were" (p. 313).

To explain such a stoic response, Chesnutt returns to his belief in environmental and hereditary determinism: "Human character is a compound of tendencies inherited and habits acquired," he insists.

> In the anxiety, the fear of disgrace, spoke the nineteenth century civilization with which Ben Davis had been more or less closely in touch during twenty years of slavery and fifteen years of freedom. In the stolidity with which he received this sentence for a crime which he had not committed spoke who knows what trait of inherited savagery? For stoicism is a savage virtue (p. 313).

Ben's retreat to "primitive" psychological methods of coping with life is hardly a failing, however, in a "sophisticated" society corrupt as that of the nineteenth-century South. After five years' slavery in the convict camps, Ben's life is ended as abruptly and meaninglessly as his dreams of prosperity and social status.

Apparently aware that his audience's response to his hopeless, ironic twist at the end of this story would probably be negative, Chesnutt indulges in what was to become a pattern for closing his books. He ends with an uplifting, hopeful, but ultimately empty, paean to God's justice:

> Some time, we are told, when the cycle of years has rolled around there is to be another golden age, when all men will dwell together in love and harmony, and when peace and righteousness shall prevail for a thousand years. God speed the day, and let not the shining thread of hope become so enmeshed in the web of circumstance that we lose sight of it; but give us here and there, and now and then, some little foretaste of this golden age,

that we may the more patiently and hopefully await its coming (pp. 322–23).

At the close of a book revealing the racist delusions and impossible dreams of Black people, Chesnutt can only assert the importance of maintaining pipe dreams. Perhaps he is merely providing the kind of ending that he knew the public demanded; or, as a mulatto who had climbed the ladder of success at least a few rungs, he might sincerely have been looking forward to a "golden age" of social justice for his brothers. It is certainly true that a cheerful optimism was as inherent a part of his personality as melancholy was of Dunbar's. Nevertheless, the ending of "The Web of Circumstance" does not develop naturally from the implications of its plot and, as the final note to *The Wife of His Youth*, is inappropriate and ineffective.

As the stories in this collection demonstrate, Chesnutt found the plight of the mulatto a particularly compelling theme. This segment of the Black population becomes the entire concern of his first novel. *The House Behind the Cedars* also introduces the popular subject of passing by African-Americans tempted by the fairness of their skin to keep their racial background secret in order to reap the benefits of their citizenship. As noted before, this was not a novel theme either in standard American literature at this time or in Black fiction. Chesnutt, however, shows a more realistic sense than most of his contemporaries of the hazards, if not the futility, of such attempts—despite his book's obvious link to the tragic mulatto genre—and is drawn closer than before to determinism and naturalism, the magnet for most experimental turn-of-the-century writers.

Both the dilemma of the person of mixed blood in a racist society and his own treatment of this theme in fictional form had haunted Chesnutt for years. Because of his own racial mixture, the fate of the educated, talented mulatto in America was continually on the writer's mind. Furthermore, it appears that he began to look upon this particular group of outcasts as representing in some prophetic way the future racial makeup of the diverse American people.

On July 31, 1875, Chesnutt, then seventeen-years old, confided to his journal, "Twice today, or oftener, I have been taken for white. . . . I believe I'll leave here and pass anyhow, for I am as white as any of them" (*CWC*, p. 15). As late as 1906, still musing on both the personal and the national problem of miscegenation, he wrote to Booker T. Washington that he did "not believe it possible for two races to subsist side by side without intermingling; experience has demonstrated this fact and there will be more experience along that line" (*CWC*, p. 199).[25] When he accepted the Spingarn Medal on July 3, 1928, an award given for outstanding contributions by an African-American, his thoughts were once again with this misunderstood group:

"My physical makeup was such that I knew the psychology of people of mixed blood in so far as it differed from that of other people, and most of my writings ran along the color line, the vaguely defined line where the two major races of the country meet. It has more dramatic possibilities than life within clearly defined and widely differentiated groups'' (Fisk University).

Chesnutt worried for ten years with turning these ''dramatic possibilities'' into fictional form. He sent the first version of the story that would become *The House Behind the Cedars* to George Washington Cable in 1889 and on September 25 of that year received his manuscript back with the discouraging note: ''Dear Chesnutt: I send back Rena Walden. You have simply the memoranda for a beautiful story'' (Fisk University).

Despite his lengthy personal commitment to Rena Walden's tale, when it finally appeared in 1900, it turned out to be his most conventional work. If *The Conjure Woman* bears the most obvious relationship to the Black literary tradition, *The House Behind the Cedars* falls most clearly in the realm of popular fiction. As in the novels and dramas of his white predecessors, Chesnutt's tragic octoroon is trotted forth to run her precarious course, suffer the discovery of her racial mixture, and, consequently, die. Appropriately, even predictably, *The House Behind the Cedars* proved to be Chesnutt's most financially successful book, selling two thousand copies in the first months of its publication and, later, even serving as the basis for a film.[26]

Praising the work's ''simple though effective plot,'' its ''presentation of a profound and perplexing problem of American life,'' and Chesnutt's ''clear style and . . . keen sense of dramatic effect,'' critics generally agreed with Joseph Chamberlain in the *Boston Evening Transcript* that ''his book is admirably worth reading.''[27] Several reviewers were perceptive enough to notice the one quality in the story that lifts it above simply a skillful retelling of a maudlin, stereotypic tale—its relentless determinism. One critic was astonished that in the story ''there is no ill-feeling betrayed. No lynchings are pictured, no tirades indulged in.'' Another remarked that the ''temper of the work is admirable. There is no touch of bitterness, of passion, or prejudice.'' The reason for Chesnutt's dispassionate tone, as both critics realized is that the ''tragedy which inevitably comes is no one's fault in particular.'' ''All concerned, white, black, and the most unfortunate of all, the 'white negroes' are the victims of their environment, the inheritors of feelings and prejudices for which the author does not hold them responsible, and from which sons of each class endeavor to free themselves.''[28] By this point in his career, it appears, Chesnutt has swapped the caldron of Black folklore for the crucible of naturalism. *The House Behind the Cedars* finally transcends its tragic mulatto stereotypes because the writer, as his critics perceived, rejects racial or political propaganda for the more compelling concept of social determinism.

On its most stereotypic level, Chesnutt's book tells the conventional story of two mulattoes, Rena and John Walden, who attempt to pass for white in upper-class southern society. Symbolic of their new, artificial life, they change their names to Rowena and Warwick. True to form, Rena becomes engaged to a dashing, aristocratic, young southerner who, through an extraordinary set of coincidences, discovers her racial identity. He rejects her, an action that leads directly to her death. Aside from a few excursions into the history of the Walden family and the development of a loyal, ever suffering Black suitor, who saves Rena's life and tries unsuccessfully at the end to repeat this act of heroism, such is the story. From its opening lines, however, Chesnutt's larger, darker interest is suggested.

The novel's first comments suggest the inescapable doom awaiting its characters. "Time touches all things with destroying hands," Chesnutt warns, "and if he seems now and then to bestow the bloom of youth, the sap of spring, it is but a brief mockery, to be surely and swiftly followed by the wrinkles of old age, the dry leaves and bare branches of winter."[29] Yet, time is fickle. In contrast to these images representing the decline and destruction of Rena's and John's youthful hopes, there is a picture of their artificial society's static continuation, maintained by the racism that is its established tradition. "And yet there are places where Time seems to linger lovingly long after youth has departed," Chesnutt remarks wryly, "and to which he seems loath to bring the evil day. . . . who has not seen somewhere an old town that, having long since ceased to grow, yet held its own without perceptible decline?" (p. 3). As the book will demonstrate, mulattoes who attempt to cheat time by rebirth into a new identity and a subsequent movement up the social scale will, inevitably, be branded with their antebellum racial identification and forced back into their unchanging, subordinate social position. In its clinging to a rigidly structured, feudal aristocracy, symbolized by its absurd jousts and tournaments, the South holds its breath, and time stands still.

The only changes in Patesville, Chesnutt's fictional version of Fayetteville, North Carolina—and there "had been some changes, it is true, some melancholy changes, but scarcely anything by way of addition or improvement to counterbalance them" (p. 4)—are empty lots where buildings had been and blackened and dismantled walls, signs of Sherman's march to the sea.[30] Such marks of the great economic and ideological struggle with the North are superficial, however; symbolic of the South as a whole, the town sports its scars like wounds honorably won in defense of noble principles and would agree almost to a man with Dr. Green, who offers a toast to the "Anglo-Saxon race: may it remain forever, as now, the head and front of creation, never yielding its rights, and ready always to die, if need be, in defense of its liberties" (pp. 123–24).

Like the town, the fate of the Waldens seems fixed. Molly Walden considers her relationship with the white father of her children a breach of God's and society's laws so serious that she and they will pay for it forever. When John comes to take Rena away to a more promising life, Molly accepts her impending loneliness with a religious stoicism: "She must lose her daughter as well as her son, and this should be the penance for her sin. That her children must expiate as well the sins of their fathers, who had sinned so lightly, after the manner of men, neither she nor they could foresee, since they could not read the future" (p. 28).

John Walden, however, bitterly resents society's limitation of his life and "felt . . . a sort of a blind anger against the fate which made it necessary that he should visit the home of his childhood, if at all, like a thief in the night" (pp. 27–28). He lives his double life with no qualms of conscience, but realizes that he must argue Rena into an acceptance of a similar new existence. "Let the dead past bury its dead," he advises her; "George Tryon loves you for yourself alone; it is not your ancestors that he seeks to marry" (p. 73). His optimistic view proves naive.

Even after Rena has left home and attended a finishing school that John chose for her, she is still self-conscious and somewhat awkward, for the "brain-cells never lose the impressions of youth, and Rena's Patesville life was not far enough removed to have lost its distinctiveness of outline" (p. 55). Chesnutt fully supports the notion of fated suffering. Rena "was yet to learn that the innocent suffer with the guilty, and feel the punishment the more keenly because unmerited. She had yet to learn that the old Mosaic formula, 'The sins of the fathers shall be visited upon the children,' was graven more indelibly upon the heart of the race than upon the tables of Sinai" (p. 69).

Nevertheless, Chesnutt cannot help but understand and support John's and Rena's subterfuge, however futile, as the only possible way in which they can hope to combat the rigidity of southern traditions:

The taint of black blood was the unpardonable sin, from the unmerited penalty of which there was no escape except by concealment. . . . To undertake what they tried to do required great courage. Had they possessed the sneaking, cringing, treacherous character traditionally ascribed to people of mixed blood, the character which the blessed institutions of a free slave-holding republic had been well adapted to foster among them; had they been selfish enough to sacrifice to their ambition the mother who gave them birth, society would have been placated or humbugged, and the voyage of their life might have been one of unbroken smoothness (pp. 116–17).

Although Chesnutt seems at some points to agree with Tryon's observation that "Circumstances make weak men; strong men mould circumstances to do their bidding" (p. 187), he fills his novel with images of the fates shuffling the cards of Rena's fortune and weaving the fabric of her future and, finally, is ambivalent about human possibility. His indecision weakens the force of his tale, and despite the critics' favorable comments, *The House Behind the Cedars* remains a thin book, as Cable had so long felt it to be.

The same cannot be said, however, about his next work, *The Marrow of Tradition,* a rich, complex, and, for the most part, nonstereotypic rendering of racial relations in North Carolina during the last part of the nineteenth century. In an almost Faulknerian examination of the tangled lives of the Black and white branches of the same family, Chesnutt concentrates on the "presentness of the past.'' To reveal his meanings, he employs three basic plots: a love triangle, a gothic mystery story involving murder and a missing will, and, as the primary focus, a tale of violent racial conflict.

The novel's germ was the actual race riot that occurred in Wilmington, North Carolina, during the November elections of 1898. Chesnutt reports to Walter Page that "in a letter received yesterday, from Wilmington, the writer characterizes the town as a place where no Negro can enjoy the blessed privilege of free speech and a free press; and where every organization, whether social, political, or industrial, undertaken by our race, must needs meet with opposition from the whites, incited by jealousy and envy" (*CWC*, p. 106). Chesnutt traveled to Wilmington to collect information for the novel, and "the people there were eager to tell him all the details of the riot, for they felt that his book might do much for the colored people of the South" (*CWC*, p. 159). Several of Chesnutt's relatives and friends were living in the town during the riot and provided Chesnutt with vivid details.[31]

The Wilmington Massacre resulted from the Bourbon Democrats' overthrowing by force and fraud the Fusion-Negro Republican coalition that had governed North Carolina since 1894. The Blacks in Wilmington were becoming too politically powerful for the comfort of the whites, holding as they did several administrative posts in the town, including representation on the Board of Aldermen. The riot resulted from a conspiracy to rob the Blacks of politial power, despite the fact that they constituted a solid majority of the population.[32] Reporting in the *Boston Evening Transcript,* Chesnutt notes,

> over fifteen hundred of the best colored citizens have left the town. Most of these have sought homes in the North. It is a curious revival of antebellum conditions. The Negroes in the South are not yet free, and social odium at the North is deemed by many preferable to the same thing at the South, with oppressive and degrading legal enactments superadded.[33]

If one leaves *The Conjure Woman* out of account, Chesnutt was correct in his assessment of *The Marrow of Tradition* as "entirely sincere, and . . . certainly a much better book than any I have heretofore written" (*CWC*, p. 172). Like *The House Behind the Cedars,* this novel opens with a genre description symbolizing southern life: "The night was hot and sultry. Though the windows of the chamber were wide open, and the muslin curtains looped back, not a breath of air was stirring. . . . The heavy scent of magnolias, overpowering even the strong smell of drugs in the sickroom, suggested death and funeral wreaths, sorrow and tears, the long home, the last sleep."[34] This oppressive, stagnant atmosphere with its scent of death and malignancy aptly represents the unchanging racial decay in postbellum Wellington. Like Griggs's South, Chesnutt's is a land in which an uneasy truce exists between the Black and white populations, a fragile coexistence that could violently explode in a moment through the ignorant heat of a lynch mob. This situation is not significantly different from that which existed in slavery times. Then, too, even with the kindest master, "there was always present, in the consciousness of the lowest slave, the knowledge that he was in his master's power, and that he could make no effectual protest against the abuse of that authority" (p. 276).

Wellington's stagnant and repressive social, political, and psychological atmosphere erupts into the riot that climaxes the novel. Ironically, in contrast to the climate of oppression and decay with which Chesnutt begins his book, the atmosphere on the day of the outbreak gives no hint of the turmoil to come:

> The Wellington riot began at three o'clock in the afternoon of a day as fair as was ever selected for a deed of darkness. The sky was clear, except for a few light clouds that floated, white and feathery, high in the air, like distant islands in a sapphire sea. A salt-laden breeze from the ocean a few miles away lent a crisp sparkle to the air (p. 274).

By nightfall, however, the fair breezes have given way to tides of violence, waves of drunken whites raging through the streets, beating and killing, spurred on by the frenzied chant: "Kill the niggers! Kill the damned niggers!" (p. 298).

Against this paradoxical background of stagnation and violence, Chesnutt juxtaposes two related families, one Black, the ambitious Millers, and the other white, the influential Carterets. Like the population of the town, these distinct branches of the same family regard each other with feelings varying from suspicion and resentment to contempt and hatred. Woven throughout this multicolored tapestry of racial relationships is the theme of the distortion of truth needed to support racial myths. Polly Ochiltree—the flower of white gentility and the sister of Samuel Merkell's first wife, Elizabeth—steals the will and wedding certificate that would have legitimized and enriched the daughter of Merkell's second wife, Julia. Clearly both sexual jealousy and an ingrained notion of white superiority lie behind her action. Like an inherited curse, the rivalry between Polly and Julia is repeated in the next generation between Olivia Merkell Carteret and Janet Miller, half-sisters and daughters, respectively, of Elizabeth and Julia, Merkell's housekeeper, whom he secretly married after Elizabeth's death.

That truth and justice are subordinated to maintain racial distinctions in southern society is clear in Polly's threat to Julia when the Black wife attempts to remove her property from Samuel Merkell's house. Julia quickly realizes that the white woman has stolen or destroyed Merkell's will as well as their marriage license. "My word is worth yours a hundred times over," Polly calmly and realistically observes, "for I am a lady, and you are—what? And now hear me: if ever you breathe to a living soul one word of this preposterous story, I will charge you with the theft, and have you sent to the penitentiary. Your child will be taken from you, and you shall never see it again" (p. 138).

Although Julia suffers a tragic, early end as a result of Polly's jealousy and treachery, Janet goes on to marry the son of a prospering member of the town's Black middle class. As a matter of fact, Janet's father-in-law buys the family mansion of Olivia's husband, Major Carteret, when the old aristocratic family falls on hard times after the war. Needless to say, there is bad blood between Janet and Olivia, who look so much alike that they could be mistaken for twins. The bad feelings are all on Olivia's side, however, for "Janet had a tender heart, and could have loved this white sister, her sole living relative of whom she knew. All her life long she had yearned for a kind word, a nod, a smile, the least thing that imagination might have twisted into a recognition of the tie between them. But it had never come" (p. 65).

When, shortly before her death, Polly reveals that Olivia's father had actually married Julia, and when Olivia later comes into possession of the missing will and marriage certificate, the younger woman's response is also dictated by her racial heritage. Predictably she burns both documents and rationalizes her action on the basis of racial dictums:

> If the woman had been white—but the woman had *not* been white, and the same rule of moral conduct did not, *could* not, in the very nature of things, apply, as between white people! For, if this were not so, slavery had been, not merely an economic mistake, but a great crime against humanity. If it had been such a crime, as for a moment she dimly perceived it might have been, then through the long centuries there had been piled up a catalogue of wrong and outrage which, if the law of compensation be a law of nature, must some time some where, in some way, be atoned for (p. 266).

Every personal act, then, becomes a racial and moral assertion. Olivia's and Janet's lives in the present are clearly determined by economic, social, and psychological decisions made generations before their births. Reverting to the determinism of *The House Behind the Cedars,* Chesnutt remarks late in the novel, "We are all puppets in the hands of Fate, and seldom see the strings that move us" (p. 304).

Once she discovers the truth of her father's past, Olivia's actions are determined not only by her own greed and antipathy toward Janet but also by a dread of being known as the daughter of a transgressor of the southern social code and even by a curious identity crisis:

> To have it known that her father had married a negress would only be less dreadful than to have it appear that he had committed some terrible crime. It was a crime now, by the law of every Southern State, for white and colored persons to intermarry. She shuddered before the possibility that at some time in the future some person, none too well informed, might learn that her father had married a colored woman, and might assume that she, Olivia Carteret, or her child, had sprung from this shocking *mésalliance*,— a fate to which she would willingly have preferred death (p. 270).

It is better in this society, then, to be a liar and a thief than to be Black; if Olivia is correct, it is better even to be dead.

Ironically, it is Janet, after her own child has been killed during the riot, who persuades her husband to save the life of this half-sister's son. She does not do so, however, until she has extracted from Olivia a recognition of their relationship and her right to a portion of the inheritance, but this admission comes far too late to breach the gap between them: "it had come, not with frank kindliness and sisterly love, but in a storm of blood and tears; not freely given, from an open heart, but extorted from a reluctant conscience by the agony of a mother's fears" (pp. 327–28). Janet rejects the inheritance and the reluctantly admitted relationship, but quixotically asks her husband to tend the desperately ill Carteret child. This generosity to the family responsible in large measure for the riot that took her own child's life seems remarkably heroic and ends Chesnutt's novel with another false, sentimental resolution. Nevertheless, the unnatural relationship between the two sisters rings true and, as in Griggs's works dealing with miscegenation, illuminates the consequences of southern racial policy.

Chesnutt is also interested in the inevitable blurring of white social classes that occurred after the war and the ironic friendships forced into existence due to racial fears. Olivia's husband is the heir of a proud, old family, one member of which "only a few generations removed, had owned an estate of ninety thousand acres of land and six thousand slaves" (p. 30). In postwar times, Carteret uses part of his wife's patrimony, which was invested in a local cotton mill, to publish the *Morning Chronicle,* the most influential newspaper in Wellington, which returns an ample income and is the means by which he intends to whip up support for the disfranchisement of the Blacks and a return to total white political supremacy:

Taking for his theme the unfitness of the negro to participate in government,—an unfitness due to his limited education, his lack of experience, his criminal tendencies, and more especially to his hopeless mental and physical inferiority to the white race,—the major had demonstrated, it seemed to him clearly enough, that the ballot in the hands of the negro was a menace to the commonwealth (p. 31).

Not all whites of Carteret's standing approve of the continuation of racial hostilities. The practical Dr. Burns, for one, believing that the Black "race must come up or drag ours down" (p. 51), is chiefly responsible for Dr. Miller's winning a medical scholarship. Dr. Price, who must lie to Miller and turn him away when, in an early episode, the latter arrives to help with the surgery on Olivia's sickly child, "liked Miller, wished him well, and would not wittingly wound his feelings. He really thought him too much of a gentleman for the town, in view of the restrictions with which he must inevitably be hampered" (p. 75). Old Mr. Delamere, the last remaining gentleman of the old school, likewise carries no animosity toward the Blacks of Wellington and, instead, thinks "they have done very well, considering what they started from, and their limited opportunities" (p. 25).

To aid him in his racist plans, then, the aristocratic Carteret must turn away from men of his own class to those of the upwardly mobile lower classes. While descended from a good family, General Belmont, the first of his confreres—a lawyer by profession, the former owner of slaves, and an individual "not without a gentleman's distaste for meanness"—nevertheless "permitted no fine scruples to stand in the way of success" (p. 34). An active politician, he is characterized by his rivals "as a tricky demagogue, which may of course have been a libel" (p. 34). Ironically, he gives the appearance of an old-style riverboat gambler or a carpetbagger, not from the North, but from Cuba or the West Indies. He was "a dapper little gentleman with light-blue eyes and a Vandyke beard. He wore a frock coat, patent leather shoes, and a Panama hat. There were crow's-feet about his eyes, which twinkled with a hard and, at times, humorous shrewdness" (p. 31).

Captain McBane, Carteret's other cohort, has none of Belmont's good humor or gentility, and Chesnutt gives him the typical poor-white villain's description:

> His broad shoulders, burly form, square jaw, and heavy chin betokened strength, energy, and unscrupulousness. . . . A single deep-set gray eye was shadowed by a beetling brow, over which a crop of coarse black hair, slightly streaked with gray, fell almost low enough to mingle with his black, bushy eyebrows. His coat had not been brushed for several days, if one might judge from the accumulation of dandruff upon the collar, and his shirt-front, in the middle of which blazed a showy diamond, was plentifully stained with tobacco juice (p. 32).

Clearly, McBane springs from the lowest segment of white society, which was rising to prominence during Reconstruction:

> No longer overshadowed by a slaveholding caste, some of this class had rapidly pushed themselves forward. Some had made honorable records. Others, foremost in negro-baiting and election frauds, had done the dirty work of politics, as their fathers had done that of slavery, seeking their reward at first in minor offices,—for which men of gentler breeding did not care,—until their ambition began to reach out for higher honors (p. 34).

Of this latter group was McBane, a former leader of the Ku Klux Klan who had derived his wealth from a contract with the state for its convict labor until the Fusion ticket carried North Carolina and the system of convict labor was abolished. McBane, moreover, is resentful of his continuing low social position: "he had never been invited to the home of either General Belmont or Major Carteret; nor asked to join the club of which they were members. . . . He had money enough to buy out half a dozen of these broken-down aristocrats, and money was all-powerful" (p. 82).

Association with white men of McBane's sort has hardened Carteret's determination against the advancement of African-Americans. "It was distasteful enough to rub elbows with an illiterate and vulgar white man of no ancestry,'' he feels, ''—the risk of similar contact with negroes was to be avoided at all cost'' (p. 87). Furthermore, his recognition of the usefulness of this new class with its growing power and wealth makes him a pawn in their hands, despite his high-flown rhetoric and traditional feeling of superiority. When it becomes clear that Wellington is on the verge of civil war, due primarily to his own incendiary editorials and the racial suspicions about the unsolved robbery and murder of old Polly Ochiltree, Carteret for the first time begins to back away from the bloody consequences of his actions. ''I would not advocate murder,'' he protests:

> ''We are animated by high and holy principles. We wish to right a wrong, to remedy an abuse, to save our state from anarchy and our race from humiliation. I don't object to frightening the negroes, but I am opposed to unnecessary bloodshed.''
>
> ''I'm not quite so particular,'' struck in McBane. ''They need to be taught a lesson, and one nigger more or less wouldn't be missed. There's too many of 'em now.''
>
> ''Of course,'' continued Carteret, ''if we should decide upon a certain mode of procedure, and the negroes should resist, a different reasoning might apply; but I will have no premeditated murder'' (p. 250).

Obviously, by this point, events are out of Carteret's hands, but he does not realize the seriousness of the fears and hatreds that he has aroused. Finally, he does understand: ''Old Jane, good old Mammy Jane, who nursed my wife at her bosom, and has waited on her and my child within a few weeks, was killed only a few rods from my house. . . . I would have defended her with my own life! We must try and stop this thing!'' (pp. 304–5). But as McBane and the Blacks know, the riot must run its course. It is spurred on unintentionally by Carteret's own cry, ''Gentlemen . . . this is murder, it is madness; it is a disgrace to our city, to our state, to our civilization!'' (p. 305). The role of the aristocrat has deteriorated from one of cautious leadership to self-delusive, mistaken rabble-rousing.

The most interesting feature of Chesnutt's tracing of this decline is the contrast between Mr. Delamere and his grandson, Tom. The old gentleman, an invalid with a short time to live, ''might be taken as the apex of an ideal aristocratic development'' (p. 96). He had been distinguished during his life ''for courage and strength of will, courtliness of bearing, deference to his superiors, of whom there had been few, courtesy to his equals, kindness and consideration for those less highly favored, and above all, a scrupulous sense of honor'' (p. 96). It is clear that Chesnutt favors these virtues as strongly as William Faulkner does in his portrayals of a dying aristocracy.

However, Tom, the representative of the present generation of Delameres, ''was merely the shadow without the substance, the empty husk without the grain'' (p. 96). Given to all the vices of the degenerate aristocrat, he lies as easily as he breathes. Because of financial worries over gambling debts, he murders and robs Polly Ochiltree while disguised as Sandy Campbell, his grand-father's faithful servant. "Courage and strength he had none," Chesnutt reports of Tom (p. 96). If "it took three or four generations to make a gentleman, and as many more to complete the curve and return to the base from which it started, Tom Delamere belonged somewhere on the downward slant, with large possibilities of further decline" (pp. 95–96). The only difference between Delamere and McBane is the former's assumption of his right to live off of others and the delicacy of his features and attire, which appropriately enough "conveyed no impression of strength, but did possess a certain element, feline rather than feminine, which subtly negatived the idea of manliness" (p. 16).

The Black community, too, has its gradations of social rank and psychological development from slavery times. The most honorable in Chesnutt's eyes is the loyal, old retainer, Sandy Campbell, an ebony copy of his master. The servant is treated occasionally with a broadly humorous touch; for instance, on a drunken trudge home he sees Tom Delamere dressed in his clothes and speculates, "Ef dat's me gwine 'long in front . . . den who is dis behin' here?" (p. 167). But Sandy's dignity, courage, and antebellum breeding as a house servant are gener-ally emphasized as his most prominent features. Such qualities prove a liability in the present-day South, however, for out of loyalty to the Delamere family, Sandy accepts an almost certain death at the hands of a lynch mob, rather than reveal what he knows about Tom's involvement in the murder. Fortunately, Sandy is rescued by the determined efforts of the old aristocrat, who refuses to place empty family pride above honor and justice.

Mammy Judy, the faithful retainer of the Carterets is not so lucky. Like Sandy, she is inordinately proud of her white folks, is supercilious to the younger Black servants who, she recognizes, do not share her feeling for the family, and, incredibly, even adopts Olivia Carteret's hatred of her Black half-sister. She is also the one who, true to the folklore, visits a conjure woman for a good-luck charm to ward off evil from Olivia's sickly infant. Despite her sincere devotion to the family of her former mistress and the Carterets' dependence on and appreciation of her services and subservience, she is killed when the riot floods Wellington.

Her most ironic and destructive function, however is to train her grandson Jerry, "ter be 'umble, an' keep in 'is place . . . an' not crowd de w'ite folks" (p. 44). Based on her own experience, she sees such behavior as a guarantee that he will get enough to eat and will live out his days in peace and comfort. Jerry is the most reprehensible Black character in the book. Like Tom Delamere, he is the corruption of an old type that had some virtue to it. Like Mammy Jane, Jerry is snobbish and comic; worse than she, however, he has no standards and princi-ples, except those associated with saving his own skin. While he neither respects nor loves the whites with whom he comes in contact, "I'm gwine ter keep my mouf shet an' stan' in wid de Angry-Saxon race,—ez day calls deyse'ves nowadays,—an' keep on de right side er my bread an' meat. W't nigger ever give me twenty cents in all my bawn days?" (p. 90). When he testifies against Sandy

Campbell and is commended by General Belmont, Jerry's obsequiosness and racial disloyalty reach a disgusting low: "Thank y', gin'l, thank y' suh! I alluz tries ter do my duty, suh, an' stan' by dem dat stan's by me. Dat low-down nigger oughter be lynch', suh, don't you think, er e'se bu'nt? Dere ain' nothin' too bad ter happen ter 'im'' (p. 184).

While Chesnutt clearly deplores pitiful pawns such as Jerry, he understands how they have been formed, as is clear from a scene between the porter and Major Carteret that satirically accounts for the young Black's behavior and at the same time indicates the depths of Carteret's self-deception. After a conversation about the necessity of returning the government of the state to the hands of whites, Jerry readily and strongly assents, assuring his employer, "I ain' gwine ter have nothin' ter do wid de 'lection, suh! Ef I don' vote, I kin keep my job, can't I, suh?" (p. 246). The major is offended by this response: "What could be expected of a race so utterly devoid of tact? It seems as though this negro thought a white gentleman might want to bribe him to remain away from the polls; and the negro's willingness to accept the imaginary bribe demonstrated the venal nature of the colored race,—its entire lack of moral principle!" (p. 246). Yet, despite Carteret's self-serving need to think otherwise, Jerry understands his situation perfectly: "He knew perfectly well that he held his job upon the condition that he stayed away from the polls at the approaching election. Jerry was a fool. . . . But while no one may be entirely wise, there are degrees of folly, and Jerry was not all kinds of a fool'' (p. 247). Both he and Carteret are unprincipled; the difference is that Jerry will admit it. Ironically, despite his allegiance to the whites, his heartfelt cry, "I wush ter Gawd I wuz w'ite!'' (p. 36), and his refusal to join with Josh Green and his determined band of desperate and angry Blacks, Jerry, like his grandmother, is killed during the riot.

Chesnutt is obviously torn between the methods of his middle-class professional, Dr. Miller, and the firebrand, Josh Green. Early in the tale Miller, at the insistence of Captain McBane, has been evicted from the first-class railroad car on his return to the South. Glancing out the window of the "negro car" while the train has stopped to take in water, Miller sees "a huge negro covered thickly with dust" crawl "off one of the rear trucks unobserved" to drink from a trough (pp. 58–59). He recognizes the stowaway as Josh Green, "an ordinarily good-natured, somewhat reckless, pleasure-loving negro," whose face is now uncharacteristically distorted with a glance of "concentrated hatred almost uncanny in its murderousness," which is directed at McBane (p. 59). The triangular interaction here is significant. Josh Green must ride the rails to return home to complete his mission of revenge against McBane, who was responsible for the destruction of his family during a Klan raid; Miller is returning full of hope and ambition, eager to resume administration of the Black hospital that he has used part of his patrimony to establish. Nevertheless, even though he travels in relative comfort in the "negro car" while Green must stow away, his position in southern society is clearly no more secure than the lower-class Black's. By the end of the novel, Green has died in his successful attempt to kill McBane; Miller's hospital lies smouldering in ruins; and the doctor's only child has been killed by a stray bullet fired during the riot.

Green and Miller clash like conflicting aspects of Chestnutt's political and artistic personality. "These are bad times for bad negroes," Miller warns. "You'd better be peaceable and endure a little injustice, rather than run the risk of a sudden and violent death" (p. 110). Thinking of McBane, Green responds, "I expec's ter die a vi'lent death in a quarrel wid a w'ite man . . . an' fu'thermo', he's gwine ter die at the same time, er a little befo' " (p. 110).

While Miller disagrees with Josh's plan for revenge, he appreciates the determination and sense of purpose that the other man's life reveals. "Miller was willing to give up his life to a cause. Would he be equally willing, he asked himself, to die for it?" (p. 113). Chesnutt is clearly as sympathetic to Josh as Griggs was to Gus, the firebrand of *The Hindered Hand*. After Miller piously reminds Josh that "the Bible says that we should 'forgive our enemies,' the more impatient man replies, "Yas, suh, I've l'arnt all dat in Sunday-school, an' I've heared de preachers say it time an' time ag'in. But it 'pears ter me dat dis fergitfulniss an' fergivness is mighty one-sided" (p. 112).

Once the riot breaks out, Josh recognizing Miller's social superiority to himself, turns to the doctor and to another middle-class Black to organize the town's African-Americans into a defensive position against the white mob. Chesnutt realizes that despite their two-to-one numerical superiority, Wellington's Black citizens cannot take a militant stance against their oppressors. Through Miller, he argues, "Suppose we made a determined stand and won a temporary victory. By morning every train, every boat, every road leading into Wellington, would be crowded with white men. . . . They would kill us in the fight, or they would hang us afterwards" (p. 282). Furthermore, the practical Miller does not have the same self-sacrificial sense of martyrdom as Josh Green:

> "I should like to arm every colored man in this town, and have them stand firmly in line, not for attack, but for defense, but if I attempted it, and they should stand by me, which is questionable,—for I have met them fleeing from the town,—my life would pay the forfeit. Alive, I may be of some use to you, and you are welcome to my life in that way,—I am giving it freely. Dead, I should be a mere lump of carrion" (p. 282).

As Chesnutt emphasizes, Miller is not heroic, but he is sensible; he will survive.

Also at issue are the different social positions of the doctor and the dock worker. Josh understands Miller's reluctance to take a suicidal stance. He even recognizes the contributions that Miller and others in his position can continue to make to the Black community. But he recognizes no such future for himself. "Dese gentlemen," he remarks as he gathers his small band of rebels about him, "may have somethin' ter live fer; but ez fer my pa't, I'd ruther be a dead nigger any day dan a live dog!" (p. 284). By the end of the novel, he is indeed dead; and Miller, at his wife's command, has trailed off behind Olivia to save the life of the Carteret heir.

Chesnutt's allegiance to life and racial cooperation at the end of his book is insufficient to overcome the bitter truths about the destructive nature of American society that the work reveals. If Miller's awareness, in the middle of the novel, of "the continuity of life, how inseparably the present is woven with the past, how certainly the future will be but the outcome of the present" (p. 112), is meant to convey one of the major meanings of the work, then the future of Chesnutt's South is a dark one, indeed. Like Miller, Chesnutt rejects the lure to fiery propagandist exposés of racism and relies, instead, on assertions of the richness of Black life to urge social reform. The political and racial realities of the first bloody year of the twentieth century render both Miller's professional dedication and Chesnutt's tempered hope graceful, but impotent, gestures.

Clearly, *The Marrow of Tradition* is hardly a militant document. Nevertheless, none of Chesnutt's works received such violent and contradictory responses from the critics. Attitudes ranged from the judgment of the reviewer in the *Nation* of March 20, 1902, that "in his statement of conditions and in criticism, Mr. Chesnutt is calm, acute, and just" to the New York *Independent'*s conclusion that the book was "written apparently by a man with a racial grievance" who presented all "the traditional virtues of the negroes" in contrast "with all the reputed vices of Southern whites with the lively distinctions of a mulatto imagination." Predictably, the harshest reviews were from the South, but even some of the comments from other areas of the country raised the question of the wisdom of producing a book that would exacerbate the violent social climate at the turn of the century (*CWC,* p. 177). Perhaps W. D. Howells's comments reflected the uncomfortable attitude of many readers. "In that republic of letters where all men are free," the naively optimistic Howells observed,

> as usual he stands up for his own people with a courage which has more justice than mercy in it. The book is, in fact, bitter, bitter. There is no reason in history why it should not be so, if wrong is to be repaid with hate, and yet it would be better if it was not so bitter . . . but he does not paint the blacks all good, or the whites all bad. He paints them as slavery made them on both sides.[35]

Although *The Marrow of Tradition* was selected by the Booklovers Library and was classed by *Outlook* among the twenty-five most important works of literature of the year, as a financial venture it fell far below the expectations of Chesnutt and his publishers: "Houghton, Mifflin and Company had been so sure of its reception by the public that they had spent a great deal of money in advertising it. Both they and Chesnutt had expected it to secure a rapid and distinct financial success and they were all terribly disappointed" (*CWC,* pp. 176–77).

This dashing of Chesnutt's hopes had become a pattern; success as a writer always appeared imminent, but never seemed to arrive. In a letter to Cable in 1894, he noted that he had managed to save ten to fifteen thousand dollars from his business as court reporter and stenographer and happily anticipated the opportunity to "devote more time, and, if necessary, some money to securing a place in literature" (*CWC*, p. 73). When *The Wife of His Youth* was well received, Chesnutt penned another heady letter to Page, exulting,

> I have been hearing from my story every day since its publication. Editors kindly send me marked copies of magazines and papers containing approving notices. I get compliments right and left from the best people of Cleveland on the Ethics, the English, and the interest of the "Wife of his Youth." I have had letters from my friends and notices in all the local papers. My autograph has been called for from "daown East," a local publisher wants to talk to me about a book, a clipping bureau would like to send me clippings; and taking it all in all, I have had a slight glimpse of what it means, I imagine, to be a successful author . . . (Fisk University).

The following month, on September 30, 1899, Chesnutt took the enormous step of closing his business office in the Society for Savings Building and setting up his literary office at home. However, despite its initial interest, the public bought neither *The Wife of His Youth* nor *The Marrow of Tradition* in anywhere near the volume necessary for Chesnutt to devote his life to letters, and by the end of 1902, he was forced to return to business; from then on, writing became his avocation.

In an essay entitled "Possibilities of the Negro," W. E. B. DuBois contrasts the careers of Paul Laurence Dunbar, who "sprang from slave parents and poverty," and Chesnutt, "who grew from free parents and thrift," and notes that to each "came his particular temptation—to Dunbar the blight of poverty and sordid surroundings . . . and to Chesnutt the temptation of money making—why leave some thousands of dollars a year for scribbling about black folks?"[36] As is clear in Dunbar's case, it was a sad fact of the nineteenth-century publishing scene, Howells's optimism notwithstanding, that a Black writer could not count on an audience to sustain him or a publisher willing to take successive risks with his work. For someone as self-sufficient and competitive in other areas as Chesnutt, who also had a family to support, it would have been completely impractical to make more than one unsuccessful attempt to support himself through his writing alone. Yet, unlike Dunbar, Chesnutt was not so eager or desperate for the questionable security of being published that he completely catered to the taste of the popular audience. Significantly, a recent critic notes that, in a sense, "Charles Chesnutt was to Paul Laurence Dunbar what W. E. B. DuBois was to Booker T. Washington."[37] By early 1904, he was hard at work on another novel.

The publication history of *The Colonel's Dream* almost duplicates the trouble that Chesnutt had with *The House Behind the Cedars*. The book was rejected by Houghton Mifflin on May 12, 1904, primarily because the company was leery of any more books from Chesnutt after the poor public response to *The Marrow of Tradition,* but also because, as with "Rena," he seemed to be writing an elongated short story. On July 1, 1904, Walter Page responded hopefully to a letter from Chesnutt, in which the author announced that he was trying to "make it a book of full grown size," and advised his friend, "Don't work the machinery of the alleged hidden treasure too hard" (Fisk University). He continued to work on the book into 1905 in what leisure time he had away from his once more thriving business and finally saw the story appear in September of that year through Doubleday, Page, and Company.

In his last published novel Chesnutt contrasts different historical periods in the South and reveals the disparities at the turn of the century between northern and southern thinking. He centers this exploration in a main character who seeks to deny such differences. Involved as well are his traditional concerns with political, economic, and spiritual stagnation and the difficulty of imposing external change upon a society.

After the reader has been led through the complexity of his themes, his usual hopeful promise at the end of the novel—"other hands have taken up the fight which the colonel dropped"—carries no conviction.[38] Nor can the reader accept the book's final flowery hope that the self-defeating racism in the South "will pass, that some day our whole land will be truly free . . . and Justice, the seed, and Peace, the flower, of liberty, will prevail throughout all our borders" (p. 294). Chesnutt is once more indulging in the empty literary formula of an upbeat ending. As a matter of fact, *The Colonel's Dream* is his most despairing look at American society. It is pessimistic not only because of its protagonist's failure to thwart the evils of the turn-of-the-century South, but, more compellingly, because it forces the reader to recognize the parallels between the hapless Colonel French and Charles Chesnutt himself.

The novel's major interest is the contrast between the gentility of antebellum ways and the materialism and vulgarity of the contemporary South. Through the frustrated attempt of Colonel French to "go home again," Chesnutt demonstrates the impossibility of denying or overcoming historical change. When French first sees Clarendon again after a career in New York, "it was all so like, and yet so different" (p. 15). He recognizes surface changes in his former home, but is blind to their deeper meanings, because his trip south is essentially a psychological journey back into his own happier past, and his nostalgia for that better time distorts the reality of the present:

> The old town, whose ripeness was almost decay, whose quietness was scarcely distinguishable from lethargy, had been the home of his youth, and he saw it, strange to say, less with the eyes of the lad of sixteen who had gone to war, than with those of the little boy to whom it had been, in his tenderest years, the great wide world, the only world he knew in the years when, with his black boy Peter, whom his father had given to him as a personal attendant, he had gone forth to field and garden, stream and forest, in search of childish adventure (p. 16).

His journey to Clarendon, then, is in quest of a long-dead world transformed through the haze of memory and imagination into "an enchanted garden, where lilac bush and jessamine vine reared their heads high, tulip, and daffodil pushed their way upward . . . all dominated by the intenser fragrance of violets'' (p. 38). This Eden, where the stars are ''brighter than in more northern latitudes'' (p. 45), exists, of course, only in Colonel French's memory. In the present-day South, the ''great forests of primeval pine'' that ''in his boyhood . . . had stretched for miles on either hand, broken at intervals by thriving plantations,'' have given way to the ''blasted trunks and stills'' of the constantly advancing turpentine, sawmill, and tar industries, ''so that the dark green forest was now only a waste of blackened stumps and undergrowth'' (p. 215). The poverty of its Reconstruction cotton economy has resulted in Clarendon's dependence upon the North for the very staples of its existence. Consequently, unemployment and lethargy are pervasive, for, as one of the Black citizens points out, ''all de fu'nicher, de shoes, de wagons, de buggies, de tinware, de hoss shoes, de nails to fasten 'em on wid—Yas, an' fo' de Lawd! even de clothes dat folks wears on dere backs, is made at de Norf'' (p. 97–98). Worst of all, like maggots in the guts of a rotting carcass, the Fetters clan is sucking dry what is left of the town's dying economy.

Josh, Bill, and Bark Fetters—early, humorless versions of William Faulkner's Snopses—are former poor whites who, like McBane in *The Marrow of Tradition*, have risen through audacity, cunning, luck, and total amorality to positions of prominence. The contrast between the Fetters and the French families is starkly symbolized in the comparison of the two monuments that Colonel French sees on a visit to the old town cemetery:

> Nearing the gate, they passed a small open space in which stood a simple marble shaft, erected to the memory of the Confederate Dead. . . . Beyond this memorial, impressive in its pure simplicity, and between it and the gate, in an obtrusively conspicuous spot stood a florid monument of granite, marble and bronze, of glaring design . . . (p. 34).

It is a monument to the memory of Joshua Fetters, the patriarch of the clan, a slave speculator in antebellum days who kept dogs to track down runaways. He had been despised by the aristocrats whose dirty work he did and, recognizing their hypocrisy, despised them in return. His grandson, Barclay, is an insolent, self-indulgent ne'er-do-well, ironically indistinguishable from the upper-class Tom Delamere in *The Marrow of Tradition*.

It is Bill Fetters, Joshua's son, who is the unscrupulous power in the new South, Bill Fetters who chains unfortunate Blacks to his pocket through his cruel use of the convict labor system, who locks tenant farmers, Black and white, to their few acres of mortgaged, depleted soil and imprisons sickly women and children for long hours of debilitating labor in his cotton mills. Slowly, Colonel French begins to realize the extent of Fetters's power: ''Fetters dominated the country and the town, and apparently the State. His name was on every lip. His influence was indispensable to every political aspirant. His acquaintance was something to boast of, and his good will held a promise of success'' (p. 76). To destroy the influence of this ''great vampire bat, sucking the life-blood of the people'' (p. 117) quickly becomes French's mission in Clarendon.

He is temporarily successful. He is on the spot, for example, to save old Peter from the chain gang and bind him to the French family again as a loyal retainer; by entertaining graciously in the old French mansion and thereby restoring ''an ancient landmark,'' he can recall, ''to a people whose life lay mostly in the past, the glory of days gone by'' and prove his ''loyalty to their cherished traditions'' (p. 102); he inspires the almost hopeless Blacks of Clarendon to contribute both their money and their labor toward building an industrial school in the town. By various endeavors, he sparks new economic life in Clarendon: ''The barber, out of his profits'' from selling back the old French homestead,

> began the erection of a row of small houses for coloured tenants. This gave employment to masons and carpenters, and involved the sale and purchase of considerable building material. General trade felt the influence of the enhanced prosperity. Groceries, dry-goods stores and saloons, did a thriving business. The ease with which the simply organized community responded to so slight an inflow of money and energy, was not without a pronounced influence upon the colonel's future conduct (pp. 88–89).

In view of his initial success, Colonel French's vague sense of purpose in returning to the South is sharpened and focused on arresting the decay of the economy and the corruption of Fetters and on transforming the town into ''a busy hive of industry, where no man, and no woman obliged to work, need be without employment at fair wages; where the trinity of peace, prosperity and progress would reign supreme'' (p. 118). This magnificent dream fails for a combination of mundane reasons. In essence, the colonel's life in the North has educated him away from the mores of southern life; it has also blinded him to the present complexity of racial and class relations.

The Clarendon to which Colonel French returns is one in which a new public library is rejected because ''the white people wouldn't wish to handle the same books'' as Blacks (p. 163); where successful African-American citizens are considered exceptions who prove the rule of their race's inferiority by the ''good,'' ''patriotic'' whites ''who would have died for liberty, in the abstract''; where, as in the Wellington of Chesnutt's earlier book, white supremacy has become the rallying cry, with the spectre of intermarriage—''Equality anywhere, means ultimately, equality everywhere'' (p. 194)—being powerful enough to launch a successful campaign for Black disfranchisement; where the old values that Chesnutt esteems—courage, honesty, respect of women, and love of culture—have given way to the raw financial force of Bill Fetters, who owns most of the white citizens of Clarendon and knows how to manipulate the prejudices of those few who are not in his debt.

Because of his own development in the North, French is unable to appreciate the seriousness of the changes in postwar Clarendon and has naively forgotten the bitterly held prejudices of antebellum days. Colonel French "had lived away from the South so long" that "an introduction to some of its customs," like the brutality of the convict labor system, "came with something of a shock. He had remembered the pleasant things, and these but vaguely . . . and in the sifting process of a healthy memory he had forgotten the disagreeable things altogether" (p. 65).

Some of the "pleasant things" still exist: old Peter's selfless loyalty; the pastoral, peaceful evenings spent with old friends; the gentility of Laura Treadwell and her mother. Yet, even the antique charm of his evening with the Treadwells was disrupted when Graciella "went to the piano and with great boldness of touch struck the bizarre opening chords and then launched into the grotesque words of the latest New York 'coon song,' one of the first and worst of its kind, and the other young people joined in the chorus" (p. 49). Having dined on sumptuous southern cooking, engaged in light-hearted conversation, and felt himself delicately intoxicated by "the perfume of lilac and violet" that "stole in through the open windows," the colonel finds himself in the mood for a "plantation song of the olden time, as he remembered it, borne upon the evening air . . . sung by the tired slaves at the end of their day of toil . . . with its simple melody, its plaintive minor strains, its notes of vague longing" (p. 49). Graciella's "coon song" more accurately represents the grotesqueness of present-day race relations in Clarendon than the colonel's comforting hymn, but he is too shrouded in memory and imagination to realize its horrible aptness.

He notes with sensuous pleasure the smooth softness of the Treadwells' fine linen, but fails to observe that the tablecloth and napkins have been carefully darned in many places; he finds charming Laura's fragile silver spoons "of fine, old-fashioned patterns," judging their continued use her preference for "the simple dignity of the past to the vulgar ostentation of a more modern time" (p. 45), unaware that the Treadwells are too poor to replace their linen or silver, so poor that Laura must accept Black as well as white music students. His solipsism becomes dangerous, moreover, when he forgets or discounts southern racism to the point that he places a Black foreman over the white bricklayers working for him. When he ignores the animosity and far-flung power of the former poor-white class and expects the old codes of chivalry and honor to prevail with men who "despised Negroes and distrusted aristocrats" (p. 264), he shows himself inadequate for his chosen role of social reformer. The blunt realization that he is hopelessly running against the tide does not come until Clarendon callously and cruelly rejects him—"We do not want to buy the prosperity of this town at the price of our principles" (p. 264)—by dishonoring his dead. The disinterment of old Peter from the French family plot in the white cemetery is the blow that causes the colonel finally to turn his back on Clarendon, on his vaguely remembered past and naively imagined future, and to return with his dead to New York.

Before this final decision, however, out of a combination of blind idealism and a hapless adoption of Fetters's standards of expediency, he precipitates acts of

violence unaccounted for in his dreams or his plans. True to his outdated code of chivalry, he responds to Laura Treadwell's wishes and does everything that he legally can to free Bud Johnson, the husband of her maid, from the chain gang. When all legal means fail, he regretfully agrees to bribe a guard to allow Johnson to slip away. "Get Johnson away," he instructs a white confidant; "I don't care how. The end justifies the means—that's an argument that goes down here" (p. 231). Having once capitulated to the standards of his enemies, French has no safe moral ground on which to stand. Significantly, he has also misread the changes in the Blacks. Bud Johnson, rather than gratefully accepting the opportunity to escape, returns to the outskirts of Clarendon intent on killing as many of his white oppressors as he can. Johnson is no loyal, timid old Peter, and French must accept responsibility for the fact that with "the best of intentions, and hoping to save a life, he had connived at turning a murderer loose upon the community" (p. 246). While vaguely aware of a new pride and a new sullenness in the Blacks, he is still living in a paternalistic past. He fails to appreciate the desperation and hatred that would lead a Bud Johnson or a Josh Green to risk an inevitable lynching to take their revenge. Furthermore, although aware that "things Southern . . . lived long and died hard" (p. 66), he is strangely shocked and disarmed by the unchanging racism of the society.

Bill Fetters, too, is an unprepared-for surprise. Although his presence broods ominously over Clarendon from the moment of French's return, he does not actually appear until a few pages before the end of the novel. When he does appear, he is startlingly different from McBane, the stereotypic poor white trash of *The Marrow of Tradition*. Colonel French

> had expected to meet a tall, long-haired, red-faced truculent individual, in a slouch hat and a frock coat, with a loud voice and a dictatorial manner, the typical Southerner of melodrama. He saw a keen-eyed, hard-faced, small man, slightly gray, clean-shaven, wearing a well-fitting city-made business suit of light tweed. Except for a few little indications, such as the lack of a crease in his trousers, Fetters looked like any one of a hundred business men whom the Colonel might have met on Broadway in any given fifteen minutes during business hours (p. 223).

The McBanes, with their grotesque vulgarity and racism, can eventually be destroyed; the Fetterses represent the much more subtle, pervasive poison of materialism that can silently and interminably manipulate the false pride and insecurity of American society.

When both Phil, French's little son, and old Peter die, the colonel's past and future in the South no longer exist; they cannot even be buried together in southern soil. Such anachronisms are he and they that they must all return to the North together. Significantly, Phil is killed trying to live out in real life one of old Peter's ghost tales. The illusory nature of the colonel's past and his inability to awaken soon enough to the reality of the present destroy his future.

Additionally, there are some larger lessons to be learned from this book, which illuminate Chesnutt's changing relationship to the tradition of Black artistry. Old Peter is a key figure here. The first embodiment of his type in Chesnutt's work was crafty, self-sufficient Uncle Julius of *The Conjure Woman,* a character who represented the African-American's capacity for survival in a murderous system, as well as symbolizing the richness of the Black literary tradition and the complex role of the Black artist. Chesnutt's identification with Uncle Julius was clear and apt. The scheming servant of "The Passing of Grandison" in *The Wife of His Youth,* who so convinces his master of his loyalty that he is able to escape with his whole family, is another trickster figure. Frank Fowler, the loyal, hopeless suitor in *The House Behind the Cedars,* however, marks the beginning of the degeneration of the type. Frank is too black to be invited to Miss Molly's party, but despite his pride and sensitivity and against the advice of his family, he devotes himself to helping Rena maintain the superior position in society that passing for white seems to promise. Although he appreciates the Fowlers' cynicism about Frank's devotion, Chesnutt also views such self-sacrifice as ennobling: Rena's "experience had dragged her through the valley of humiliation," while Frank's "unselfish devotion had reacted to refine and elevate his own spirit" (p. 255). Nevertheless, Frank plays a secondary role in the novel, just as he does in his society and in Rena's interest. He is used essentially as a device to further the plot. Chesnutt's portrayal of this antebellum type reaches almost stereotypic proportions in *The Marrow of Tradition,* with Sandy Campbell, who is not only comic but also willing to die for a murder that he did not commit, rather than expose the heir of the family whom he has served all his life. Sandy is brave, but as inappropriate a role model for Black readers as Chesnutt judges Josh Green, the suicidal firebrand, to be.

Most anachronistic of all these figures, however, is beloved old Peter of *The Colonel's Dream*. Like Sandy, he revels in the past glory of his white folks: "If Peter could be believed, there were never white folks so brave, so learned, so wise, so handsome, so kind to their servants, so just to all with whom they had dealings" (p. 144). But much more so than Sandy, Peter is childlike, "undeveloped," "though by nature faithful, . . . never unduly bright" (p. 143). There is obviously no identification between Chesnutt and old Peter; there can be none, because unlike Uncle Julius, the artist, the trickster, Peter is as impotent as Colonel French's memories of the South. Significantly, the link in this last novel is between Chesnutt and his white protagonist.

In 1905, Chesnutt was forty years old, approximately the same age as French. Like the Colonel, he

had looked forward to the time . . . when he might retire from business and devote his leisure to study and travel, tastes which for years he had subordinated to the pursuit of wealth; not entirely, for his life had been many-sided; and not so much for the money, as because, being in a game where dollars were like counters, it was his instinct to play it well (pp. 17–18).

Like his fictional counterpart, Chesnutt had left the South at an early age and was almost immediately successful in business in New York. Moreover, his "dream," too, was to use his particular influence to help bring about a society in which "each man, in his little life in this our little world might be able to make the most of himself" (pp. 280–81). Like his hero, Chesnutt sprang from the aristocracy of his society; his parents were free mulattoes, and, as numerous critics have pointed out, he continued throughout his life to be interested in and committed to the South. Commented one scholar, the "North Carolina environment helped to shape his literary aims before he began his career; moreover the course of North Carolina history significantly determined the content and trend of his imaginative writing from beginning to end."[39]

Like French, Chesnutt's success occurred in the North. Besides building a business career that permitted him to send his son to Harvard, two daughters to Smith, and one to Western Reserve University in Ohio, he was able to provide his family with a large, comfortable home in Cleveland and to take his wife on trips abroad. In addition, he achieved some measure of the scholarly reputation to which he had aspired as a boy. Besides substituting as a lecturer for Walter Hines Page, becoming the first African-American writer published consistently in leading literary journals like the *Atlantic,* being elected to the Cleveland Council of Sociology, and appearing in the 1901–02 edition of *Who's Who in America,* he was also one of the select group of 150 American writers invited to attend the December 5, 1905, dinner honoring Mark Twain at Delmonico's in New York City. Ironically, all these marks of similarity between Chesnutt and his white hero only emphasize their insurmountable differences in American society.

When Mr. French, successful New York businessman, returns South, "where titles are seldom ignored" and where he "could hardly have escaped his own, even had he desired to do so" (p. 18), he becomes Colonel French; the South also had an identity for Charles Chesnutt. Like Dr. Miller in *The Marrow of Tradition,* Chesnutt, despite his accomplishments, was only a "nigger" in turn-of-the-century southern society. He was fortunate to be educated, surprisingly successful, but—on southern soil—still inferior to the McBanes and the Fetterses. Not since antebellum times had the African-American's lot looked so desperate as in the bloody years of the first decade of this century. Chesnutt's dream of awakening America's slumbering conscience and of changing the climate of his Southland through his fiction's undeniable truths was dashed for good by the poor reception of *The Colonel's Dream.*

Like a bad omen, the first copies of the book spelled Chesnutt's name incorrectly on the cover (*CWC,* p. 21). Although this error was quickly remedied, with apologies from the editors, the mistake seems a portent that the work would fail to gain for Chesnutt the literary recognition that had so long eluded him. In contrast with the handling of his other books, his new publishing company of Doubleday, Page did not publicize this one very heavily. Chesnutt wrote to the publisher, Marcowson, on October 14, 1905, asking, "Is 'The Colonel's Dream' catching on at all? . . . I have not seen the book advertised anywhere, except about half an inch in the last number of the 'World's Work,' and I fear that a number of my friends around Cleveland have not yet been advised of the fact that I have published a new book." Plaintively, he adds, "I am willing to cooperate" (Fisk University). But no amount of cooperation could have sparked the sale of a book that insisted, in 1905, on a realistic appraisal of racial conditions. It was a time when feelings against Blacks were hardening into murderous attacks in parts of the country far removed from the South.

After *The Colonel's Dream* failed to bring him acclaim, Chesnutt returned in earnest to his more successful career as a public man. During the year of its publication, he was elected to membership in the Committee of Twelve for the Advancement of the Negro Race, which had been formed in 1904 in response to the increasing racial violence in the country. From this period until his death in 1932, his energies were divided between active participation in the worlds of business and politics and peripheral literary concerns.

In 1910, he was delighted by the publication of "The Wife of His Youth" in the *Journal de Genève,* translated into French by Marie Louise Press of Geneva. In December of that year, he became a member of the Rowfant Club, a nationally known organization of men who collected books and enjoyed meeting to discuss literature.[40] However, it was also in 1910 that he addressed the annual meeting of the National Negro Committee, which later became the NAACP. In the fall of 1911, he was elected president of the Council of Sociology of Cleveland; and during the mayoral campaign for the term 1912–14, he accompanied the successful candidate, Newton D. Baker, and reported his speeches to the newspapers. He was unanimously elected to membership in the Cleveland Chamber of Commerce in 1912 and in 1913 was awarded an honorary LL.D. from Wilberforce University. In March 1916, he appeared before a Senate committee in Washington to testify against the Shipstead Anti-Injunction Bill, which would have strengthened the hand of labor unions that were discriminating against Blacks. Clearly, his field of battle had shifted from the realm of art to that of politics.

Although he had not been published as a fiction writer for twenty-three years, in June 1928, Chesnutt received a telegram from James Weldon Johnson informing him that he had been awarded the coveted Spingarn Medal for his contributions to the advancement of African-American life. Honored and inspired by recognition from a generation that he was surprised knew of his work, Chesnutt turned his hand one last time to another novel, "The Quarry," which, because of his failing energies, he was never to complete.[41]

Shortly before his death, Chesnutt commented happily, "I have lived to see, after twenty years or more, a marked change in the attitude of publishers, and the reading public in regard to the Negro in fiction."[42] His own literary career spanned the painful emergence of the African-American writer after the Civil War to the post-Harlem-Renaissance submersion of Black expression in the economic doldrums of the 1930s. Despite his ultimate reliance on success in the white world of business, Chesnutt's artistic contributions clearly define the traditions upon which the early Black writers drew and suggest the difficulties facing later spokesmen in America's racist climate. In 1926, Chesnutt lamented that "the really epical race novel, in which love and hatred, high endeavor, success and failure, sheer comedy and stark tragedy are mingled, is yet to be written, and let us hope that a man of Negro blood may write it."[43] Chesnutt was not to be that man, but his accomplishment "illuminate[s] the blackness of [his] invisibility" and that of all his artistic kinsmen.[44]

A Final Perspective

In 1853, the year that *Clotel* was published in London, heralding the birth of the African-American novel, the National Council of Colored People was founded in Rochester, New York. Frederick Douglass was in attendance and appears as one of the signers of a declaration that protested that "with the exception of the Jews, under the whole heavens, there is not to be found a people pursued with a more relentless prejudice and persecution than are the free colored people of the United States."[1] This statement was in response to the recent racial animosity in the North and West that had frequently exploded into riots, the most serious of which erupted in Pennsylvania in the 1830s. The year 1857 saw the London publication of *The Garies and Their Friends* and also an African-American convention in Philadelphia, the setting of Webb's novel, to protest the Dred Scott decision, by which the Supreme Court upheld the right of masters to transport slaves into nonslave territory and to retain ownership of them. In the last sixteen years of the nineteenth century, at least twenty-five hundred individuals were lynched in the United States, the majority of them Black; and in the first year of the new century, more than one hundred Blacks were killed by mobs.[2] At the call of W. E. B. DuBois in the summer of 1905, "some of the ablest and most earnest men in the Negro race" met at Niagara Falls, Canada.[3] A year later they issued a manifesto asserting,

> Never before in the modern age has a great and civilized folk threatened to adopt so cowardly a creed in the treatment of its fellow citizens, born and bred on its soil. Stripped of verbiage and subterfuge and in its naked nastiness, the new American creed says: fear to let black men even try to rise lest they become equals of the white.[4]

In September 1905, *The Colonel's Dream*, a book that, with *Pointing the Way*, rounds off the earliest period of African-American fiction, appeared and began to gather dust in the nation's bookstores. Clearly, despite the trauma of the Civil War and the hope engendered in many by the abolition of slavery, little of substance had occurred in race relations in the United States in the fifty-two years separating Clotel and Colonel French.

In that half-century, America's national will was tested and defined by events as seemingly contradictory as the threatened, then actual, secession of the Confederate states and the victory of the new Republican party in 1860, with Abraham Lincoln as its standard bearer. With the Confederate surrender at Appomattox, the abolition of slavery, and the establishment of the Freedman's Bureau, 1865 appeared to mark the beginning of a new era in the fortunes of America's Blacks. However, such premature hopes were quickly dashed.

As James D. Hart notes, "A predatory class of capitalists emerged as ultimate victors of the Civil War."[5] The North increased its industrialization with a vengeance and spread the influence of big business via the railroads into the West in acquisition of raw materials and new markets to build production and profits. The newly subjugated South was also fertile ground for exploitation, for "Northerners were as anxious to sell to ex-Confederates as they were to have customers in the North."[6] The need to rebuild the South and bring it within the political and economic goals of the country, defined largely by special interest groups with influence in Washington, finally determined the course of Congress's relationship with the rebels and ultimately permitted white home rule, which plunged southern Blacks into an economic situation as bad as that of prewar times. "The wages paid to freedmen in 1867 were lower than those that had been paid to hired slaves,"[7] most of the Blacks gradually being bound to the land as sharecroppers, sinking deeper into debt each year. The Reconstruction Act of 1867, which disfranchised the majority of white southerners and gave the ballot to the former slaves, infuriated the whites, but offered little beyond temporary political representation for some of the Blacks. Predictably, "in failing to provide adequate economic security for the freedmen, Reconstruction left no alternative but to submit to their old masters, a submission that made easier the efforts of Southern whites to overthrow Reconstruction and restore a system based on white supremacy."[8]

As historians have noted, in order for significant changes in the lives of African-Americans to have occurred during the decades after the war, the entire country would have needed "reconstructing." Instead, Americans had grown weary of the race problem and were turning their attention to expanding the nation's influence and suturing regional differences. "Politics and high finance continued to walk arm in arm," checked only occasionally by such steps as the Interstate Commerce Act, passed in 1887 to curb the power of the railroads, and the 1890 Sherman Antitrust Act against monopolies.[9]

Despite such legal measures, the rift between rich and poor widened as the century drew to a close: "Capitalist economy, controlled by the cities, moved onto the farms in the shape of mortgages or such expensive implements as reapers and harvesters, putting farmers into big business or in the grip of it."[10] It was a short step from the industrial giants' dominating groups within the country to their following the example of other Western nations of the period and turning to foreign fields for additional resources and markets.

Twenty-two Blacks were among those killed on board the battleship *Maine* when it was blown up in Havana harbor in 1898, precipitating the war with Spain that led directly to the United States' taking control of Cuba, Puerto Rico, the

Philippines, and islands in the West Indies, thus entering the ranks of the major imperialist nations of the world. Commented John Hope Franklin,

> Before the end of the century . . . the United States had acquired an empire composed primarily of darker peoples—Polynesian, Japanese, Chinese, and others. In so doing, the leading power in the Western hemisphere was conforming to the prevailing pattern of imperialism that had swept the world: the injection of the spirit of industrialism into a program to dominate the backward areas of the world. Invariably, these backward people were dark, and frequently they were Negroid. The United States was well on her way to the development of an empire of darker peoples.[11]

Significantly, the Wilmington race riot during the 1898 elections in North Carolina, the fiery background of *The Marrow of Tradition*, shared local headlines with the Spanish-American War.

Countering the heady atmosphere of world domination was the continued political turmoil at home, fed not only by racial clashes but also by the widening class and economic gap. The American scene was further troubled by the flood of hopeful or desperate poor, Black and white, sweeping off the farms and pouring into cities that were unable to begin to absorb them. Seventy-five percent of the Blacks in the United States were still in the nonurban South in 1880, but by the end of the century, in increasing numbers they were abandoning their dead-end rural life, so that between 1890 and 1900, at least 107,796 southern Blacks moved north and west.[12] As Gilbert Osofsky notes in *Harlem: The Making of a Ghetto*, "The rapid growth of Negro New York in these years created social problems and racial tensions unequaled since slavery days. The poverty, violence and segregation of these years were typical of the difficulties Negroes confronted in every major northern urban area in the twentieth century."[13]

After the threat of national dissolution that the Civil War represented, the country's pride had been aroused and kept afloat by the series of centennial celebrations stretching from 1875 to 1890. This nationalist chauvinism was not to be deflated, even by the growing social, political, and economic troubles culminating in the financial crisis of 1893. The Gilded Age comforted itself with an optimistic outlook and genteel self-image, ignoring as much as it could the "concentration of industrial and commercial power, the drive toward imperialism, the sharp cleavage in classes, the insecurity of the many and the arrogant certainty of the few, the dominance of business ethics over civic responsibility."[14] Overwhelmed by these complex problems, some of the threatening implications of which were already apparent in the violent birth of the labor movement—which also discriminated against Blacks—the majority of people in the country chose to rationalize most of what they saw and to seek escape from the rest. Nowhere was this desire more apparent than in the kinds of books that they bought.

In 1901, twenty-two hundred new works of fiction were published; the novel-reading public numbered into the hundreds of thousands. It was "in large part a public anxious to emulate the taste of the wealthy or share vicariously through fiction in the pleasures presumably granted to those with ample funds."[15] Because of the recently aroused interest in America's founding, historical romances set around important incidents in the country's history, costume dramas situated on the western and southern frontiers, and nostalgic local color tales placed among simple country folk, considered representative of America's rural values, were especially popular. As James Hart notes,

> The socially conscious Americans who planned to improve the cities were far fewer than the gently discontent who dreamed of a better life close to nature and folksy ways of the country. Muckrakers might startle people with their exposés of corruption in politics and big business, but a book like Lincoln Steffen's *The Shame of the Cities*, published in 1904, could not compete with such fiction as that year's best sellers, *The Little Shepherd of Kingdom Come* and *Rebecca of Sunnybrook Farm*.[16]

Obviously, then, the isolated position of early African-American writers grew even more pronounced after the abolitionist fervor of the prewar years gave way to increasing racial, economic, and class tensions after the war. With very few exceptions (*Uncle Tom's Cabin* springs almost solely to mind), novels do not change the progress of a country; art, finally, is a window, not a weapon. However vehemently and perceptively writers may attack society's evils, fiction most often reflects or, possibly, rejects a culture, but does not rewrite it. What makes the earliest African-American novels the illuminating documents that they are is their paradoxical shaping by the very culture that most of them were attempting to change. Moreover, as has been seen, most of their authors were forced to look for acceptance and understanding from the same people whose morality and humanitarianism they were questioning.

Their audience was dual, and their purpose was correspondingly twofold: to inspire pride and determination in Black readers and to educate and arouse sympathy and desire for reform in whites. Their successes depend upon the extent to which they rejected dehumanizing stereotypes, replacing them not with counterstereotypes, but with characters rooted in the realities of their people's history. Their failures demonstrate the limitations not only of the individual writers, in terms of talent and imagination, but of an American society that prescribed which art was acceptable, which culture, which people, and blinked at the consequences of such dogmas.

The majority of the early Black artists were clearly assimilationists, wishing success according to the artistic and social standards of their day. Sutton Griggs's trusted protagonists are neither stereotypes nor counterstereotypes, but they are definitely middle-class, nonviolent aspirers to the establishment. There is obviously a connection between the characterizations and plots in these novels and their authors' own hopes of achieving the promises of the American dream.

Significantly, the books mirror attempts occurring in the Black community on the economic front, where the establishment of innumerable kinds of businesses, especially short-lived banking firms, marked the end of the century. Speaking of the "real significance" of these banks, John Hope Franklin concludes that "they represent an effort on the part of Negroes to adopt the business ideals and social values of the rest of America and, thus, to assimilate themselves more completely."[17]

Despite this frequently thwarted drive to blend, like more recent immigrants, into the yeasty brew of American life, from the first African-American fiction through the writings of Griggs and Chesnutt the fertility of Black culture and the potency of Black energy are emphasized. With the exception of most of Dunbar's fiction, the importance of recognizing Black cultural vitality, its life-giving influence throughout the race's American experience, and a rejection of racist, degrading definitions of Black individuals are repeatedly sounded. Yet, by the turn of the century, everywhere could be seen a denial of that richness, mirrored in disfranchisement, segregation, violence, and the country's growing exploitation of darker nations. Discussing the political ineffectiveness of this early body of Black protest literature, Addison Gayle, Jr., concludes, "The fault lies not in the genre itself, but upon the flimsy premise upon which the writer based his protest—that America wanted and desired an equalitarian society in which man opted for truth and beauty over narrow interests, material gain, and selfish pursuits."[18] Even a brief survey of America's national and international endeavors in the last half of the nineteenth century quickly corrects that misapprehension.

Notes

Introduction: The Tensions and the Traditions

1. Don L. Lee, "Black Poetry: Which Direction?" *Negro Digest* 17 (September–October 1968): 27–32.

2. Ibid., p. 29.

3. See Nathaniel Hawthorne, *The Scarlet Letter* (Boston, 1850); Mark Twain, *The Adventures of Huckleberry Finn* (New York, 1885); Henry James, *The Ambassadors* (London, 1903).

4. See Booker T. Washington, *Up From Slavery* (New York, 1901); W. E. B. DuBois, *The Souls of Black Folks* (Chicago, 1903).

5. Ralph Ellison, *Shadow and Act* (New York, 1953), "Introduction."

1 Popular Myths and the Audience

1. Unless otherwise indicated, all information presented in this study about the sales, editions, and popularity of American novels during the nineteenth century is taken from James D. Hart, *The Popular Book: A History of America's Literary Taste* (New York, 1950).

2. Herbert Ross Brown, *The Sentimental Novel in America, 1789–1860* (Raleigh, N.C., 1940), p. 176. Characterizing the overall intent and technique of this type of fiction, Brown observes,

> The sentimental formula was a simple equation resting upon a belief in the spontaneous goodness and benevolence of man's original instincts. . . . It was informed throughout with a moral purpose to which all its other elements were subordinated. Into its capacious framework were poured the stock characters and situations dear to popular story-tellers of every generation. The final solution was neatly reserved for the last chapter where the punishment was made to fit the crime, and the reward to equal the virtue. To achieve it, authors subjected the long arm of coincidence to the rack of expediency where it was stretched and fractured to suit every need of the plot. The reader, meanwhile, was made to cry—and to wait. As a "true feeler," he was expected to match pang for pang, and sigh for sigh with the persecuted victim; he was mercilessly roasted over the slow fires of suspense (p. 176).

The adaptability of this "formula" to the uses of anti-slavery propaganda was being proved by the white abolitionists, and it was only a short step further to its acceptance by Black writers who wished to tell firsthand about Black life.

3. Walter Stowers and William H. Anderson, *Appointed* (Detroit, 1894), pp. 67–68. Hereafter, following bibliographic identification, all quotations from the nineteenth-century African-American novels will be followed by the page number in parentheses.

4. Herbert Ross Brown, *Sentimental Novel in America*, p. 169.

5. For a detailed description of early Black portraiture in American literature, see Seymour L. Gross and John Edward Hardy, eds., *Images of the Negro in American Literature* (Chicago, 1966); Wade Hall, *The Smiling Phoenix: Southern Humor from 1865–1914* (Gainesville, Fla., 1965);

Sterling Brown, *The Negro in American Fiction* (New York, 1937); Jean Fagan Yellen, *The Intricate Knot: The Negro in American Literature, 1776–1863* (New York, 1971).

6. Sterling Brown, *Negro in American Fiction,* p. 17.

7. Herbert Ross Brown, *Sentimental Novel in America,* p. 254.

8. Hugh M. Gloster, *Negro Voices in American Fiction* (Chapel Hill, N.C., 1948), p. 12.

9. Hall, *Smiling Phoenix,* p. 228.

10. Ibid., p. 212.

11. Theodore L. Gross, "The Negro in the Literature of the Reconstruction," in Gross and Hardy, *Images of the Negro,* p. 78.

12. Sterling Brown, *Negro in American Fiction,* p. 2.

13. Robert Bone, *The Negro Novel in America* (New Haven, Conn., 1958), p. 21.

14. Kennett Young, *Selene* (Nashville, 1898), p. 17.

15. Even Howard's friend Mr. Hardy, although appearing only briefly, is a model student, who "shone with brilliancy in the literary circles" and who, after a successful lecturing career, "laid aside this role of honor, gathered to himself laurels won in many fiercely contested debates," and headed West to find adventure in the Indian Wars.

16. Two Black novelists, Amelia E. Johnson and Emma Dunham Kelley, actually wrote books containing no Black characters at all. *The Hazeley Family* (Philadelphia, 1894) concerns Flora, an orphan girl raised by a stern aunt. Flora returns to live with her disorganized family and, in the course of about 150 pages, reforms her mother, her aunt, and her brother, matches up another brother with a childhood friend, finds a set of long-lost grandparents for a next-door neighbor, and lives happily ever after in this best of all possible worlds. While there is the barest possibility of racial overtones in one relationship depicted in which a daughter is disinherited for marrying against her parents' wishes, it is never made explicit. Johnson's earlier novel, *Clarence and Chlorine; or, God's Way* (Philadelphia, 1890), is a heart-tugger that follows the fortunes of two children victimized by a violent, drunken father and an apathetic, non-Christian mother. Luckily, the children are soon orphaned and begin their uphill trudge from rags to riches through a tale heavily laced with Biblical quotations and "good" advice.

Kelley's *Megda* (Boston, 1892) tells of the religious conversion of a skeptical, but beautiful and—of course—talented, schoolgirl and all of her friends. It contains a particularly sentimental deathbed scene in which Megda is "bequeathed" the fiancé of a dying classmate.

So far, I have been unable to locate Clarissa Thompson's *Treading the Wine Press* (1886), mentioned in Richard Barksdale and Keneth Kinnamon, *Black Writers of America* (Carbondale, Ill., 1972), as one of the early Black novels that "enjoyed considerable popularity during their day." I suspect that it is of the same sort as Johnson's and Kelley's works.

17. John Hope Franklin, *From Slavery to Freedom* (New York, 1947), p. 403.

18. William Wells Brown, *Clotelle; or, The Colored Heroine* (Boston, 1867), pp. 57–58. This is the fourth version of Brown's novel, originally published in London in 1853.

19. Frederick Douglass, *The Heroic Slave* (1853), in Ronald T. Takaki, comp., *Violence in the Black Imagination* (New York, 1972), p. 40.

20. Frederick Douglass, *Narrative of the Life of Frederick Douglass, an American Slave* (Boston, 1845).

21. Sterling Brown, *Negro in American Fiction,* p. 2.

22. J. McHenry Jones, *Hearts of Gold* (Wheeling, W. Va., 1896).

23. Jerome's militancy is, however, given a more conventional outlet in this version of Brown's tale. He and Clotelle return to America at the outbreak of the Civil War. He responds to General Butler's call for enlistment in the Black Union battalion known as the "Native Guard" and, as a member of the "First Louisiana," is killed while retrieving an officer's body after the siege of Port Hudson on May 27, 1863.

24. Mike Thelwell, "Back with the Wind: Mr. Styron and the Reverend Turner," in John Henrik Clark, ed., *William Styron's Nat Turner: Ten Black Writers Respond* (Boston, 1968), p. 80.

25. Frances E. W. Harper, *Iola Leroy; or, Shadows Uplifted* (Philadelphia, 1892), pp. 28–29.

26. William Wells Brown, "Narrative of William Wells Brown, a Fugitive Slave," in William Loren Katz, ed., *Five Slave Narratives,* (New York, 1968), pp. 1–108.

27. Benjamin Botkin, comp., *Lay My Burden Down: A Folk History of Slavery* (Chicago, 1945), pp. 5–6.

28. Other comic examples of minor Black characters are Old Tony in *Clotelle;* Jim Seabury and Uncle Jack in James H. W. Howard, *Bond and Free* (Harrisburg, Pa., 1886); and Aunt Comfort, Kinch, and Caddie Ellis in Frank Webb, *The Garies and Their Friends* (Philadelphia, 1857).

29. Carl Van Doren, *The American Novel, 1789–1939* (New York, 1940), p. 116.

30. Victoria Earle, *Aunt Lindy* (New York, 1893).

31. Van Doren, *The American Novel,* p. 107.

32. James Weldon Johnson, "The Dilemma of the Negro Audience," *American Mercury* 15 (December 1928): 477–81.

33. Paul Laurence Dunbar, *The Best Stories of Paul Laurence Dunbar,* ed. Benjamin Brawley (New York, 1938), p. xv.

34. Saunders Redding, "The Negro Writer and His Relationship to His Roots," in *The American Negro Writer and His Roots* (New York, 1960), p. 4.

35. Ellison, *Shadow and Act,* p. 171

36. Ibid., p. 18.

37. Wallace Thurman, "Negro Artists and the Negro," *New Republic* 52 (August 31, 1927): 37–39.

A more recent critic, Harold Cruse, reaches the same conclusion in *The Crisis of the Negro Intellectual* (New York, 1967): "Middle-class Negroes have rejected the basic art expressions of the Negro folk in music, dance, literature and theater. This was first noticeable during the 1920's at the height of the Negro literary and artistic renaissance" (p. 34).

38. Sterling Brown, "Our Literary Audience," *Opportunity* 8 (January 1930), pp. 42–46.

39. James Weldon Johnson, "Dilemma of the Negro Audience," p. 480.

40. Griggs managed the Orion Press in Nashville, Tennessee, which printed and promoted four of his novels. The copy of *The Hindered Hand* in the Schomburg Collection of Negro Literature in the New York Public Library contains a dedication in Griggs's hand to Mr. Jos. Q. Battle, "the efficient foreman of the bindery whose skill as a workman puts him clearly in the forefront of Negro book makers."

41. Langston Hughes, quoted in Lloyd L. Brown, "Which Way for the Negro Writer?: II," *Masses and Mainstream* 4 (April 1951): 50–59.

42. Charles W. Chesnutt, "Post-Bellum—Pre-Harlem," *Crisis* 38 (June 1931): 193–94.

43. Ibid., p. 94.

44. Gloster, *Negro Voices in American Fiction,* p. 261.

2 Black Sources

1. J. Noel Heermance, *William Wells Brown and Clotelle: A Portrait of the Artist in the First Negro Novel* (Hamden, Conn., 1969), p. 27.

2. Ibid., p. 29.

3. Ibid., p. 142.

4. Lloyd L. Brown, "Which Way for the Negro Writer?: I," *Masses and Mainstream* 4 (March 1951): 55.

5. Heermance, *Brown and Clotelle,* p. 142.

6. Keneth Kinnamon recounts a grisly real-life companion piece to Jones's fictional lynching, in which the murder was advertised on the front page of the May 22, 1917, *Memphis Commercial Appeal* and drew a crowd of approximately five thousand spectators. Afterwards, the victim's head was placed on display in a local barbershop. See Kinnamon, *The Emergence of Richard Wright* (Carbondale, Ill., 1972), p. 9.

7. Katz, *Five Slave Narratives,* p. 6.

8. For a contemporary nonfictional revelation of the evils of the southern convict system, see George Washington Cable, *The Silent South* (New York, 1885).

9. Henry Bibb, "Narrative of the Life and Adventures of Henry Bibb," in Gilbert Osofsky, ed., *Puttin' On Ole Massa,* (New York, 1969), p. 118.

10. Solomon Northup, "Twelve Years a Slave: Narrative of Solomon Northup," in Osofsky, *Puttin' On Ole Massa,* p. 292.

11. Franklin, *From Slavery to Freedom,* pp. 395, 397.

12. Bone, *Negro Novel in America,* p. 21.

13. Gross, "The Negro in the Reconstruction," pp. 71–83.

14. Ellison, *Shadow and Act,* p. 172.

15. Langston Hughes and Arna Bontemps, eds., *The Book of Negro Folklore* (New York, 1958), p. ix.

16. Botkin, *Lay My Burden Down,* p. 2. A recent version of this folk character and his attitude can be seen in the elusive and indestructible protagonist of Melvin Van Peebles's film *Sweet Sweetback's Baaaad Assssss Song.*

17. Howard, *Bond and Free,* pp. 196–97.

An interesting historical account that substantiates this view is offered by Frances Anne Kemble, an Englishwoman who married a Georgia planter and moved to the South in the early nineteenth century:

> . . . certain is the fact . . . that the worst of all tyrants is the one who has been a slave; and for that matter . . . the command of one slave to another is altogether the most uncompromising utterance of insolent truculent despotism that it ever fell to my lot to witness or listen to. "You nigger—I say, you black nigger,—you no hear me call you—what for you no run quick?" (*Journal of a Residence on a Georgia Plantation in 1836–1839* [London, 1863], p. 110).

18. A revealing early twentieth-century treatment of color prejudice among Blacks is Wallace Thurman, *The Blacker the Berry. . . .* (New York, 1929).

19. James Weldon Johnson's nameless hero in *The Autobiography of an Ex-Colored Man,* first published in 1912 and long mistakenly considered the first Black novel to deal with this theme, chooses "passing" as the lesser of two evils, although he wonders finally whether or not, "after all, I have chosen the lesser part, that I have sold my birthright for a mess of pottage" (in John Hope Franklin, ed., *Three Negro Classics,* [New York, 1965] 6 p. 511).

20. Martin R. Delany, *Blake; or, The Huts of America,* ed. Floyd J. Miller (Boston, 1970).

21. Ibid., p. ix.

22. Takaki, *Violence in the Black Imagination,* p. 98.

3 Sutton Griggs: The Dilemma of the Black Bourgeoisie

1. Novels by Sutton Elbert Griggs are *Imperium in Imperio* (Cincinnati, 1899); *Overshadowed* (Nashville, 1901); *Unfettered* (Nashville, 1902); *The Hindered Hand* (Nashville, 1905); and *Pointing the Way* (Nashville, 1908). In addition, he wrote *Life's Demands: or, According to Law* Nashville, 1916).

2. The term is Griggs's and is used several times in his works. It has a primarily political and economic connotation and should not be confused with the New Negro and the renaissance of artistic creativity based in Harlem in the 1920s.

3. Sutton E. Griggs, *Triumph of the Simple Virtues; or, The Life Story of John L. Webb* (Hot Springs, Ark., 1926), p. 9.

4. Thomas Oscar Fuller, *History of the Negro Baptists of Tennessee* (Memphis, 1936), pp. 75–78.

5. Ruth Marie Powell, *Lights and Shadows: The Story of the American Baptist Theological Seminary, 1924–64* (Nashville, 1964), p. 156.

6. Fuller, *Negro Baptists,* pp. 76–77.

7. Griggs's fund-raising activities had much to do with the construction of the American Baptist Theological Seminary in Tennessee. One of the buildings on the campus is called Griggs Hall.

8. Half of his male protagonists are mulattoes, the same proportion found in the books of the earlier Black novelists, but only half of his major female characters are also of mixed blood, indicating Griggs's greater acceptance of the idea of Black beauty. While all of the protagonists are articulate, particularly about racial concerns, their speech seldom displays the artificiality found in the elaborate diction of the earlier novelists. All the main characters are educated and are portrayed as teachers, ministers, politicians, or other professionals; therefore, their command of the language seems more natural than that of the high school boys and field hands of *Appointed* and *Clotelle*. He slips occasionally, it is true, into the familiar quicksand of sentimental speech, but aside from a few aberrations, like Morlene and Dorlan of *Unfettered*, Griggs's major characters speak naturally.

9. An exception is the traditionally sentimental conception of the power of female beauty in *Overshadowed*. A hired killer fails to carry out his mission when he gazes upon his intended victim's lovely face and becomes transfixed.

10. Griggs dedicated a treatise, *Wisdom's Call* (Nashville, 1911), to Texas:

The one dear life which, in all the on going of time, I shall
  be allowed to live upon this planet, came to me
    within the borders of the imperial state
      of Texas. Whatever others
may say, shall I not, therefore, love her? Well, I do; and
  to Texas soil which fed me, to Texas air which
    fanned my cheeks, to Texas skies which
      smiled upon me, to Texas stars
        whose fiery orbs searched
My soul, chased out the germs of slumber and bade me come
  to them, this volume is affectionately dedicated by

THE AUTHOR.

11. Griggs's novels do contain two white characters treated in the traditional manner. The Hon. Thomas Barksdale, a hypocritical politician in *Pointing the Way,* sits

tilted back in a chair, a great, sickly, soulless smile upon his face. . . . His smile disclosed the ragged remnants of his teeth and at the same time allowed two slight streams of tobacco juice to ooze out of the corners of his mouth, anointing the ends of his sandy mustache, which, shaped like the claws of a crab, nestled near his jaws (p. 134).

Another politican, Congressman Bloodworth in *Unfettered,* a man of "sallow" complexion, "very coarse" skin, and "exceedingly tame" eyes, is more ridiculous than repulsive. He is actually early Black literature's vain, stupid, "comic whitey."

12. LeRoi Jones, [Imamu Baraka], "The Changing Same (R&B and New Black Music)," in Addison Gayle, Jr., ed. *The Black Aesthetic* (Garden City, N.Y., 1972), pp. 114–15.

13. Griggs presents a similar character in *Imperium in Imperio,* a rural parson who, in keeping with the folk tradition, is a glutton, eating up all the Sunday dinner. See "The Two Ducks" in Hughes and Bontemps, *Book of Negro Folklore,* p. 160.

14. Griggs's indebtedness to Booker T. Washington for the focus of his class concerns is indicated by the similarity between his treatment of Margaret and Aunt Molly and Washington's observation in *Up From Slavery* (1901):

In Washington I saw girls whose mothers were earning their living by laundrying. These girls were taught by their mothers, in rather a crude way it is true, the industry of laundrying. Later, these girls entered the public schools and remained there perhaps six or eight years. When the public-school course was finally finished, they wanted more costly dresses, more costly hats and shoes. In a word, while their wants had been increased, their ability to supply their wants had not been increased in the same degree. On the other hand, their six or eight years of book education had weaned them away from the occupation of their mothers. The result of this was in too many cases that the girls went to the bad (in Franklin, *Three Negro Classics*, p. 77).

See Hugh M. Gloster, "The Negro in American Fiction: Sutton E. Griggs, Novelist of the New Negro," *Phylon* 4 (Fourth Quarter 1943): 335–45, for an opposing view of Griggs's attitude toward Washington.

15. Another white quality that Griggs admires and considers essential for racial progress is a chivalric attitude toward women. Belton Piedmont faces not only embarrassment, but, in Griggs's eyes, racial retrogression by placing his date in the position of having to pay her own cab fare:

Woman now occupied the same position in Belton's eyes as she did in the eye of the Anglo-Saxon. There is hope for that race or nation that respects its women. It was for the smile of a woman that the armored knight of old rode forth to deeds of daring. It is for the smile of woman that the soldier of today endures the hardships of the camp and braves the dangers of the field of battle.

The Negro race had left the last relic of barbarism behind, and this young Negro, fighting to keep that cab driver from approaching the girl for a fee, was but a forerunner of the Negro, who, at the voice of a woman, will fight for freedom until he dies, fully satisfied if the hand that he worships will only drop a flower on his grave (*Imperium in Imperio*, p. 82).

16. Like J. McHenry Jones in *Hearts of Gold*, Griggs makes use of this turn in the plot to dramatize and document the dreadful conditions in convict labor camps. The following note closes this section:

It would be nothing short of a crime against humanity for an author to allow his imagination to create such a picture as is here drawn, unless the portraiture was true to life. In simple justice to himself, the writer cites as his authority the July 1, 1899 issue of *The Missionary Review of the World* (p. 198).

17. Wilbur J. Cash, *The Mind of the South* (New York, 1941), p. 60.

18. Griggs is not nearly as optimistic about the young whites in the North, however. He prophesies that mass Black migration to northern cities, a desire for national unity, and economic interests will increasingly align northerners with white southerners against the African-Americans. See the discussion between Ensal and Earl in *The Hindered Hand*, pp. 142–43.

19. The murder of Alene Dalman introduces the most mysterious subplot in all of Griggs's novels. Griggs apparently intends this tale of southern gothicism to mirror the political plot in which Gus Martin kills Percy Marshall in the mistaken belief that he was seducing Tiara. The effect of all this mystery and intrigue is the creation of an atmosphere of unrelieved tension and foreboding that is inextricably bound up in the complexities of subconscious incestuous desires on the personal level and racial exploitation in the public arena.

20. Griggs's concern with the plight of rural Blacks is reflected in Bud and Foresta Harper's dedication to solving the problems of the sharecroppers in Mississippi. A few years later, W. E. B. DuBois would focus on the Black sharecropper and the entire plantation economy of the South in his novel *The Quest of the Silver Fleece* (Chicago, 1911).

21. See Ronald T. Takaki's essay, "War upon the Whites" in Takaki, *Violence in the Black Imagination*, pp. 79–101, for an interesting assessment of Martin Delany's ambivalence about Africa.

4 Paul Laurence Dunbar: The Triumph of the Tradition

1. Addison Gayle, Jr., *Oak and Ivy: A Biography of Paul Laurence Dunbar* (Garden City, N.Y.,

1971), p. xiii. See also Darwin T. Turner, "Paul Laurence Dunbar: The Rejected Symbol," *Journal of Negro History* 52 (January 1967): 1–13; Houston A. Baker, Jr., "Paul Laurence Dunbar: An Evaluation," *Black World* 21 (November 1971), pp. 31–37; Victor Lawson, *Dunbar Critically Examined* (Washington, D.C., 1941).

2. James Weldon Johnson, ed., *The Book of American Negro Poetry,* rev. ed. (New York, 1931), p. 36.

3. Lida Keck Wiggins, *The Life and Works of Paul Laurence Dunbar* (Naperville, Ill., 1907), p. 64.

4. Wiggins, *Life of Dunbar,* p. 16.

5. Gayle, *Oak and Ivy,* p. xiii.

6. James B. Stronks, "Paul Laurence Dunbar and William Dean Howells," *Ohio Historical Quarterly* 67 (April 1958): 215

7. Saunders Redding, *To Make a Poet Black* (Chapel Hill, N.C., 1939), p. 59.

8. William Dean Howells, speaking sarcastically of popular fiction, in *Criticism and Fiction* (New York, 1891), p. 106.

9. Edward F. Arnold, "Some Personal Reminiscences of Dunbar," *Journal of Negro History* 17 (April 1932): 400–8.

10. Paul Laurence Dunbar, *In Old Plantation Days* (New York, 1903), "The Brief Cure of Aunt Fanny," pp. 203–16, and "The Memory of Martha," pp. 152–63. Hereafter cited as *IOPD.*

11. Paul Laurence Dunbar, *The Heart of Happy Hollow* (New York, 1904), "Cahoots," pp. 145–59. Hereafter cited as *HHH.*

12. Paul Laurence Dunbar, *The Strength of Gideon and Other Stories* (New York, 1900), "The Strength of Gideon," pp. 3–24. Hereafter cited as *SOG.*

13. Jovial and juvenile Master Morduant is victimized not only by his imitative butler; both Aunt Tempe, the mammy of his children, and Aunt Fanny, his cook, continually manipulate him. When Morduant and his wife attempt to install Maria, a much younger woman, in the kitchen to help her, Fanny rebels:

> "Nemmine, I see you want to git rid o'me; nemmine, M'ria kin have de kitchen." The old woman's voice was trembling and tears stood in her eyes, big and glistening. Morduant, always gentle-hearted, gave in. "Well, confound it, Fanny," he broke in, "do as you please; I've nothing more to say. I suppose we'll have to go on eating your burned biscuits and tough batter-cakes as long as you please. That's all I have to say" (*IOPD,* "The Brief Cure of Aunt Fanny," p. 207).

The crafty, old woman is finally retired, but not without the help and trickery of another old retainer, Mam Henry.

Aunt Tempe, the mammy, is so certain of her importance in the big house and of Morduant's lack of nerve that her antics cause him to burst out helplessly, "The fact is, half the time I don't know who's running this plantation, you or I. You boss the whole household round, and 'the quarters' mind you better than they do the preacher. Plague take my buttons if I don't think they're afraid you'll conjure them!" (*IOPD,* "Aunt Tempe's Triumph," pp. 1–11).

14. "Across the Colour Line," unsigned review of *The Uncalled, Bookman* 8 (December 1898): 339.

15. Paul Laurence Dunbar, *Folks From Dixie* (New York, 1898), "The Colonel's Awakening," pp. 69–79. Hereafter cited as *FFD.*

16. In "The Tragedy at Three Forks" (*SOG,* pp. 269–83), a grim tale of revenge and violence set in central Kentucky after the Civil War, two innocent Blacks are lured into confessing to a barn burning and are then lynched. Dunbar's interest is equally divided between this injustice and his portrayal of the torment of Jane Hunster, the white girl who set the fire. Only one obscure newspaper editor speaks out against the murder. The rest "warned the negroes that the only way to stop lynching was to quit the crimes of which they so often stood accused" (pp. 282–83).

17. Dunbar's only other reference to the class distinctions between house servants and field hands occurs in "The Strength of Gideon," when a fellow slave observes, "Brothah Gidjon is de nicest

house dahky dat I ever hyeahd tell on. Dey jes' de same diffunce 'twixt him an' de othah house-boys as dey is 'tween real quality an' strainers—he got mannahs, but he ain't got aihs'' (*SOG*, p. 11).

18. In contrast, there is the occasional Black belle who causes intense rivalries in the quarters and whose qualities do not set her apart from the counterstereotypes employed by the early African-American novelists. The best of several examples is Miss Sophiny, the heroine of "The Trouble About Sophiny," *IOPD*, pp. 83–94, who was

> in the whole State the prettiest girl, black, brown, or yellow that had ever tossed her head, imitated her mistress and set her admirers wild. She was that entrancing color between brown and yellow which is light brown if you are pleasant and gingerbread if you want to hurt a body's feelings. Also, Sophiny had lustrous, big black eyes that had learned from her mistress the trick of being tender or languishing at their owner's will (p. 84).

19. For two recent opposing studies of Black family life during slavery, see Eugene D. Genovese, *Roll, Jordan, Roll: The World the Slaves Made* (New York, 1974), and Herbert G. Gutman, *The Black Family in Slavery and Freedom* (New York, 1977).

20. Dunbar shows the happiest alternative for a slave mother with Susan, whose "cup of earthly joy was full" (*IOPD*, "A Blessed Deceit," p. 192) when she was ordered to clean up her son and to bring him up to the big house to live, and with Gideon's mother, whose "master discovered his worthiness and filled Cassie's breast with pride by taking him into the house to learn 'mannahs and 'po'ment'" (*SOG*, "The Strength of Gideon," p. 7).

21. While isolated elements of folklore appear in several of the tales, very rarely—despite his heavy hand with dialect—does Dunbar employ poetic Black speech similar to that found in Griggs and Frances Harper. One rare example is the following exchange between the old couple in "The Memory of Martha": " 'I reckon you couldn't jine in de hymn to tek de wickedness outen dis ol' banjo?' . . . 'I don't know 'bout j'inin' in, but you go 'long an' play anyhow. Ef I feel lak journeyin' wid you I fin' you somewhar on de road' " (p. 156).

Scenes of slave festivities somewhat more believable than his pictures of Christmas celebrations appear often in these tales. But Dunbar does not appear comfortable with this subject. For example, the song of Juba started by the field hands in "A Dinner by Proxy" when they discover that the Morduants have left the plantation is not nearly as effective as many of the songs included in his poetry collections; it is certainly not as rhythmic. Perhaps the difference between this verse attributed to the slaves and Dunbar's own songs is due to his desire to portray the people of the quarters as rude and rough in order to contrast them with his "dark aristocrats of the region."

Tricks developed to aid runaways escape capture appear a few times, and Dunbar was aware enough that superstition and conjure were surefire subjects of interest to include two such stories, "The Conjuring Contest" (pp. 130–41) and "Dandy Jim's Conjure Scare" (pp. 142–51), in his third volume of short stories, *In Old Plantation Days*. Although he is sympathetic to the superstitious characters whom he portrays and is amused by the predicaments that he imagines them getting into because of their fears, Dunbar's final attitude toward conjuring seems close to that of the white plantation owner who remarks on "these great overgrown children . . . still frightened by fairy tales." His most effective and sympathetic presentation of Black superstition is the following scene from "The Easter Wedding":

> . . . the strange, weird wedding song of the Negroes . . . died away into the night, a low minor sob, as much of sorrow in it as of joy, as if it foreshadowed all that this marriage was and was not. Just as the last faint echo died away into the woods that skirted the lawn and the waiting silence was most intense, the hoot of an owl smote upon their ears and Eliza turned ashen with fear. She gripped Ben's arm; it was the worst of omens. . . .
>
> As their feet touched the ground of the lawn, the owl hooted again, and ever and anon, his voice was heard as the procession wound its stately way to the place of the next festivities.

In a few days, of course, the couple will be separated on the auction block.

22. Douglass, "A Parody," in *Life of Frederick Douglass,* p. 124.

23. Despite his burlesque treatment, Parker is clearly one of Dunbar's favorite characters. "The Last Fiddling of Morduant's Jim" (*IOPD*, pp. 60–70) fondly narrates the circumstances of the old preacher's death, the result of a cold caught when he ventured out in bad weather to try to persuade an unregenerate slave to give up his "sinful" fiddling. A similar character given a like treatment is the aged minister in "The Fruitful Sleeping of the Rev. Elisha Edwards" (*SOG*, pp. 75–86).

24. Another good example of such satire appears in "The Trial Sermons on Bull-Skin" (*FFD*, pp. 83–109).

25. Fear of the big city seems to have been deep-seated in Dunbar. Lida Keck Wiggins tells of his apprehension before leaving for the World's Columbian Exposition in Chicago, where he was destined to meet Frederick Douglass: "and the hour had come to say good-bye, he leaned on the mantlepiece and sobbed like a child, saying: 'Oh, ma, I don't want to go—it is such a wicked city: I know I shall learn a great deal but I'm afraid to venture. I don't want to go'" (*Life of Dunbar,* p. 39).

26. Tom's father, Deacon Swift, "a great, white-haired, rugged, black figure . . . heroic in his very crudeness," is loyal to the Republicans who guaranteed his freedom from slavery. He could have been simply one of a score of comic preacher figures in these stories, for he "wore a long, old Prince Albert coat, which swept carelessly about his thin legs. His turn-down collar was disputing territory with his tie and waistcoat . . . his hands fumbled at the sides of his trousers in an embarrassment which may have been pretended or otherwise" (p. 247). Despite this traditional humorous description, he is used to reinforce Dunbar's mistrust of the Democrats' motives. "Forty years ago," he says scornfully to his son, "I brung fifteen hun'erd, an' dat was only my body, but you sell body an' soul fu' fi' dollahs!" (p. 252).

27. During the same year that this book appeared, 1901, Dunbar published a series of five short stories, dubbed "The Ohio Pastorals," in *Lippincott's Monthly Magazine.* "The Mortification of the Flesh," "The Independence of Silas Bollender," "The White Counterpane," "The Minority Committee," and "The Visiting of Mother Danbury" concentrate upon white rural and small-town characters similar to the inhabitants of Dorbury in *The Fanatics.* The first two stories are humorous accounts of the doings of two eccentric farmers, Silas Bollender and Nathan Foster. The others, less genial, reveal the religious quarrels and family jealousies prone to develop and flourish in rural communities.

28. Lawson, *Dunbar Critically Examined,* pp. 120–21; italics mine.

29. Gayle, *Oak and Ivy,* p. 11.

30. Ibid., p. 65.

31. Saunders Redding, "The Negro Author, His Publisher, His Public, and His Purse," *Publisher's Weekly* 167 (March 24, 1945), pp. 1284–88.

32. Paul Laurence Dunbar, *The Uncalled* (New York, 1901), p. 33.

33. Paul Laurence Dunbar, *The Love of Landry* (New York, 1900), p. 73.

34. Paul Laurence Dunbar, *The Fanatics* (New York, 1901), p. 13.

35. This ambivalence is reinforced in his picture of slaves fleeing the South in the wake of the Union Army:

> Many indeed, found employment as the servants of officers, where their traditional qualifications as cooks or valets came into full play. But for the most part, they simply hung on, worrying and embarrassing the soldiers with their importunities, sickening and dying from fatigue and exposure, and conducting themselves altogether, like the great, helpless, irresponsible children that they were. . . .
>
> They were not all a burden, though. In the gloom of the dark hours, their light-heartedness cheered on the march; their pranks, their hymns and their ditties made life and light (pp. 155–56).

The effect of the sudden increase of Blacks in Dorbury intensifies the tensions between those of conflicting political persuasions. Even the free Blacks begin to resent the newly arrived slaves, feeling that their presence will make conditions worse for all of them. The local Black church refuses to grant them membership.

> One aged woman, trembling with anger and religious excitement, tottered up, and, starting for the door, hurled this brief condemnation of the culprits who dared desire membership in her church: "W'y befo' I'd see dis chu'ch, dis chu'ch dat we free people built give up to dese conterbands, I'd see hit to' down brick by brick" (p. 163).

36. Paul Laurence Dunbar, *The Sport of the Gods* (New York, 1902), p. 1.

5 Charles Waddell Chesnutt: Art or Assimilation?

1. Sylvia Render, "Eagle with Clipped Wings: Form and Feeling in the Fiction of Charles Waddell Chesnutt" (Ph.D. diss., George Peabody College for Teachers, Aguust 1962).

2. In his rejection of the "mediocrity of what has been called 'Negro Literature,' " Imamu Baraka charges Charles Chesnutt with "inverted paternalism" attributable to his and other Black writers' membership in the "Negro middle class, a group that has always gone out of its way to cultivate *any* mediocrity, as long as that mediocrity was guaranteed to prove to America . . . that they were now really who they were, i.e., Negroes" (LeRoi Jones [Imamu Baraka], *Home: Social Essays* [New York, 1966], p. 106).

The only African-American art form that Baraka values is Black music, because "it drew its strengths and beauties out of the depth of the black man's soul, and because to a large extent its traditions could be carried on by the lowest classes of Negroes." Yet, his definition of high art—that which must issue "from *real* categories of human activity, *truthful* accounts of human life and not fancied accounts of the attainment of cultural privilege by some willingly preposterous apologists for one social 'order' or another" (p. 109)—applies very well to Chesnutt's conjure stories, in which a former slave outwits his wealthy, white employer and educates the employer's wife.

3. In addition to Sylvia Render's dissertation, in this regard, see Margaret Just Butcher, *The Negro in American Culture* (New York, 1969); Jules Chametzky, "Regional Literature and Ethnic Realities," *Antioch Review* 3 (Fall 1971): 385–96; Russell Ames, "Social Realism in Charles W. Chesnutt," *Phylon* 14 (Second quarter 1953): 199–206.

4. He is later to pay tribute to these tokens of Reconstruction, to the enormous importance of education for the newly freed Blacks, and to the "brigade of Yankee schoolmasters and ma'ams" who invaded the South on the heels of the Union troops. See "Cicely's Dream" in *The Wife of His Youth and Other Stories of the Color Line* (New York, 1899), pp. 132–67.

5. Helen Chesnutt, *Charles Waddell Chesnutt: Pioneer of the Color Line* (Chapel Hill, N.C., 1952). Hereafter cited as *CWC*.

6. Charles Waddell Chesnutt, *Frederick Douglass: The Beacon Biographies,* ed. M. S. DeWolfe Howe (Boston, 1899), p. ix.

7. Samuel Sillen, "Charles W. Chesnutt: A Pioneer Negro Novelist," *Masses and Mainstream* 6 (February 1953): 9. This work was "Lost in a Swamp." Two years earlier, this weekly had serialized an essay by Chesnutt, in which he condemned the reading of dime novels.

8. "He received his first rejection slip in 1882, before he left Fayetteville. Many more came before the McClure Syndicate paid him ten dollars for 'Uncle Peter's House,' which appeared in the *Cleveland News and Herald* in December, 1885" (Sylvia Lyons Render, ed., *The Short Fiction of Charles Waddell Chesnutt* [Washington, D.C., 1974], p. 10). All but four of Chesnutt's anecdotes, short stories, and tales, exclusive of those collected in *The Conjure Woman* (New York, 1899) and *The Wife of His Youth,* were published together for the first time in this volume. Render's introduction provides biographical details of Chesnutt and a helpful discussion of the literary qualities of this little-known material.

9. From a letter in the Charles Waddell Chesnutt Collection of the Erastus Milo Cravath Memorial Library, Fisk University, Nashville, Tennessee. Hereafter, all citations to this collection will be indicated parenthetically by reference to their location, Fisk University.

10. Sylvia Lyons Render, "Tar Heelia in Chesnutt," *College Language Association Journal* 9 (September 1965): 39.

11. Charles W. Chesnutt, "Superstitions and Folk-Lore of the South," *Modern Culture* 13 (May 1901): 232.

12. Ibid., p. 233.

13. Julian D. Mason, Jr., "Charles W. Chesnutt as Southern Author," *Mississippi Quarterly* 20 (Spring 1967): 80.

14. Ibid., p. 79.

15. Charles W. Chesnutt, "The Free Colored People of North Carolina," *Southern Workman* 30 (May 1901): 139.

16. For an unusually perceptive and helpful reading of these stories, see Richard E. Baldwin, "The Art of *The Conjure Woman*," *American Literature* 43 (1971–72): 385–98.

17. Sterling Stuckey, "Through the Prism of Folklore: The Black Ethos in Slavery," in Jules Chametzky and Sidney Kaplan, eds., *Black and White in American Culture* (Boston, 1969), p. 186.

18. Ibid., p. 188.

19. Chametzky, "Regional Literature and Ethnic Realities," p. 394.

20. Charles W. Chesnutt, *The Conjure Woman,* "The Goophered Grapevine," pp. 9–10.

21. From the beginning, William Dean Howells appreciated and recommended Chesnutt's writing. In extravagant praise, the leading American proponent of realism ranked the Black writer with Maupassant and Turgenev: "He belongs in other words, to the good school, the only school, all aberrations from nature being so much truancy and anarchy" (W. D. Howells, "Mr. Charles W. Chesnutt's Stories," *Atlantic* 85 (May 1900): 700). In contrast to Dunbar's plantation, Howells identified Chesnutt's province as

> those regions where the paler shades dwell as hopelessly, with relation to ourselves, as the blackest negro. He has not shown the dwellers there as very different from ourselves. . . . they are like us because they are of our blood by more than a half, or three quarters, or nine tenths. It is not, in such cases, their negro blood that characterizes them . . ." (p. 701).

Although his optimistic assertion that in literature "there is, happily, no color line" is myopically naive, Howells sees clearly enough to predict the development of a viable African-American middle class:

> Bound in that sad solidarity from which there is no hope of entrance into polite white society for them, they may create a civilization of their own, which need not lack the highest quality. They need not be ashamed of the race from which they have sprung, and whose exile they share; for in many of the arts it has already shown, during a single generation of freedom, gifts which slavery apparently only obscured" (p. 701).

Howells's review of *The Marrow of Tradition,* if less laudatory, is equally optimistic. Lamenting the lack of simplicity in the novel, however, he observes, "Mr. Chesnutt, it seems to me, has lost literary quality in acquiring literary quantity" ("A Psychological Counter-Current in Recent Fiction," *North American Review* 72 (December 1901): 882). He praises Chesnutt's courage and fairness in the book, deplores its bitterness and characteristically concludes that "no one who reads the book can deny that the case is presented with great power, or fail to recognize in the writer a portent of the sort of negro equality against which no series of hangings and burnings will finally avail" (p. 883). In his relationships with both Dunbar and Chesnutt, then, Howells appears to have been appreciative of their artistic attempts, but blind to the implications of their careers and deepest meanings of their art.

22. Charles W. Chesnutt, *The Wife of His Youth and Other Stories of the Color Line,* "The Wife of His Youth," p. 1.

23. William E. B. DuBois, "Postscript: Chesnutt," *Crisis* 15 (January 1933): 20. By way of a eulogy for his old acquaintance, DuBois wrote,

> Chesnutt was of that group of white folk who because of a more or less remote Negro ancestor identified himself with the darker group, studied them, expressed them, defended them, and

yet never forgot the absurdity of this artificial position and always refused to admit its logic or its ethical sanction. . . . Merit and friendship in his broad and tolerant mind knew no lines of color or race, and all men, good, bad and indifferent, were simply men.

24. Writing on "The Negro in Cleveland" for the *Clevelander* in November 1930, Chesnutt reveals that in his chosen city, "Negroes as a class live on a low economic plane. Most of them are poor, some of them very poor; many of their children go to school undernourished and insufficiently clad" (p. 3). He finds no wealthy men among them and estimates that the middle class or upper middle class, like himself, who "own handsome, well-furnished homes with many evidences of taste and culture" (p. 3), approximately 10 percent of the Black population. White and Black social and professional interaction he finds woefully lacking, the only African-Americans accepted in white homes and civic clubs being a few "close to the color line" (p. 24). Chesnutt's awareness of political rumblings two years before his death is evident in his warning that racist treatment "might conceivably make the colored people a fertile soil for socialist or communist propaganda; for whatever the weaknesses of communism, it teaches human equality, which makes an irresistible appeal to those who are denied it" (p. 27).

25. The personal and national problem of miscegenation, necessarily a central theme for the earliest African-American writers, formed the subject of much of Chesnutt's nonfiction. See "What is a White Man?" in the *Cleveland Independent,* May 30, 1899; the series entitled "The Future American Race" during the late summer 1900 in the *Boston Evening Transcript;* his address of June 25, 1905, "Race Prejudice: Its Causes and Its Cure," before the Boston Literary and Historical Association; and his address before the Dunbar Forum in Oberlin, Ohio, "The Negro in Present Day Fiction."

26. This conclusion is based upon Chesnutt's ironic comment in "The Negro in Art, How Shall He Be Portrayed," *Crisis* 33 (November 1926): 28–29: "My most popular novel was distorted and mangled by a colored moving picture producer to make it appeal to Negro race prejudice." The producer was Oscar Micheaux, who, over a thirty-year period, produced thirty-four pictures, most of which were intended for a Black audience.

27. Quotations are taken, respectively, from unsigned review, *Southern Workman* 29 (1900); unsigned review, *Cleveland Plain Dealer,* November 4, 1900; unsigned review, *Pittsburgh Post,* December 2, 1900; review by Joseph Chamberlain, *Boston Evening Transcript,* October 31, 1900.

28. Quotations are taken, respectively, from unsigned review, *Pittsburgh Post,* December 2, 1900; unsigned review, *Cleveland Plain Dealer,* November 4, 1900; *Pittsburgh Post,* December 2, 1900; *Cleveland Plain Dealer,* November 4, 1900.

29. Charles W. Chesnutt, *The House Behind the Cedars* (New York, 1900), p. 3.

30. For comments about Chesnutt's use of the actual geographical locale and real personages of North Carolina as prototypes for the novel's characters, see Render, "Tar Heelia in Chesnutt," and John Parker, "Chesnutt as a Southern Town Remembers Him," *Crisis* 56 (July 1949): p. 205.

31. Again, see Render, "Tar Heelia in Chesnutt," for parallels between events in the novel and political events in Wilmington.

32. Ames, "Social Realism in Chesnutt," p. 199.

33. Charles W. Chesnutt, "The White and the Black," *Boston Evening Transcript,* March 20, 1901.

34. Charles W. Chesnutt, *The Marrow of Tradition* (New York, 1901), p. 1.

35. Howells, "Psychological Counter-Current in Fiction," p. 882.

36. DuBois, "Possibilities of the Negro—The Advance Guard of the Race," *Booklover's Magazine* 2 (July 1903): 13.

37. Robert Farnsworth, "Testing the Color Line—Dunbar and Chesnutt," in C. W. C. Bigsby, ed., *The Black American Writer,* Vol. 1 (Deland, Fla., 1969).

38. Charles Chesnutt, *The Colonel's Dream* (New York, 1905), p. 293.

39. Render, "Tar Heelia in Chesnutt," p. 49.

40. It was before this group that Chesnutt at last received the opportunity to indulge his penchant for scholarship. Although he satirized the club in "Baxter's Procustus," *Atlantic Monthly,* June

1904, pp. 823–30, considered by many critics to be one of his best short stories, he was also an active participant at their Saturday night meetings. As Helen Chesnutt notes, "His first paper entitled 'Who and Why was Samuel Johnson' was read in November 1911. Then followed in April, 1914, 'The Life and Works of Alexander Dumas,' and in March, 1915, 'François Villon, Man and Poet.'" Chesnutt had for several years been devoting his spare time to the study of French poetry and had been collecting editions of François Villon's works, both in the original French and in translation. " 'George Meredith,' 'The Diary of Philip Hone,' 'The Autobiography of Edward, Baron Herbert of Cherbury' were titles of other papers that he presented as the years went on" (*Charles Waddell Chesnutt,* p. 289).

41. The Special Collections at Fisk University contain the manuscripts of six unpublished Chesnutt novels: "The Rainbow Chasers" (ca. 1900), "Evelyn's Husband" (ca. 1900), "A Business Career" (n.d.), "Paul Marchand, F.M.C." (n.d.), "Mandy Oxedine" (n.d.), and "The Quarry" (1928).

42. Chesnutt, "Post-Bellum—Pre-Harlem," p. 194.

43. Chesnutt, "The Negro in Art," p. 29.

44. Ralph Ellison, *Invisible Man* (New York, 1952), p. 16.

A Final Perspective

1. Franklin, *From Slavery to Freedom,* p. 237.

2. Ibid., p. 439.

3. Kelly Miller, *Race Adjustment: Essays on the Negro in America* (New York, 1908; rptd., Miami, 1969), p. 16.

4. Barksdale and Kinnamon, *Black Writers of America,* p. 377; "Resolution at Harpers Ferry, 1906," pp. 377–78.

5. Hart, *The Popular Book,* p. 157.

6. Franklin, *From Slavery to Freedom,* p. 298.

7. Ibid., p. 311.

8. Ibid., p. 323.

9. Hart, *The Popular Book,* p. 159.

10. Ibid., p. 202.

11. Franklin, *From Slavery to Freedom,* p. 416.

12. Gilbert Osofsky, *Harlem: The Making of a Ghetto,* 2d ed. (New York, 1971), p. 18.

13. Ibid., p. ix.

14. Hart, *The Popular Book,* p. 200.

15. Ibid., p. 183.

16. Ibid., p. 205.

17. Franklin, *From Slavery to Freedom,* p. 403–4.

18. Addison Gayle, Jr., *The Way of the New World: The Black Novel in America* (Garden City, N.Y., 1976), pp. 377–78.

Selected Bibliography

"Across the Color Line." Unsigned review of Paul Laurence Dunbar, *The Uncalled. Bookman* 8 (December 1898): 338–41

The American Negro Writer and His Roots. New York, 1960.

Ames, Russell. "Social Realism in Charles W. Chesnutt." *Phylon* 14 (Second quarter 1953): 199–206.

Arnold, Edward F. "Some Personal Reminiscences of Dunbar." *Journal of Negro History* 17 (April 1932): 400–8.

Baker, Houston A., Jr. "Paul Laurence Dunbar: An Evaluation." *Black World* 21 (November 1971): 31–37.

Baldwin, Richard E. "The Art of *The Conjure Woman*." *American Literature* 43 (1971–72): 385–98.

Barksdale, Richard, and Kinnamon, Keneth, eds. *Black Writers of America.* Carbondale, Ill., 1972.

Bigsby, C. W. C., ed. *The Black American Writer,* vol. 1. Deland, Fla., 1969.

Bone, Robert. *The Negro Novel in America.* New Haven, Conn., 1958.

Botkin, Benjamin, comp. *Lay My Burden Down: A Folk History of Slavery.* Chicago, 1945.

Brown, Herbert Ross. *The Sentimental Novel in America, 1789–1860.* Raleigh, N.C., 1940.

Brown, Lloyd L. "Which Way for the Negro Writer?: I." *Masses and Mainstream* 4 (March 1951): 53–63.

———. "Which Way for the Negro Writer?: II." *Masses and Mainstream* 4 (April 1951): 50–59.

Brown, Sterling. *The Negro in American Fiction.* New York, 1937.

———. "Our Literary Audience." *Opportunity,* January 1930, pp. 42–46.

Brown, William Wells. *Clotel; or the President's Daughter; A Narrative of Slave Life in the United States.* London, 1853.

———. *Clotelle: A Tale of the Southern States.* Boston, 1864.

———. *Clotelle; or the Colored Heiress: A Tale of the Southern States.* Boston, 1867.

———. *"Miralda; or, the Beautiful Quadroon: A Romance of American Slavery, Founded on Fact."* New York, December 1, 1860–March 16, 1861. Serialized in the *Weekly Anglo-African.*

Butcher, Margaret Just. *The Negro in American Culture.* New York, 1969,

Cable, George Washington. *The Silent South.* New York, 1885.

Cash, William. *The Mind of the South.* New York, 1941.

Chametzky, Jules. "Regional Literature and Ethnic Realities." *Antioch Review,* Fall 1971, pp. 385–96.

Chesnutt, Charles Waddell. "A Business Career." Unpublished novel, n.d. Fisk University Special Collections.

———. *The Colonel's Dream.* New York, 1905.

———. *The Conjure Woman.* New York, 1899.

———. "The Disfranchisement of the Negro." *The Negro Problem.* New York, 1903.

———. "Evelyn's Husband." Unpublished novel, ca. 1900. Fisk University Special Collections.

———. *Frederick Douglass: The Beacon Biographies.* Edited by M. S. DeWolfe Howe. Boston, 1899.

———. "The Free Colored People of North Carolina." *Southern Workman* 30 (May 1901): 136–41.

———. "The Future American Race." *Boston Evening Transcript,* July 2, 1900– August 31, 1900.

———. *The House Behind the Cedars.* New York, 1900.

———. "Mandy Oxedine." Unpublished novel, n.d. Fisk University Special Collections.

———. *The Marrow of Tradition.* New York, 1901.

———. "The Negro in Art, How Shall He Be Portrayed." *Crisis* 33 (November 1926):28–29.

———. "The Negro in Cleveland." *Clevelander,* November 1930, p. 3.

———. "The Negro in Present Day Fiction." Address to the Dunbar Forum at Oberlin, Ohio, n.d. Fisk University Special Collections.

———. "On the Future of His People." Review of Booker T. Washington's *Future of the American Negro. Saturday Evening Post* 172 (January 20, 1900).

———. "Paul Marchand, F.M.C." Unpublished novel, n.d. Fisk University Special Collections.

———. "Post-Bellum—Pre-Harlem." *Crisis* 38 (1931): 193–94.

———. "The Quarry." Unpublished novel, 1928. Fisk University Special Collections.

———. "Race Prejudice: Its Causes and Cure." Address to the Boston Literary and Historical Association, June 25, 1905. Fisk University Special Collections.

———. "The Rainbow Chasers." Unpublished novel, ca. 1900. Fisk University Special Collections.

———. *The Short Fiction of Charles Waddell Chesnutt.* Edited by Sylvia Lyons Render. Washington, D.C., 1974.

———. "Superstitions and Folk-Lore of the South." *Modern Culture* 13 (May 1901), 231–35.

———. "A Visit to Tuskegee." *Cleveland Leader,* March 31, 1901, p. 19.

———. "What is a White Man?" *Cleveland Independent,* May 30, 1899.

———. "The White and the Black." *Boston Evening Transcript,* March 20, 1901.

———. *The Wife of His Youth and Other Stories of the Color Line.* New York, 1899.

Chesnutt, Helen. *Charles Waddell Chesnutt: Pioneer of the Color Line.* Chapel Hill, N.C., 1952.

Clark, John Henrik, ed. *William Styron's Nat Turner: Ten Black Writers Respond.* Boston, 1968.

Cruse, Harold. *The Crisis of the Negro Intellectual.* New York, 1967.

Delany, Martin R. *Blake; or, The Huts of America.* Edited by Floyd J. Miller. Boston, 1970. Originally published in the *Weekly Anglo-African,* November 1861 to May 1862.

Douglass, Frederick. *Narrative of the Life of Frederick Douglass.* Boston, 1845.

DuBois, William E. B. "Postscript: Chesnutt." *Crisis* 15 (January 1933): 20.

———. *The Quest of the Silver Fleece.* Chicago, 1911.

———. *The Souls of Black Folks.* New York, 1903.

Dunbar, Paul Laurence. *The Best Stories of Paul Laurence Dunbar.* Edited by Benjamin Brawley. New York, 1938.

———. *The Fanatics.* New York, 1901.

———. *Folks From Dixie.* New York, 1898.

———. *The Heart of Happy Hollow.* New York, 1904.

———. *In Old Plantation Days.* New York, 1903.

———. *The Love of Landry.* New York, 1900.

———. "The Ohio Pastorals." *Lippincott's Monthly Magazine* 68 (July–December, 1901).

———. *The Sport of the Gods.* New York, 1902.

———. *The Strength of Gideon and Other Stories.* New York, 1900.

———. *The Uncalled.* New York, 1901.

Earle, Victoria. *Aunt Lindy.* New York, 1893.

Ellison, Ralph. *Invisible Man.* New York, 1952.

———. *Shadow and Act.* New York, 1953.

Franklin, John Hope. *From Slavery to Freedom.* New York, 1947.

Fuller, Thomas Oscar. *History of the Negro Baptists of Tennessee.* Memphis, 1936.

Gayle, Addison, Jr. *Oak and Ivy: A Biography of Paul Laurence Dunbar.* Garden City, N.Y., 1971.

———. *The Way of the New World: The Black Novel in America.* Garden City, N.Y., 1976.

———, ed. *The Black Aesthetic.* Garden City, N.Y., 1972.

Genovese, Eugene D. *Roll, Jordan, Roll: The World the Slaves Made.* New York, 1974.

Gloster, Hugh M. "The Negro in American Fiction: Sutton E. Griggs, Novelist of the New Negro." *Phylon* 4 (1943): 335–45.

———. *Negro Voices in American Fiction.* Chapel Hill, N.C., 1948.

Griggs, Sutton Elbert. *The Hindered Hand.* Nashville, 1905.

———. *Imperium in Imperio.* Cincinnati, 1899.

———. *Life's Demands; or, According to Law.* Nashville, 1916.

———. *Overshadowed.* Nashville, 1901.

———. *Pointing the Way.* Nashville, 1908.

———. *Triumph of the Simple Virtues; or, The Life Story of John L. Webb.* Hot Springs, Ark., 1926.

———. *Unfettered.* Nashville, 1902.

———. *Wisdom's Call.* Nashville, 1911.

Gross, Seymour L., and Hardy, John Edward, eds. *Images of the Negro in American Literature.* Chicago, 1966.

Gutman, Herbert G. *The Black Family in Slavery and Freedom.* New York, 1977.

Hall, Wade. *The Smiling Phoenix: Southern Humor from 1865–1914.* Gainesville, Fla., 1965.

Harper, Frances E. W. *Iola Leroy; or, Shadows Uplifted.* Philadelphia, 1892.

Hart, James D. *The Popular Book: A History of America's Literary Taste.* New York, 1950.

Heermance, J. Noel. *William Wells Brown and Clotelle: A Portrait of the Artist in the First Negro Novel.* Hamden, Conn., 1969.

Howard, James H. W. *Bond and Free.* Harrisburg, Pa., 1886.

Howells, William Dean. *Criticism and Fiction.* New York, 1891.

———. "Mr. Charles W. Chesnutt's Stories." *Atlantic* 85 (1900): 699–701.

———. "A Psychological Counter-Current in Recent Fiction." *North American Review* 72 (December 1901: 881–83.

Hughes, Langston, and Bontemps, Arna, eds. *The Book of Negro Folklore.* New York, 1958.

Johnson, Amelia. *Clarence and Chlorine; or, God's Way.* Philadelphia, 1890.

———. *The Hazeley Family.* Philadelphia, 1894.

Johnson, James Weldon. *The Autobiography of an Ex-Colored Man.* In *Three Negro Classics,* edited by John Hope Franklin. New York, 1965.

———. "The Dilemma of the Negro Audience." *American Mercury* 15 (1928): 477–78.

———, ed. *The Book of American Negro Poetry.* New York, 1931.

Jones, J. McHenry. *Hearts of Gold.* Wheeling, W.Va., 1896.

Jones, LeRoi [Imamu Baraka]. *Home: Social Essays.* New York, 1966.

Katz, William Loren, ed. *Five Slave Narratives.* New York, 1968.

Kelley, Emma Dunham. *Megda.* Boston, 1892.

Kemble, Frances Anne. *Journal of a Residence on a Georgia Plantation in 1836–1839.* London, 1863.

Kinnamon, Keneth. *The Emergence of Richard Wright.* Carbondale, Ill., 1972.

Lawson, Victor. *Dunbar Critically Examined.* Washington, D.C., 1941.

Lee, Don L. "Black Poetry: Which Direction?" *Negro Digest* 17 (September–October 1968): 27–32.

Mason, Julian D., Jr., "Charles W. Chesnutt as Southern Author." *Mississippi Quarterly* 20 (1967): 77–89.

Miller, Kelly. *Race Adjustment: Essays on the Negro in America.* New York, 1908; reprinted, Miami, 1969.

Osofsky, Gilbert. *Harlem: The Making of a Ghetto.* 2d ed. New York, 1971.

———, ed. *Puttin' On Ole Massa.* New York, 1969.

Parker, John. "Chesnutt as a Southern Town Remembers Him." *Crisis* 56 (1949): 205.

Powell, Ruth Marie. *Lights and Shadows: The Story of the American Baptist Theological Seminary, 1924–64.* Nashville, 1964.

Redding, Saunders. "The Negro Author, His Publisher, His Public, and His Purse." *Publisher's Weekly,* No. 167 (1945), pp. 1284–88.

―――. *To Make a Poet Black*. Chapel Hill, N.C., 1939.

Render, Sylvia Lyons. "Eagle With Clipped Wings: Form and Feeling in the Fiction of Charles Waddell Chesnutt," Ph.D. diss., George Peabody College for Teachers, August 1962.

―――. "Tar Heelia in Chesnutt." *College Language Association Journal* 9 (September 1965): 39–50.

Sillen, Samuel. "Charles W. Chesnutt: A Pioneer Negro Novelist." *Masses and Mainstream* 6 (February 1953): 8–14.

Stowers, Walter, and Anderson, William H. [Sanda]. *Appointed*. Detroit, 1894.

Stronks, James B. "Paul Laurence Dunbar and William Dean Howells." *Ohio Historical Quarter.* 67 (April 1958): 95–108.

Takaki, Ronald T., comp. *Violence in the Black Imagination*. New York, 1972.

Thompson, Clarissa. *Treading the Wine Press*. 1886.

Thurman, Wallace. *The Blacker the Berry . . .* New York, 1929.

―――. "*Negro Artists and the Negro*." *New Republic* 52 (August 31, 1927): 37–39.

Turner, Darwin T. "Paul Laurence Dunbar: The Rejected Symbol." *Journal of Negro History* 52 (January 1967): 1–13.

Van Doren, Carl. *The American Novel, 1789–1939*. New York, 1940.

Washington, Booker T. *Up From Slavery*. New York, 1901.

Webb, Frank. *The Garies and Their Friends*. Philadelphia, 1857.

Wiggins, Lida Keck. *The Life and Works of Paul Laurence Dunbar*. Naperville, Ill., 1896.

Yellen, Jean Fagan. *The Intricate Knot: The Negro in American Literature 1776–1863*. New York, 1971.

Young, Kennett. *Selene*. Nashville, 1898.

Index

About the Author

ARLENE A. ELDER is associate professor of English at the University of Cincinnati, Ohio. Her articles have appeared in such journals as *Phylon* and *The Old Northwest.*